THE NEW PARENT

THE NEW PARENT

MIRIAM STOPPARD

DORLING KINDERSLEY
London • New York • Sydney • Moscow
www.dk.com

A DK PUBLISHING BOOK
www.dk.com

For Cressida and Henry

Managing Editor: Jemima Dunne
Senior Managing Art Editor: Lynne Brown

Senior Editor: Nicky Adamson
Project Editor: Dawn Bates
US Editor: Jill Hamilton

Senior Art Editor: Carole Oliver
Designer: Maria Wheatley

Production: Antony Heller

Special Photography: Susanna Price

First American edition, 1998
2 4 6 8 10 9 7 5 3

Published in the United States by DK Publishing, Inc.
95 Madison Avenue, New York, New York 10016

Library of Congress Cataloging-in-Publication Data
Stoppard, Miriam.
    New Parent/by Miriam Stoppard.--1st American ed.
        p. cm.
    Includes index.
    ISBN 0-7894-1997-1
    1. Infants. 2. Infants--Care. 3. Parent and infant. 4. Parenting. 5. Pregnancy. 6. Childbirth. I. Title.
HQ774.S85 1998
649'.122--dc21   97-50087
                                                                                         CIP

Reproduced by Colourscan, Singapore.
Printed and bound in China by L.Rex Printing Co., Ltd.

CONTENTS

INTRODUCTION

TODAY'S NEW PARENTS have many advantages over their predecessors, but they also face many new challenges. Knowledge of the way babies grow and develop both before and after birth has increased enormously in the past few years. But this knowledge in itself creates new pressures, worries, and anxieties for parents. If you are a couple thinking of starting a family, how do you know where to turn? I hope that this book will help you to find out what best suits you, and what makes you feel comfortable and confident enough to follow your own instincts.

There's much evidence to indicate that the unborn baby benefits from having a relaxed, calm mother who can take setbacks in her stride. Other research demonstrates that the most important factor in determining whether a pregnant woman is tranquil or not, is a caring, interested, supportive partner. And here we have come to the reason for my writing this book. It is not just for first-time mothers, but for couples – mothers *and* fathers. I've included basic advice on caring for your baby during her first year of life, but it's just as important to emphasize how a baby will affect your relationship.

— THE IMPACT ON YOUR RELATIONSHIP —

Few couples think about the impact their new baby will have on their lives, their work, their emotions, and their feelings for one another. With the care of their baby as the top priority, parents can easily give too little consideration to looking after themselves. Both new mothers and new fathers will find their world turned upside down by the advent of a baby. This may create tensions and strains, which, if unspoken and unresolved, could drive a wedge between them.

It's a huge leap from being a couple to becoming a family. A man is very different from a father, and different things are expected of him. If they're honest, most men admit to experiencing difficulties in making the transition to fatherhood. By the same token, a mother is a very different person from a woman, who was probably self-confident and independent before she became pregnant. Now she may be apprehensive and come to feel isolated. She has to cope with a baby who is completely dependent upon her, which can bring with it a perceived loss of identity. This in turn may lead to confusion, resentment, and irritation toward her partner.

The good news is it's possible for both of you to pick your way through this minefield of new feelings and responsibilities. But it isn't always easy and it requires a lot of give and take to smooth the path. Perhaps now, more than at any other time, each of you has to be aware of and sensitive to the needs of the other and actively look for ways of showing that you care.

— ADVICE AND REASSURANCE —

While my main aim is to give new parents the confidence to follow their own instincts in fashioning their particular brand of family life, and to be open and loving with one another so that their relationship is enriched by their new baby, there's no doubt that first-time parents find bits of advice quite useful. So I've tried to be helpful in matters with which most young families have problems.

Issues like where to have your baby, how to stay healthy during pregnancy, what to expect during labor, how to establish breast-feeding, and ways to cope with broken nights or a fretful baby are all covered. While love for your baby can begin from the moment of birth, her care is a skill that you'll be learning throughout this first year of life, and understanding how she develops is a crucial part of it. All new parents feel anxious and inept to begin with, but if you share the worries as well as the joys, you're less likely to strain your relationship.

——— Making room for fathers ———

Throughout the book, I approach pregnancy, birth, and baby care as a joint venture. Fathers are addressed on every page because mothers and babies need involved, active fathers. Men are as good at fathering as women are at mothering; there's no qualitative difference between the two. Fathering instincts are strong and just need a little encouragement to flower. Babies love being nurtured by fathers as well as mothers; it follows that parenting should be equal and shared.

On the face of it, following this principle may seem fraught with obstacles, but not so. Parents can share all the elements of baby care with a little planning and a generous heart. After all, baby care means loving your baby, encouraging your baby, teaching your baby, watching your baby grow and develop, and establishing bonds with your baby that in all probability will be the strongest you ever make with anyone. Who in their right mind would miss out on it?

Men should try not to allow themselves to be deprived of this unique relationship. And when they're fully involved with their baby, a little miracle occurs along the way: their relationship with their baby's mother flourishes, too.

—— Making parenting a partnership ——

To help both parents become fully involved, I've included special panels that give the mother's point of view on one side of the page and the father's point of view on the other. Arranging information in this way has a special purpose: it can help you gain insight into what your partner may be feeling about a particular topic, or might want to say but is reluctant to make demands. Looking at this information together may help you get a discussion going. Communication is the key to a successful relationship, so hopefully these panels will enable you to talk things through and be generous about the other's way of looking at things.

Above all, couples whose relationship is on a sound footing and who enter into parenthood as a true partnership are doing the best for their baby, who will grow up secure in the love of both parents. Shared care means there'll be time for your baby, time for yourselves, and time when, as well as being a family, you're just a couple – but with the knowledge that together you have produced and nurtured a wonderful baby.

7

DECIDING ON PARENTHOOD

When you decide to have a baby, you are also making the decision to become a parent. This is probably the most important step you'll ever take in your life, because bringing a child into the world isn't something that you can simply add on to your current lifestyle. You're creating a completely new person, and taking on a responsibility that is lifelong. You're also creating a new unit – from being two individuals, you are becoming a family – something that both cements and strains your existing relationships with each other, your friends, and family. This is equally true whether you're a lone parent or if you have children from a previous relationship: your new baby is going to create a new family grouping. So it's well worth looking at all the implications of parenthood and the different forms that the modern family takes, and to ask yourselves some searching questions about how you see parenting and how it's going to affect your everyday needs and your emotions.

THE CHANGING FAMILY

HOW ROLES ARE CHANGING

At their most basic, the terms "mother" and "father" describe a range of biological facts. A mother produces ova (eggs) and gives birth to children. A father's sperm fertilize the ova and contribute half of his child's genes. But these are obviously not the only differences. Human beings belong to a species where there is fairly clear "sexual dimorphism," in which the physical differences between men and women evolved to enable men (being bigger and stronger) to protect women.

NO NEED FOR BRUTE STRENGTH
For thousands of years, men used their biological role to claim privilege and authority, but today the traditional roles of mother and father are about as relevant to modern parents as flint tools and mammoth traps. Those roles evolved to adapt to circumstances that simply don't exist any more. Modern technology has done away with the need for brute strength and nowadays women and children generally don't need their menfolk to protect them from incoming marauders.

INVOLVING MEN IN PARENTING
Since the 1970s it has been increasingly recognized that men should be more involved in the upbringing of their children. This is sometimes seen as a spin-off from the women's movement, but this oversimplification misses the point. The equal investment of men in the rearing of their children shouldn't just be the result of women refusing to be captive to outmoded social conventions, but also the outcome of men's determination to claim their right to one of the most humanizing of human activities: the nurture, guidance, and bringing to independent maturity of a child.

WHEN YOU DECIDE TO HAVE A BABY, you are creating a new social unit; instead of being two people who may have made a commitment to each other, but who essentially keep their individuality, you become a family. Human babies need constant protection because of their long infancy and helplessness: the family has evolved to make sure that happens. Although there are many variations in family structure, there is nowhere in the world where it doesn't exist. But a child knows nothing about structure – all she knows is the quality of care, interest, and love she receives from within her family.

HOW IT USED TO BE

Until two or three generations ago, the family was usually based on the extended model. People were part of a large group of three or four generations, extending outward to include cousins. When people's lives were less mobile, and they lived and worked in one small area, face-to-face contact was possible on a daily basis. This larger family unit could act as a support group for its members, particularly in the case of child rearing.

THE EXTENDED FAMILY
Four generations were gathered together for this photograph – an example of the traditional extended family that was already becoming a rarity by the 1920s, when this photograph was taken.

THE FAMILY TODAY

In the past fifty years, this extended family grouping has largely broken down. Increasingly rapid technological change produced a labor market that demanded mobility; people wanted to go where the jobs were, or were forced to do so through economic necessity. Leaving home meant leaving the extended family network and possibly settling where there were no relations at all to lean on for financial and emotional support. At the same time, increased prosperity allowed people to set up their own homes, whereas in the past they may have remained in the family home, even when married. This broad social movement saw the rapid spread of the isolated nuclear family: just mother, father, and children. Even when embedded within an extended family, this unit can be a hothouse of troubled emotions; on its own, its long-term survival is more likely to be precarious.

NEW FAMILY GROUPINGS

Since the 1960s, women have increasingly developed a degree of financial independence that made them less likely to hang onto the last remnant of a marriage just because they didn't think they could provide for themselves and their children on their own. Liberal attitudes to welfare have also played their part in the transformation of the traditional family; as the nuclear family – detached from its older members or more tenuous branches – became the norm rather than the exception, the divorce rate increased, giving rise to a variety of less orthodox family structures.

DIVORCE AND REMARRIAGE

Many divorced or separated people have not turned their backs on marriage or partnership as such, but only on the one they found intolerable. A good proportion of them is prepared to have another try, thus often creating a stepfamily (see p. 123). As with the nuclear family, the stepfamily has been around for a long time (and hasn't always had a very good press), but its recent growth has been quite dramatic.

SINGLE PARENTS

The one-parent family is a much maligned institution. It is true that it has often grown out of unhappy situations and the pressures, not least financial, on the lone parent are great. But many single-parent families are thriving and vigorous units that are bound by particularly close ties, and that offer the children involved continuity, stability, and happiness (see p. 120).

A NEW KIND OF PARENTING

Not only has the composition of the traditional family changed in recent times, but also the way in which it functions. Whereas fathers used to be protectors, having little direct involvement in day-to-day child care, their importance as equal partners is now being recognized – side by side with women's increasing role as an equal or even the primary financial provider. In recent years an alternative family arrangement has developed where the father cares for home and family by choice, while his partner earns the daily bread (see p. 154). One reason why such families are often strong and successful units is that they take account of both partners' talents and generally come out of careful discussion and planning. But whatever the practicalities of any individual family unit, providing a stable, loving, and open environment in which to bring up children is probably the only important constant.

THE NUCLEAR FAMILY
The majority of modern families plan the number of children they have, and both parents want to become involved, to a greater or lesser degree, in child care.

WHAT IS A FATHER?

No one has a problem in defining a mother's role. Mothers care for children: they feed, comfort, dress, and bathe; they encourage, teach, carry, undress, put to bed, and maybe sing to sleep. We know this because it's what we experienced as children. Defining the role of a father is more problematic.

FINDING A ROLE MODEL
Much as we may love our fathers, the way we experienced them as children is not necessarily how we hope our own children will experience their fathers. Men are constantly being exhorted to become fully involved in nurturing their children, but few have any role model to demonstrate what this actually means. To put it bluntly, what we want is for fathers to be more like mothers.

BABIES DON'T DIFFERENTIATE
Babies and young children don't see any difference in male and female nurturing. They experience comfort, warmth, and security from two adults and, although they soon learn to tell them apart, they don't make value judgments based on a notion of what mothers' and fathers' roles ought to be. Apart from breast-feeding, there is nothing a woman can do for a baby that can't be done by a man.

THE NEED FOR PARENTING
Babies don't need mothering and fathering, they need parenting. They need the most important adults in their lives to be models of what parents do for their children; when this is achieved, the next generation of fathers will not be at a loss as to what a father's role should be. Care for a child is indivisible; she will only compartmentalize her needs if this is what she learns from her experiences.

11

WHY BE A PARENT?

MOTHER

While it's recognized that a mother's role has changed, unfortunately it's taking longer to break down stereotypes of fathering. It's a good idea to be clear about your own attitude to make sure it doesn't reinforce these traditional ideas.

ATTITUDES TO FATHERING

■ In the past it was assumed that fathers came home from work expecting the home to be clean, the children ready for bed, and a meal on the table. It's a myth that's died hard, but it's difficult to believe that many modern mothers would entertain it.

■ Many women still expect their partners to handle all the family finances, sometimes to their disadvantage. However, couples should find an equitable way to share their financial burdens.

■ It's often assumed that men do all the heavy work associated with parenthood. However, while a man must do this when his partner is pregnant and the baby is young, women are fitter and stronger than they used to be and these tasks can be shared.

■ Women still tend to take on the chores while their partners play with the baby, even when both parents work. But both of you should try to find time to play with your baby, and share the housework equally.

■ Some women hide behind their partners when disciplining their children, but, "I'll tell your father when he gets home" is both outdated and a cop-out. Attitudes to discipline should be agreed and consistently applied by both parents (see p. 157).

YOU MAY NEVER do anything more important than bringing up a child. However satisfying your career, however important your job, whatever prowess you have achieved in sport or leisure activities or in volunteer work, your achievement in bringing up a happy child is matchless; what's more, no one else can claim the credit. As your child's first – and lifelong – caregiver, teacher, coach, supporter, counselor, trainer, promoter, and fan, you have an enormous responsibility. If you approach parenthood realistically, you'll find it's a role that is rewarding in a way that is unlike anything else.

FOLLOWING YOUR INSTINCTS

The instinct to bear children is a strong one, and luckily the joy and fulfillment felt by the majority of parents far outweigh some of the inconveniences and compromises they may have to accept. Although this isn't always so, making the decision to have a child usually comes from within a close, loving relationship between two people who decide that they would like to express their mutual affection in having a baby. This is just as well – you're unlikely to have made the decision because you're attracted by the notion of reduced free time, never being able to put yourself first, sleeplessness, going everywhere with a baby survival kit, or forking out for designer infant sneakers! If you think carefully about the changes brought about by parenthood, you'll realize that it's your genes that are pushing you relentlessly toward re-creating yourselves in the form of children. Today, people don't like to admit that they might be at the beck and call of basic urges and tend to dress them up as something more refined. That's fine, as long as we remember that we can also push back and say no to parenthood. For some, that can be the best decision, because having a baby is a commitment like no other.

MORE THAN JUST NATURE

Aside from the biological reasons, people also want to have a baby for fulfillment and personal achievement. Human beings are social animals, and the way they think and act always has a social element. This is shown most clearly in human parenthood in the case of adoption where (usually) two people voluntarily make a commitment to assume all the rights and duties of natural parents, while being genetically unrelated to the child (see p. 122). Adoption also illustrates the depth of the emotional need that people feel to nurture, educate, and, above all, love a child. What you give to your babies and children in time, love, understanding, and example will constantly be repaid as you watch them grow and develop over the months and years. Every child is genetically the sum of his parents, but he is also a unique personality in his own right, and knowing that you have been the primary influences and educators in allowing that personality to take shape and mature is deeply enriching as well as being a major achievement.

SOCIAL AND ECONOMIC PRESSURES

In a society where everyone goes to school, everyone expects to go to school. Similarly, when everyone except a small minority has children, people expect to have children. It's as though a person has to have a reason for remaining childless, rather than the opposite. In the past, when families tended to live close together, in the same street or village if not actually in the same house (see p. 10), there were quite important economic reasons for having children. As soon as they were old enough to work, children made a vital contribution to the family's economic welfare, and parenthood was also a guarantee of being cared for in old age.

CHANGING DEMANDS

In the much more fragmented society in which we live today, children aren't expected to contribute to the family income (at least until they have finished their education), and the state has taken over some of the basic responsibilities for the elderly, or people make their own provision for old age. As a result, the economic demands of the family are now directed downward, from parents to children, instead of the other way around. Bringing up children today can be a costly business, and not just financially. For the first time in history, large numbers of women can achieve a whole range of satisfactions outside parenthood and the home; and with safe methods of contraception, they can also choose when and whether they want to have children. This doesn't mean that large numbers of women are opting out of motherhood, although some are; but what they are doing is fitting having and bringing up children into lives where work and a career are also seen as theirs by right.

A QUESTION OF UPBRINGING

Having begun to consider parenthood seriously, the first thing to realize before you go further is that having a baby is just the overture to bringing up a child. It isn't too difficult to imagine having a baby – the excitement, the celebrations, the delighted grandparents, the supportive friends and family. It is almost impossible to visualize bringing up a child if you haven't done it. The demands in time, energy, and emotion are almost limitless, unless of course the first thing you're going to teach your toddler is how to use the remote control for the TV and VCR. This isn't an option for most people because, even before you become parents, you'll have some idea of the kind of people you hope your children will grow up to be, and of the upbringing that will make this idea a reality.

A FIRM FOUNDATION

Upbringing begins from the moment of birth. For a baby or young child, everything is a learning experience, so how you care for your baby is influential from day one. It's worth looking at the background of someone you know who is independent but has a large capacity to love and interrelate with others, who is effective and confident, who recognizes that there is such a thing as the general good and wants to contribute to it. You'll probably find that person found the world an accepting, loving, encouraging, reasonable, and respectful place from birth. His parents made him feel that way, and the foundation for everything he has become was provided by them in his first year of life.

FATHER

When you're considering whether you're ready to be a parent, it is worth questioning your own ideas of parenthood, and whether what you think of as a mother's role isn't just as applicable to fathers.

ATTITUDES TO MOTHERING
■ While it's true that most of the people who stay at home with children are still women, many are now returning to work within months of the birth. In addition, a significant minority of fathers are becoming primary caregivers of their children (see p. 154).

■ Recent surveys continue to show that women, even full-time working mothers, do most of the chores in the home. Ask yourself if this is fair; cooking is increasingly seen as genderfree, and in any partnership day-to-day cleaning should always be shared.

■ As the children grow up, tasks like dealing with caregivers and teachers, taking and picking up from school, used to be seen exclusively as the mothers' responsibility. But most fathers realize that being involved in their child's life and education is important, and they're fitting activities like the car pool, helping in the classroom, or taking their child to the doctor into their day.

■ It used to be thought that mothers put children to bed, but most fathers know that the bath and story routine is enjoyable, especially if they've been away from their children all day.

■ The idea – prevalent not so long ago – that it was somehow demeaning for a man to push a stroller is now laughable. Not only are men happy to be seen doing this, but they are also more than happy to take their children to the supermarket to do the weekly shopping without their partners.

13

YOUR ATTITUDE TO PARENTING

However right it may seem at the time, the decision to have a child needs the same reasoned evaluation you would give to buying a house or a new car. It may be quite illuminating to ask yourselves the following questions, even if, in the event, your pregnancy is unplanned. If the answer to more than five questions is "yes," you may need to think about your whole attitude to parenting:

■ Do you already have ambitions for your children's future?

■ Are you uncertain about how parental actions affect children?

■ Do you still have to work out some of your views on parenting?

■ Do you think that after the birth, instinct will take over and you'll know exactly how to behave toward your child?

■ Are you worried that your partner sees parenting roles differently to you?

■ Do you believe in a strict routine for newborn babies?

■ Do you think a baby would benefit from such a routine?

■ Can you spoil a young baby?

■ Do you believe that babies cry for no reason?

■ If you're both intending to work after the birth, will you leave investigating child care until then?

■ Are your views on baby care at odds with those of your partner?

■ Will you find it difficult to tolerate the measure of disorder a new baby may bring to your home?

■ Do you foresee any conflict with grandparents or other relatives about the way you intend to care for your baby?

All of these topics are discussed elsewhere in this book. Parenting is not an exact science, but the advice given here should help you to clarify your own thinking.

TIMING IT RIGHT

IF YOU ARE WAITING for everything to be just right before you have your baby, you may as well give up now and take up a hobby instead. It's rare for a couple to feel that the perfect moment has arrived to have a child, but now that men and women have control over their fertility, it gives time for all the options to be considered.

MAKING THE DECISION

For many people, finance and accommodation may be the most pressing issues when making the decision whether or not to become parents. Others may look at their personal freedom, and how having a child may affect it. In today's society, where more and more women are finding satisfaction in the progress of their careers, making the decision to break off and have a child can be extraordinarily difficult. Although many companies – and countries – are providing increasingly generous maternity leave and benefits, this may not compensate for the fact that having a baby could delay your career prospects, especially if you want to spend more than a few months at home with your baby. This is one reason why many women, particularly those with satisfying or high-powered jobs, are waiting to start a family at least until their thirties, when they feel that they've reached a level of achievement that enables them to stand back from their careers with confidence.

MAKING SPACE FOR PARENTHOOD
Men also need to think about how their work commitments may affect their relationship with their children. Many older men who become parents for a second time in a new relationship have acknowledged that they regretted having missed out on their first family's childhood because pressures of work effectively separated them from their children. Childhood passes quickly and you only have one chance with any child, so think about how much time you will be able to give to her.

PRACTICAL CONSIDERATIONS

It's quite feasible to bring up a child in anything upward from a two-room apartment – if there's a separate space for the baby, that's ideal. If you're thinking of moving into a larger home to accommodate future children, try to move before you become pregnant; otherwise, it's best to wait until after your baby is born. You don't want the double pressure of a new baby and moving house. No one pretends there isn't a financial implication to parenthood, but the cost of having a baby is largely dependent on what a couple see as essential. Be assured that no baby in a bassinet with one or two loving parents ever lay awake wondering why she didn't have an elaborate crib with Brahms' lullaby wafting from the attached electronic musical box. Nevertheless, it makes good sense to make the best of what's available. Look at your likely overall income and expenditure once the baby is born, taking account of benefits (see p. 160), and plan accordingly. Whenever the state of your finances allows you to shop, invest in the basic minimum (see p. 68); leave luxuries until you can really afford them.

PARTNERSHIP OR MARRIAGE

If you're in a long-term stable relationship but unmarried, you probably had good reason for choosing this kind of partnership. Now that you are considering parenthood, is there a case for reconsidering your position? Do either or both of you have anything to gain from marrying and, more importantly, does your prospective child? One of the reasons most commonly given by prospective parents for marrying before the baby is born is that it ensures that the father is the legal parent of his child. The legal situation may vary from country to country, so formal marriage may not necessarily be the only option for you, but clearly neither of you would want to encounter problems in gaining access to your child in the event of your relationship breaking down and leading to a split. However unlikely this may seem at present, no one can foretell the future and most couples would want to guarantee that their baby always has the equal benefit of both parents, even if at some time they may not live together anymore.

CHANGING RELATIONSHIPS

Sometimes new parents have not bargained for the fact that their relationship with family and friends will change. More importantly perhaps, the dynamics of their own relationship will also change. No time is better spent before you even start trying for a baby than in exploring together what these differences might be (see p. 108). Policies that are made in advance needn't be written in stone, but if you don't have a policy, you don't have a starting point for tackling problems.

Grandparents You both know the personalities of the prospective grandparents and you may already see difficulties ahead because their views and attitudes may not be the same as yours. You'll find later on that agreement with grandparents about how you're going to set limits for your child is invaluable. It's also a good idea to agree that you'll both gently but firmly resist any attempt by them to dictate methods of parenting to you. You can, however, ask them to help you to implement yours. But it's also wise to listen to their views or you may be passing up good advice based on real experience. It's also true that many grandparents find it easier to have a relaxed and freer relationship with their grandchildren than they had with their own children, to the benefit of all concerned.

Your friends If you want to hang onto your childfree friends or those who have older children, look at their relationship with others who have recently become new parents. Keep a weather eye out for the vacant, glazed look that lets you know they find a baby's wicked way with biscuits less than fascinating. Once you have children you may not be available to your friends as much as you were before, so they'll appreciate it if you retain your identity as a friend rather than a parent while you're with them. Bear in mind also that you'll meet other people with babies with whom you'll forge new friendships, based on the shared experience of new parenthood.

The impact at work Try also to rehearse in advance what difference the advent of the baby may have at work. You may never have clock-watched in your life before now, but it's difficult not to when you're aching to get back to your baby – and this is just as true for fathers as it is for mothers. However, your colleagues, no matter how sympathetic, have the right to assume that you'll be as good an employee as you were before. If you can see possible pitfalls, be up front and negotiate; you won't always be a new parent and lost trust is difficult to reestablish.

QUESTIONING YOUR REASONS

When making any decision, it can be useful to put into words some of the half-formulated thoughts and questions that lurke in the corners of the mind. Even if you think you both really want a baby because you love each other and it's the natural thing to do, it's still sensible to think about all the issues. The following questions don't have right or wrong answers, but provide what I hope will be a useful starting point for you:

■ Does the idea of having a baby seem to be the instinctive next step for you both, arising from your positive commitment to each other as a couple?

■ Have you always taken it for granted that one day you would have children?

■ Do you just want a child, or do you want a child specifically with your partner?

■ Does one of you want this baby more than the other? If so, what effect has this had on your relationship?

■ Do you want to have a baby because you think it will cement your relationship with your partner?

■ What images do you conjure up when thinking about life with your baby? Do they include sleepless nights and dirty diapers?

■ What will you miss most about being a couple rather than a trio?

■ Do you have any firm personal ambitions that could be compromised by having a baby?

■ Do you want a baby to make up for areas in your life that you find unsatisfactory?

■ Is any part of your motivation to please family members, such as grandparents?

■ Are you and your partner quite clear about the commitment each of you will make to the baby?

PREGNANCY IS AN EXCITING TIME FOR YOU BOTH, BUT YOUR EXCITEMENT CAN ALSO BE TINGED WITH APPREHENSION, UNCERTAINTY, AND – IF THE PREGNANCY IS A SURPRISE – EVEN DISMAY. EACH PERSON'S REACTION TO THE KNOWLEDGE THAT HE OR SHE IS GOING TO BECOME A PARENT IS DIFFERENT, BUT LUCKILY NATURE HAS MADE SURE THAT THERE IS PLENTY OF TIME TO GET USED TO THE IDEA DURING THE FORTY OR SO WEEKS FROM CONCEPTION TO BIRTH. PREGNANCY IS NOT A DISEASE BUT IT DOES PUT A LOT OF STRAIN ON A WOMAN'S BODY. SO IF YOU'RE PLANNING TO BECOME PARENTS IT MAKES SENSE TO THINK ABOUT YOUR FITNESS WELL BEFORE YOU CONCEIVE AND TO LOOK AFTER YOURSELF DURING THE PREGNANCY. ONCE THE PREGNANCY IS CONFIRMED YOU WILL BOTH FEEL HAPPIER IF YOU FOLLOW ITS PROGRESS BY ATTENDING PRENATAL CHECKS AND FINDING OUT AS MUCH AS POSSIBLE ABOUT HOW YOUR BABY DEVELOPS IN THE WOMB. IT WILL HELP YOU BOTH TO UNDERSTAND THE MINOR DISCOMFORTS AND EMOTIONAL UPS AND DOWNS THAT A PREGNANT WOMAN SOMETIMES FEELS, AND TO FACE UP TO THE SLIGHT POSSIBILITY OF SOMETHING UNEXPECTED HAPPENING.

PREPARING FOR PARENTHOOD

PLAN FOR PREGNANCY

W HEN YOU MAKE THE DECISION to become parents, it makes sense to prepare yourselves in advance. To have a healthy baby, research shows that by far the most important factors are your own fitness and nutrition. This means fathers too: every baby is 50 percent her father and so that half has to be the healthiest and best that it can be.

MOTHER

It's sensible to think ahead about the best time to conceive (see right). Once you're pregnant, your baby's due date will be calculated as 40 weeks from the first day of your last period, so you need to take that into account when planning prepregnancy fitness.

WHY FITNESS IS IMPORTANT
There is a phenomenal buildup over the 40 weeks of pregnancy; the statistics are staggering. Here are a few: the womb increases in volume (muscle) 1,000 times; the womb increases in weight (protein) 30 times; individual muscle fibers of the womb increase 40 times in length; the work done by a mother's heart increases 50 percent; the volume of a mother's blood increases by one-third; a mother's kidneys filter 50 percent more blood than before.

PREVENTING ANEMIA
If you're anemic, your heart is overworked, which can affect your baby. A blood test would reveal anemia and it may be necessary to take iron supplements.

AVOIDING BIRTH DEFECTS
Folic acid has been found to reduce the risk of some birth defects such as spina bifida. It's advisable to start increasing folic acid intake three months before you stop contraception, and for three months after you conceive. Good food sources are green leafy vegetables, cereals, and bread; or, alternatively, take supplements.

IF YOU HAVE A MEDICAL PROBLEM
If you take regular medication for a medical condition, let your doctor know before you try for a baby; the dose may have to be changed once you're pregnant (see p. 33).

TIMING THE BIRTH

If you're serious about starting a family, ideally you should begin to think about it at least a year before the time you'd like your baby to be born. It's a good idea to allow at least three months to get your bodies to peak preconception fitness (see opposite). There are other issues you may want to take into account as well, such as the timing of the birth. If you're planning to move, or know that work commitments are going to take you away from home at a specific time of year, you'll want to avoid allowing these to clash with the possible arrival of your baby. Some parents may even want to take account of whether their baby is born in winter or summer: most education systems involve a fall start to the academic year and there is evidence to suggest that some children born in the summer, the youngest in their grade level, may not achieve as well academically as the older and more mature children who are born in the winter. This doesn't just affect the early years; it can sometimes last well into the teens.

DELAYING PARENTHOOD
More and more women are now delaying childbearing into their thirties or even early forties. A pregnant woman over 35 will be monitored more closely, but women's general health and fitness has improved enormously in recent years and the older pregnant mother is no longer likely to have the same risks of earlier generations. In addition, couples starting a family in their thirties are more likely to have planned the baby, be in a stable relationship, and be financially secure. However, leaving conception until your mid-thirties or later does increase the time you might have to wait to conceive – an average of six months when you're 35, as opposed to four months when you're 25 (see p. 20).

WHEN TO STOP CONTRACEPTION

If you've been using straightforward barrier methods such as the condom or diaphragm, you can safely conceive as soon as you stop using them. However, most doctors recommend at least one normal period after ceasing other forms of contraception, before you try to conceive.

The pill The best plan is for you to stop taking the pill three months beforehand, but a month would do, as long as you have one normal period before you get pregnant.

Intrauterine device (IUD) The same timescale would apply to an IUD, so have it removed three months before you intend to get pregnant. Have at least one normal period before stopping all contraception – use a barrier method in the meantime.

18

HOW FITNESS HELPS BOTH OF YOU

As a prospective mother, the fitter you are, the more easily your body will be able to cope with the stresses and strains of pregnancy (see box opposite). But fitness and lifestyle may also change a man's ability to father a child, by affecting sperm production (see box below). Try to think about your general health and lifestyle at least three months before you're planning to stop contraception. As well as helping to improve your fitness, it will increase your chances of conceiving without delay and of having a healthy baby.

A HEALTHY DIET

Adjusting your diet shouldn't require uncomfortable changes. Your staple diet should include good-quality carbohydrates such as wholewheat bread, rice, and potatoes. Keep your animal fat intake down by changing to skim milk and low-fat cheeses, and use olive or safflower oil for cooking. Eat lots of fresh fruit and vegetables every day (see p. 34). Don't skip meals; avoid processed foods; outlaw the liquid lunch; and eat a hearty breakfast, although not a fried one.

EXERCISING

Exercise makes a contribution to becoming a healthy potential parent, so if you don't already do so, start a gentle exercise program together, such as jogging, swimming, or aerobics. Try for 20 minutes' exercise that increases your heart rate at least three times a week. However, bear in mind that very strenuous training or dieting may reduce fertility.

ROUTINE HEALTH PRECAUTIONS

WHAT TO LOOK AT	HOW TO IMPROVE
SMOKING	Smoking reduces fertility, especially in men since it lowers their sperm count. Give up before you try to conceive; smoking during pregnancy – direct or passive – harms your unborn child.
ALCOHOL	Alcohol can damage both sperm and the ovum, so prospective parents should consume no more than five units a week for women, 10 for men. (One unit=one small glass of wine or a half pint of beer.)
DRUGS AND MEDICATION	Many medicinal and street drugs affect fertility or cause birth defects. Cannabis reduces sperm production; the effects can take months to wear off. Consult your doctor if you take regular medication.
PREPREGNANCY SCREENING	Well before conceiving, check for rubella (German measles) immunity and get immunized if necessary; have a cervical smear test and any treatment; check for sexually transmitted diseases.
ENVIRONMENTAL FACTORS	Before conceiving, and after you stop contraception, make sure you avoid X rays, hot saunas, and pollutants such as dioxins and PCBs (found in many garden and household products).

FATHER

It may seem obvious to you that your partner's fitness and lifestyle will have a bearing on her ability to conceive, but you need to be aware that your own fitness is also a crucial factor. If you aren't fit, you may not donate the best genetic material to your child in your sperm, so it's a responsibility you can't shirk.

WHY YOUR LIFESTYLE MATTERS
Whatever you think about your sexual prowess, it may bear no relation at all to your ability to father a child. Male fertility not only depends on the number of sperm produced, but also on the health of that sperm. This is affected by all sorts of lifestyle factors, such as smoking, alcohol, and drugs (see left), and also stress. Try to reorder your life if it's stressful, and look at your diet and physical fitness.

19

GENETIC COUNSELING

Seek advice and have tests in advance if a genetic disorder runs in your family. Examples of heritable conditions include cystic fibrosis, thalassemia, muscular dystrophy, and hemophilia.

WHAT HAPPENS IN COUNSELING
The counselor explains the condition and your family background and shows you the pattern of inheritance through past generations. Not all carriers of a defective gene get the condition: if it's recessive it can be masked by a healthy version, whereas a dominant gene will always show up. With a dominant gene the chances of your baby being affected are one in two, with a recessive gene they are one in four.

INCREASING CHANCES OF CONCEPTION

Once you've stopped using contraceptives and your periods are normal (see p. 18), the following tips might help you conceive more quickly:

■ Try to have intercourse during your most fertile period (see right).

■ Your fertile period is signalled by the texture of your cervical mucus, which becomes clear, thin, and slippery, making it easier for the sperm to swim up through your cervix. Ovulation usually occurs 24 hours after this type of mucus is at its most profuse.

■ Avoid making love for a couple of days before your fertile period to help build up to an optimum number of sperm.

■ The "missionary position" (man on top) is thought by some to be most effective for conception, particularly if you lie down for half an hour or so after you've had intercourse.

■ Cut down on your intake of caffeine – there's some evidence to suggest that it can interfere with the ability of the embryo to implant in the wall of the uterus.

CONCEPTION

CONCEIVING A BABY is the ultimate expression of a loving sexual relationship between partners, who have made the decision together, without pressure from each other. You could conceive within a few months of making the decision to stop using contraception, especially if you have intercourse at your most fertile time of the month.

WHEN YOU'RE FERTILE

A woman is fertile only when she is ovulating – when an egg has been released from her ovum. This is nearly always 14 days after the first day of the last menstrual period. You can therefore predict ovulation by tracking your periods in a diary, or you can do an ovulation test on your urine, which may be helpful if you don't have a regular 28-day cycle. Three-quarters of all couples who have unprotected intercourse will conceive within nine months, and 90 percent in 18 months, but from the age of about 25, the fertility of both men and women does start to wane.

WHAT HAPPENS WHEN YOU CONCEIVE

Since the ovum can survive for 36 hours and sperm for 48 hours, your fertile period can last for about three days. When ovulation and intercourse overlap, sperm swim up through the cervix and uterus to meet the ovum, and fertilization with one sperm usually happens in the upper end of the fallopian tube. It then takes 3–4 days for the fertilized cell (called a zygote) to reach the uterus and implant in the endometrium – the specially prepared uterine lining. The process of implantation is called nidation; the fertilized egg, now called a blastocyst, burrows into the lining and quickly forms a primitive placenta; seven days after ovulation, the blastocyst is embedded and growing.

Fertilized egg (zygote) begins to divide as it travels down the tube

Zygote continues to divide, forming a sphere of cells

Dividing zygote forms a solid ball of cells called a morula

The ball of cells becomes hollow. Now known as a blastocyst, it reaches the uterus after three days

One sperm fertilizes the egg when they meet in the fallopian tube

Fimbriae (fingerlike fronds at the end of the fallopian tube) collect the ripe egg into the tube

Hormones stimulate the ripening of an egg follicle. The egg is released from the follicle at ovulation

Follicle containing developing egg

Degenerated empty follicle from earlier ovulation

Ovary, containing eggs (ova), which are released at every menstrual cycle

About seven days after fertilization, the blastocyst implants in the uterine wall

CONCEPTION

Every month a woman's body prepares itself for conception through the action of hormones that ripen the ovum and cause the lining of the womb to thicken in order to nourish the tiny embryo.

FINDING OUT IF YOU'RE PREGNANT

Many women suspect that they are pregnant within days of conception, but the single most obvious indicator is a missed period, and anyone who has a regular menstrual cycle will realize something has happened once they are three or four days late. Other women may not realize for two or three weeks, especially if they continue to have so-called "withdrawal" bleeding, where prepregnancy hormones still present in the body cause a weak menstrual bleed; these women may suspect that they are pregnant from other physical signs (see below). Either way, you'll probably want to confirm it as soon as possible with a pregnancy test.

PREGNANCY TESTS

Commercially produced pregnancy tests are now widely available – although often expensive – and can confirm whether or not you are pregnant from the day your period is due. However, if you can wait a day or two longer, you'll obtain a more reliable result; a false positive is unlikely, but you may wrongly test negative if you try too early. You can also ask your doctor to do the test.

OTHER SIGNS OF PREGNANCY

You may experience other signs within days of missing your period that will alert you to the possibility of successful conception:
● Tender, heavy breasts that may tingle a little. Your bra may seem a bit too tight, the veins on your breasts more prominent than usual, and your nipples and areolae may seem redder than usual.
● A feeling of nausea. Although often called "morning sickness," it may happen at any time of the day.
● A supersensitive sense of smell, and a metallic taste in your mouth.
● The need to pass urine more frequently than usual.
● Feeling incredibly tired, especially in the evening.

WAITING A LONG TIME TO CONCEIVE

If you've been trying to conceive for 12 months without success (or eight months if you're over 35), you could approach your doctor to talk about being referred for investigations into your fertility. Finding out that you are unable to conceive without help can be very stressful, but many couples discover that taking this first step is in itself an antidote to stress and they may go on to conceive before their appointment with the specialist.

PREPARING YOURSELVES FOR FERTILITY INVESTIGATIONS

The test process can be long and difficult, so both partners must enter willingly into the investigation. Before you embark on it, you should think carefully about the strain (including perhaps financial) of what you are about to do. Many relationships have crumbled under the stress of infertility investigations, and living with the uncertainty, and the unpleasant and invasive tests, can be extremely hard.

SHARING THE RESPONSIBILITY

Be aware that your ability as a couple to conceive – your fertility – is the sum of both your fertilities. Investigations may indicate a problem that will probably be treatable, and it's worth remembering that in as many as half of infertile couples, the problem lies with the man. Infertility is nobody's fault, you share it. Don't apportion blame or feel resentment or guilt, or you'll drive a wedge between you two that may make conception even more elusive.

BOY OR GIRL?

I'm not in favor of trying to select a boy or girl baby. Nature does very well in maintaining a balance of about 103 boys to 100 girls and we shouldn't interfere with that. With advances in ultrasound and fetal cell investigations, you may be able to find out the sex of your baby during pregnancy, although this deprives you of the lovely surprise of finding out your baby's sex at the birth.

WHAT DETERMINES A BABY'S SEX?
Men produce sperm with 22 chromosomes plus either one X (female) or one Y (male) sex chromosome. Women's ova also have 22 corresponding chromosomes, but they only produce an X sex chromosome. A zygote fertilized by an X sperm grows up to be a girl, a Y sperm results in a boy.

IS IT POSSIBLE TO INFLUENCE A BABY'S SEX?
Although no method with any scientific validity has been developed, by noting the different characteristics of X and Y sperm, it's possible to suggest a way of increasing your chances of conceiving the gender you want:

■ X sperm are larger and slower than Y sperm.

■ X sperm live longer than male Y sperm.

■ To increase the chances of an X sperm fertilizing the ovum and conceiving a girl, intercourse should be two to three days prior to ovulation, since only female sperm survive long enough to meet the ovum when it's finally released.

■ There's a higher chance that a Y sperm will fertilize an ovum on the day of ovulation because it will reach the ovum more quickly, and the baby will be a boy.

■ Frequent ejaculation lowers the proportion of Y sperm, so a girl is likely. Infrequent sex increases the proportion of Y sperm and the chances of a boy.

21

PREGNANCY AFTER MISCARRIAGE

The trauma of a miscarriage, stillbirth (see p. 33), or even a termination in the past can affect how you both feel about your current pregnancy.

REKINDLING GRIEF
Even if your earlier pregnancy or pregnancies were some time ago, you may find being pregnant again rekindles your need to grieve. Talk through your feelings with your partner or a close friend: if you work through this old grief now, you'll find it easier to welcome your new baby when she's born.

RELIVING THE PAST
If you had a miscarriage, you'll both find it very difficult to be relaxed about the new pregnancy. In particular, you may find the weeks around the time you lost your last baby very difficult to get through. Take heart from the fact that the vast majority of women who miscarry go on to have a healthy child next time around.

AFTER A TERMINATION
If you had a termination due to abnormality, you're likely to be offered diagnostic tests in this pregnancy as early as possible. Again, take heart from the fact that many such problems are extremely unlikely to recur. If your termination was for other reasons, you may suffer feelings of guilt that you're going ahead with this pregnancy. It's important to talk about this rather than bottling up feelings that may adversely affect your relationship with your new baby.

AFTER A STILLBIRTH
If you had a stillbirth, you'll probably be wondering whether or not this baby is alive and find the end of your new pregnancy almost unbearable. Although you'll be monitored carefully, talk your fears through with your consultant – you may very well be able to have the baby some days or even weeks before the due date.

ADJUSTING TO PREGNANCY

THE CHANGE FROM BEING AN INDIVIDUAL to becoming a parent is one of the most profound you'll ever experience; a woman is different from a mother; a father is not the same as a man. It's an essentially positive and deeply satisfying experience – but you're going to find it shattering, exhausting, and incredibly hard work too.

THINKING AHEAD

Your pregnancy is a time to ponder the great changes ahead – for each of you as individuals and for you both as a couple. In many ways it's impossible to describe exactly what's ahead in pregnancy until you're there, but it's certainly true that you can be as prepared as possible by asking questions, reading, and talking to friends who've already gone through it.

YOUR DIFFERING REACTIONS

Men and women respond differently to the news of pregnancy; elation may fade into fear, anxiety, or depression at the thought of the looming responsibilities and the unavoidable changes. Changes in relationships can be threatening at the best of times. Those that take place in early pregnancy are particularly taxing because they have to be played out when the mother is feeling tired and possibly anxious, and the father may be feeling ambivalent about the new situation (see p. 24). Use the months ahead to prepare, as much as possible, for what's in store, but try to enjoy your pregnancy, too. Life will, after all, never be the same again. If you can, go away for a weekend or have a vacation when you're between four and seven months pregnant – it will give you plenty of time and space to share your feelings together, and in the years ahead you'll probably look back on it as the end of your old way of life, in the run-up to the exciting new times ahead.

FEELINGS ABOUT PREGNANCY

You have approximately nine months to examine your feelings as dispassionately as possible, and following the progress of the pregnancy is helpful here (see p. 30). At first, the physical changes common to most pregnant women may color your view of the pregnancy. Many women find the physical discomforts of the first three months – tiredness, nausea, tender breasts – occur almost as soon as the pregnancy has been confirmed, sometimes within a few days of missing a period (see p. 20). This can take couples by surprise, turning initial delight into apprehension and uncertainty. However, this reaction is usually temporary, lasting about 12 weeks; after this you'll suddenly realize that you're not waking up with nausea and a fuzzy head, that you're full of energy, and that instead of just looking thicker around the waist, you're developing a recognizable "bump" that announces your pregnancy to the rest of the world, and of which you can be proud!

PLANNED OR UNPLANNED

Whether the pregnancy was planned or not has a bearing on your attitude to it. An unplanned pregnancy may be welcomed by one partner more than the other (and this is often the father rather than the mother), or both of you could be ambivalent about it, especially if you have financial concerns. Whether your pregnancy is planned or unplanned, there may well be implications for your career, especially if you work for a company that doesn't have a sympathetic attitude to parenthood. This is more important for working women than men, but experience shows that it is possible to resume a career even when you've had a long break for birth and child care (see p. 148). Once you know you're pregnant, talk to your employer about the options as soon as possible to find out what maternity leave is offered (see p. 160). This will help allay any fears you have about your future career prospects that might tarnish how you feel about your pregnancy as a whole.

IF YOUR PREGNANCY WAS ASSISTED

Your attitude to your pregnancy is bound to be affected if you've waited a long time to conceive, and perhaps had treatment to assist conception. You'll feel an enormous sense of relief that your longed-for baby is at last on the way, but may worry about doing anything that could lead to miscarriage, so that there's a tendency to treat the pregnancy like an illness. Try to avoid this; most specialists in assisted conception will hand their patients over to the normal maternity services once the pregnancy is established – if anything will go wrong, it is most likely to happen in the first eight to ten weeks, and you'll have been warned about this. Even if you've had to endure quite lengthy and invasive treatments to achieve the pregnancy, try not to dwell on them and look forward instead to the birth of your healthy baby.

GIVING THE NEWS

You might both want to tell everyone immediately that you're having a baby; on the other hand you might want to keep your secret to yourself for a while. You may surprise yourself at how it comes out, depending on who you're telling, because many people find admitting they are about to become parents to a third party seems to make it real for the first time. The unqualified support of friends and family can help overcome any feelings of doubt; alternatively you may find yourself confessing to your closest friend your ambivalence about the whole thing, even though on the surface you appear to be delighted. Once the news is out, bear in mind that in the event of a miscarriage, the more people you have told, the more distressing it may be for you if you have to explain that you've lost the baby (see p. 33).

PREBIRTH BONDING

Although it's wonderful to be able to see your baby moving when you have your first scan (see p. 29), most women feel that the bonding process really begins once they feel it. Although this may not happen until about 16 weeks in a first pregnancy, it's an advantage you have that your partner lacks – so share your feelings as much as possible and encourage him to feel your tummy. First sensations of movement often coincide with a change in energy levels, so you'll probably be feeling better about yourself and the baby than you ever thought possible to start with.

FATHER

The physical changes of pregnancy can affect your partner's attitude to it. Being prepared for what may happen should help you deal with the low moments she may have as they crop up.

YOUR PARTNER'S FEELINGS

■ Exhaustion is a common feature of early pregnancy – it's probably caused by all the hormones your partner's body is suddenly having to deal with. Encourage her to take things easy, and look forward to the middle months when she'll probably feel incredibly energetic and wide awake; the "bloom" of pregnancy at this time will make your partner look wonderful – so make sure you tell her!

■ The effect of pregnancy hormones combined with the whole idea of becoming a parent could make her much more emotional than usual; she'll cry easily at a "weepy" movie or a tragic story in the news. Don't mock her – be sympathetic.

■ She may worry about the fact that she'll inevitably be gaining weight. Don't draw attention to this; be positive about how she looks and compliment her. It is a very bad idea to diet in pregnancy, but she doesn't need to eat for two either. Most of the fat laid down in pregnancy is stored to nourish breast-feeding, and is burned off remarkably quickly once she starts feeding after the birth; encourage her with this information (see p. 70).

■ Your partner may feel that she's lost control of her life by getting pregnant because there's always someone else with ideas on what's best for her. Don't add to this – she knows her body best and when it comes to decision time, she has the last word.

23

THE EXPECTANT FATHER

MOTHER

You may not think your relationship with your partner will change before the baby is born, but it will, so you should be prepared for this.

UNDERSTANDING YOUR PARTNER

■ It is very easy for men to feel left out so make sure you involve your partner as much as possible.

■ Don't expect him to feel the same way as you. Expecting a baby is an external experience for him and it may be very difficult for him to empathize with the invisible changes taking place within you. Remember, his day-to-day life will be much the same and there won't be such an obvious change for him until after your baby is born.

■ Talk to your partner about how you are feeling. You may have big mood swings and go through periods of feeling insecure and unattractive. Don't take it out on him – it's not his fault. Rather than bottling it up and allowing it to come out in an argument, sit down with your partner and explain how you feel.

AFFECTION AND SEX

■ Your partner may be anxious about your well-being and treat you as if you are ill. This kind of attention can be suffocating, so tell your partner if you don't like it. Also, remind him that you are as anxious as he is not to do anything to endanger the baby. Equally, if your partner is not giving you enough attention, tell him when you need a hug.

■ Your desire to have sex may change at different stages of your pregnancy. If you do not feel like intercourse, tell your partner.

ONE OF THE MOST EXCITING MOMENTS of your life will probably be when you find out that you are going to be a father. The emotional impact for you will be just as real as it is for your partner, but it's often underestimated and you are likely to find that once the initial excitement has worn off, people stop asking you how *you* are feeling. It is, however, important to talk about your emotions, even if it is only to your partner, and to get involved in the pregnancy and birth plans. Make it as big a part of your life as you can – it is, after all, something that is happening to both of you, not just your partner.

UNDERSTANDING YOUR CONFLICTING EMOTIONS

The pregnancy may not seem real for the first couple of months – not least because your partner will physically look the same. Don't worry if you feel differently from her about the pregnancy; it is an internal experience for her and an external one for you, and you don't suddenly become one person with one set of feelings just because you are having a baby together. However, once you see that your partner's body has begun to change and, later, when you have felt the baby move, the idea of having a baby will become more real. It is at this time that your feelings of joy and excitement may be replaced by fears and worries; whatever your family set-up, it is normal for a man to begin to worry about being able to provide for his family. Having a child can be an extra financial burden, especially if your partner is going to give up her job, but try not to make life-changing decisions, such as getting a new job or seeking promotion. It's difficult to know whether you'll want extra responsibility a year down the line, once you are a parent. Remember that, as a father, you have more than just material possessions to offer your child.

HOW YOU CAN PARTICIPATE

Being an expectant father is the one time in your life when you are quite likely to feel out of control. This feeling of being an outsider will not be helped by the way other people treat you: well-meaning female friends and relatives may unconsciously push you out of what they see as their territory. You may also find that the professionals, such as obstetricians and midwives, direct their conversations at your partner more than you.

TAKE THE INITIATIVE

Don't step back and allow your female relatives and friends to be more involved than you. Tell your own friends and colleagues: you may be subject to a certain amount of teasing but, equally, people may view you as more responsible and mature. Try to find out as much as you can about the pregnancy so that you can understand the changes taking place in your partner's body. If possible, go with her to the scans so that you can see your baby developing, talk about the fact you are going to be a father, and ask as many questions as you want – most of all, enjoy it!

24

TAKING AN ACTIVE ROLE

WHAT TO DO	HOW IT CAN HELP YOU
TALK TO YOUR PARTNER	The best way to understand how your partner is feeling, and what is going on in her body, is to talk to her. Ask her what it feels like when the baby moves; discuss your plans for the birth together; find out if she has particular discomforts. She'll appreciate your interest.
GO TO PRENATAL CLASSES	If you go to prenatal classes (especially father-only sessions), you will have an opportunity to learn about the birth and talk through your own concerns. This will help you to work out the best way to support your partner and enable you to be more involved in birth choices.
TALK TO OTHER FATHERS	Get to know the other expectant fathers at prenatal classes – they will probably be feeling the same as you and be glad to have someone to talk to. Talk to friends and colleagues who have babies; find out what their experience was like and ask their advice.
READ ABOUT PREGNANCY AND PARENTING	Read pregnancy and parenting books and any leaflets you are given. The more you understand about what's going on during the pregnancy, the more familiar it will become and it can help you to understand how your partner is feeling. It will also enable you to ask the right questions.
ASK QUESTIONS	Go to prenatal appointments with your partner so that you can meet the professionals and be present at the examinations. As a first-time parent, there will be things you don't understand and need to know about. If you ask questions of professionals, they are more likely to involve you.

PLAN FOR THE BIRTH TOGETHER

You will need to discuss with your partner the type of birth she wants (see p. 26) and decide what your involvement will be. You will also need to talk to your employer about taking time off to go to the prenatal appointments as well as the birth, and to enable you to spend some time at home after the baby is born.

THE BIRTH PLAN

Discuss the issues raised by the birth plan (see p. 27) with your partner, but don't impose your views. If your partner feels strongly about certain issues, for example, she wants to try for a drugfree labor (see p. 41), try to respect her feelings, but insist on discussing the advantages and disadvantages. Look forward to being present at the birth. Remember, witnessing the birth of your child is probably one of the most precious things you will ever experience and holding your baby in the first few seconds of life is proven to help with future bonding between father and child.

PRENATAL BONDING

You can never start bonding with your baby too early. Babies can hear sounds outside the womb by five or six months; if you talk to your baby, he will bond to your voice while he is still in the womb and, in fact, he can hear your low-pitched voice more clearly than his mother's. Don't feel awkward – think about the life you've created and love it. To help you to bond with your baby:

■ Gently massage your partner's tummy and feel your baby move.

■ Talk and coo softly to your baby, and kiss and nuzzle him through your partner's skin.

■ Use the inner tube of toilet-paper rolls to listen to the heartbeat.

■ Go to scans with your partner to see your baby develop (see p. 29).

25

BEING INVOLVED

It's your baby too. You have every right to be involved in all aspects of the pregnancy and to:

■ Be open about your feelings.

■ Express your concerns without fear of misinterpretation.

■ Talk candidly to your partner about sex so that it does not become an issue.

■ Be party to all arrangements and plans for the birth.

■ Go to prenatal classes.

■ Go to prenatal appointments so that you can hear your baby's heartbeat and see him move on the ultrasound monitor.

■ Visit the hospital and delivery room with your partner.

■ Contribute to the birth plan.

■ Meet any professionals involved.

■ Be present at the birth.

PRENATAL CLASSES

It's immensely helpful and supportive for you both to attend a series of prenatal classes.

WHAT CLASSES DO
They will help explain a lot of the choices available before, during, and after the birth of your baby. In addition to telling you about labor, birth, and baby care, you'll meet other expectant parents with due dates near yours, with whom you can share experiences.

WHERE TO FIND CLASSES
If you're planning a hospital delivery, hospital-based classes can be useful because they'll help familiarize you with procedures and will include a tour of the labor ward. Community classes may be run by midwives, providing "shared" care (see right) in your local health or community center or at your doctor's office. Parent education networks or active birth groups (see p. 163) are usually run in the teachers' own homes and are much more likely to focus on natural childbirth and alternative birth options than classes that are run by hospitals or midwives.

PREPARATION FOR BIRTH
Prenatal classes give you a chance to learn techniques to prepare you for labor and birth well in advance.

Your partner can practice different techniques for relieving pain

Lean on a pillow over a chair-back

Experiment at classes with different labor positions

OPTIONS FOR PRENATAL CARE

Nowadays, choice is the watchword of maternity care, although how wide the choice is will depend on what's available in your area. Looking at your prenatal options also involves looking ahead to your birth options. Although the majority of births do take place in hospital, this needn't automatically mean a high-tech managed labor.

WHO CAN DELIVER CARE?

Once you know you're pregnant, your first call will probably be to your family doctor. He or she may confirm the pregnancy with another test, take your blood pressure, and ask you when your last period was, to work out the due date. Your doctor will tell you the different options for prenatal care available in your area and you can also talk through where the baby will be born since these are often linked. Don't feel you have to make your mind up on any of these issues immediately: go away and think about the possibilities before finalizing the details.

Shared care Prenatal care may be offered by your family doctor, in association with midwives and the hospital. Routine checks will be done by your doctor and the midwife, and you'll go to the hospital for special tests such as ultrasound. This type of care is helpful if you live some distance from the hospital. However, you may not have met the midwife who delivers your baby in the hospital before the event.

Midwife care In some places, prenatal care is given almost entirely by midwives working in teams, or with a hospital (see opposite). They are based either at a local health center or hospital and can also arrange home births. You'll be able to build up a relationship with the midwives who will also deliver your baby.

Independent midwives If you want to be cared for solely by midwives, you might want to consider hiring an independent one. Although this option is expensive, it does enable you to arrange your care, labor, and birth exactly as you want it.

Hospital care In some areas this may still be the only option. You'll receive your care from hospital-based doctors and midwives. It will be competent, but may lack the informality of other options. However, if you have any complications, have an existing medical condition, or are having twins, it's probably the wisest option.

WHERE TO HAVE YOUR BABY?

Thinking about prenatal care also involves deciding where you want your baby to be delivered. Whatever type of prenatal care you're having, you'll be booked into the hospital at the first appointment (see overleaf). If you want to have a home birth, it may need a certain amount of negotiation with your doctor or midwives. Either way, you need to look at the options side by side with those for prenatal care.

HOSPITAL BIRTH

Having a first baby in the hospital feels right to many couples, and is usually the recommendation of the medical profession. There's plenty of backup on hand if things aren't straightforward, and in most hospitals there's access to the full range of pain relief.

Advantages Having your baby in the hospital doesn't necessarily mean opting for high-tech: many hospitals have special low-tech birthing rooms where you'll be free to walk around during labor and where intervention will be kept to a minimum. Many hospitals have pools for pain relief (see p. 41), although it's difficult to make sure you'll get to use one since it is not usually possible to prebook them. In some areas, a midwife comes to your home once you're in labor, accompanies you to the hospital, delivers your baby, and then returns with you to your home as little as four hours later. If you like the idea of being back at home with your family as soon as possible after delivery, but want the medical backup for the delivery itself, this option could be ideal for you.

Disadvantages It's important to realize that having a baby in the hospital does mean agreeing to childbirth policies that may cramp your style. You will, for example, be required to have your baby's heartbeat electronically monitored, at least for a time, which may make it difficult for you to remain active and upright throughout, if that's what you'd hoped for.

HOME BIRTH

Although numbers are rising, only a tiny percentage of births happen in the home, and much depends on the attitude of your own doctor and midwives. Despite evidence showing that a planned home birth is as safe as a hospital birth, some doctors are reluctant to cooperate and you may have to seek out an independent midwife to help you achieve it (see opposite).

Advantages Home is a more relaxed place to have a baby than the hospital. You're far less likely to need emergency treatment if you remain active as far into labor as you can. Your chances for a straightforward, problem-free delivery at home are good, even if this is your first child.

Disadvantages You don't have immediate access to emergency treatment, so if anything unusual happens or your labor fails to progress, you might need to be transferred to the hospital. You also won't have access to pain relief such as an epidural and, in some countries, pethidine (see p. 41).

DELIVERY IN A BIRTH CENTER

Birth centers are usually located near hospitals, but are completely self-contained and designed to have a less medical feel. They may be staffed by family doctors and midwives or run solely by midwives. Staff often don't wear uniforms, and you'll probably be given your own room in which to spend your labor, give birth, and then remain after the delivery. These centers can provide an excellent intermediate approach, giving you the informality of a home birth with the safety net of high-tech care nearby.

YOUR BIRTH PLAN

Once you've considered all your prenatal care and birth options, and have some clear ideas of what you would like to happen during your labor and birth, it's worth preparing a simple birth plan in consultation with your doctor and midwife. This should be kept with your hospital notes. It's probably best to wait until you're about 32–36 weeks pregnant before discussing the details; by that time you'll probably have discovered whether there are any special factors associated with your pregnancy that might make some of your requests difficult to achieve. You also need to be prepared to be flexible because things may not go according to plan on the day. Your birth plan might include the following:

■ Who you want to be present at the birth with you.

■ Your views on interventions such as induction, the artificial speeding up of labor (see p. 48), and fetal monitoring (see p. 42).

■ Your views on active labor, and whether you would like the possibility of using a birthing pool to help cope with labor (see p. 41).

■ Your preferences for pain relief (see p. 41), and the use of breathing and relaxation techniques you've been practicing during your pregnancy.

■ Whether you mind student doctors or midwives being present during your labor and birth, if it is a teaching hospital.

■ What position you might adopt to deliver your baby (see p. 44).

■ Whether you would prefer not to have an episiotomy (see p. 45) if the delivery is normal.

■ Whether you mind if the delivery of your placenta is speeded up with a hormonal injection or whether you'd prefer it to be delivered naturally (see p. 46).

YOUR PRENATAL CARE

THE PHYSICAL EXAMINATION

At every prenatal appointment, various checks will always be done to rule out potentially dangerous medical conditions.

BLOOD PRESSURE
A rise in blood pressure could mean you're at risk of preeclampsia, a potentially serious circulatory disorder (see p. 32).

URINE TEST
A urine sample will be tested for the presence of protein, which could mean an infection or, later in pregnancy, preeclampsia; glucose or sugar, which could signal diabetes; and ketones, chemicals which indicate you're not eating enough.

ABDOMINAL CHECK
The midwife will feel your abdomen to check the size of your uterus. She'll also listen to your baby's heartbeat, using either a Pinard stethoscope or a sonicaid, an electronic stethoscope that amplifies the baby's heartbeat so you can hear it (see below).

YOUR BABY'S HEARTBEAT
It's a thrill the first time you hear your baby's heartbeat amplified through a sonicaid.

The midwife locates the heartbeat with an external probe

WHICHEVER KIND OF PRENATAL CARE you choose, there will be certain procedures that any midwife or doctor will follow throughout your pregnancy when caring for you. In general, prenatal checks are done to make sure that all is going well with your pregnancy – that you are healthy, and that your baby is growing properly.

YOUR FIRST APPOINTMENT

Often known as the registration appointment, your first prenatal session may be quite long, lasting as much as an hour. It may be at your home, at the local health center or doctor's office, or at a hospital clinic. A midwife will take a detailed medical history, and will ask a long list of questions about your general health, your family's health, and your gynecological and obstetric history. She will also ask whether or not this baby was planned, how long ago you stopped using contraceptives or what contraceptive you were using when you got pregnant, and the date of the first day of your last menstrual period. The midwife will also talk to you generally about how your pregnancy is going and ask you how you are feeling. She'll offer you advice – often backed up by booklets you can take away to digest at home – on issues like diet, exercise, and maternity benefits. You will also be able to discuss your thoughts on what kind of delivery you'd like, although it's still early days and nothing will have to be decided at this time unless you're absolutely sure (see previous page). You'll probably be asked to bring a urine sample to each appointment.

THE BLOOD TEST
You'll probably have some blood taken, which will be sent to the laboratory for analysis. Ask the midwife exactly what your blood will be checked for and why; it's routinely checked for iron content, blood group and rhesus factor, rubella immunity, blood sugar levels, and sexually transmitted diseases. Other tests, such as one to check whether you've been exposed to toxoplasmosis (a parasitic disease that may affect your unborn baby), may also be available. Blood isn't usually tested at every appointment, but in certain situations you will be asked to give blood again at later appointments (see opposite), and many hospitals test routinely at 28 and 36 weeks.

FUTURE APPOINTMENTS

Your routine prenatal check-ups will generally be shorter than your registration appointment, but if you're attending them at a hospital clinic you may need to set aside a couple of hours each time because lines can easily build up if another appointment overruns. Between appointments, it's a good idea to write down any questions you may have as you think of them, and keep them with your other records; otherwise you're likely to forget them. You'll be given a schedule of appointments, but you can always ask for an additional appointment if you have any worries.

ULTRASOUND SCANS

Ultrasound is now offered routinely to almost all pregnant women because it enables the baby's gestational age to be measured very accurately and can also detect visible abnormalities. Many hospitals offer two scans, one at about 12 weeks and the other at 16 to 20 weeks. The scans are carried out at the hospital, and your partner should be allowed into the examination room with you; this is a wonderful opportunity for a father to relate to his growing baby since you'll be able to see it moving about. The operator slowly scans across your abdomen with a hand-held instrument called a transducer that detects sound waves bounced off your uterus and baby's body. These are transmitted to a computerized monitor for visual interpretation. After the scan you may be offered a picture – your first photo of your baby!

HAVING AN ULTRASOUND SCAN

As you lie comfortably on a bed, gel is spread over your abdomen. The transducer is passed gently back and forth across the abdomen and the image transmitted to a nearby visual monitor.

Image of the baby shows on a screen from which measurements can be taken

Gel helps the transducer to pass smoothly across the abdomen

29

THINKING AHEAD

If you are offered any of the tests for abnormalities (see chart below), you are likely to have mixed feelings about them. Although it may seem very difficult, you really should ask yourselves the question: what would we do if we found our baby did have Down syndrome or spina bifida? If the answer is that you wouldn't do anything, but continue with the pregnancy, it may not be worth having the tests. If you know you would have a termination, or think you wouldn't be able to make up your mind until you had the information, then you may want to go ahead. Before any test, find out:

■ Exactly what your baby is being tested for.

■ Whether the test involves risk.

■ How accurate it is.

■ What information the test will actually provide.

■ Whether there's an alternative.

SPECIALIST SCREENING AND DIAGNOSTIC TESTS

TEST	HOW IT IS DONE	WHAT IT CAN TELL YOU
NUCHAL SCAN	A fairly new noninvasive screening scan done at 11–13 weeks, measuring the thickness of the "nuchal pad" in the baby's neck.	A thick nuchal pad may mean a higher risk of chromosomal defects, so you'll be offered a test such as amniocentesis later.
TRIPLE (OR BART'S) TEST	This blood test (noninvasive to the baby) screens you for the risk of Down syndrome. It is done at 15–16 weeks along with a scan.	Hormone levels indicate the risk of your baby being affected; if it is greater than 1 in 250, you'll be offered a diagnostic test.
AFP TEST	A screening blood test that checks the level of alpha-fetoprotein (AFP) at about 15–18 weeks.	A higher or lower level than usual may indicate Down syndrome or spina bifida.
CHORIONIC VILLUS SAMPLING	A diagnostic test, in which a cannula (tube) is passed through the cervix at about 10–12 weeks to take cells from the developing placenta.	The cells are examined to check the baby's chromosomes for any abnormalities. This technique carries a small risk of miscarriage.
AMNIOCENTESIS	A diagnostic test done at about 15 weeks. Guided by ultrasound, a needle takes a sample of amniotic fluid through the abdominal wall.	Chromosomes in fetal cells can be checked for abnormalities such as Down syndrome. There's a small risk (1 in 200) of miscarriage.
FETAL BLOOD TEST (CORDOCENTESIS)	This rare diagnostic test is carried out after about 18–20 weeks. It takes blood from the umbilical cord.	Blood is tested for abnormal chromosomes or infections. There's a miscarriage risk of about 1–2 per cent.

MOTHER

The knowledge that your baby is growing inside you is really exciting, so don't let minor complaints get you down.

COPING WITH COMMON COMPLAINTS

■ Feeling nauseous is most common in the first three months. It may happen in the morning, but by no means always, and you may also vomit. Eating little and often rather than big meals helps. Avoid foods that make you feel nauseous. If you're vomiting incessantly, consult your doctor.

■ You're more likely to get cramps in your legs or feet. It's not known exactly why, but you can relieve it by pulling your toes up hard toward your ankles.

■ Constipation is a common problem, caused by the presence of hormones that slow down the workings of the large intestine. Make sure you eat plenty of fiber, exercise regularly, and drink plenty of water. Iron pills may make it worse.

■ Later in pregnancy, you may suffer from indigestion or heartburn because your enlarging womb is pressing on your stomach. You can prevent this by eating smaller meals more often, sitting up straight when eating, and avoiding spicy foods. Sipping milk, especially at night, can help if you have heartburn.

■ Hemorrhoids – swollen varicose veins that protrude from the rectum – occur during pregnancy due to pressure from the baby, especially if you're constipated and strain to open your bowels. Eat plenty of fiber and avoid standing for long periods. Apply an ice pack or cold wet washcloth to ease discomfort. Consult your doctor if they become very painful or prolapse.

THE PROGRESS OF PREGNANCY

H AVING A BABY GROWING INSIDE YOU is like being part of a real-life miracle. Sometimes you'll pat your bump and feel you can hardly believe your child is in there – it seems so amazing and extraordinary. Take time to ponder on the wonder of what's happening; you'll both be laying the foundations for a baby who feels secure and wanted.

FOLLOWING YOUR PREGNANCY

No part of a woman's body escapes when she's carrying a baby, and you both need to keep that in mind. For instance, tender breasts that are getting ready for breast-feeding need to be treated gently by a father when he caresses them; the growing uterus pressing on your internal organs, so you must never be too far from a toilet during the last three months of pregnancy. The guide that follows is only a brief outline of the complex changes going on inside your body.

WHAT'S HAPPENED BY THREE MONTHS

The first three months of pregnancy (the first trimester) are tremendously important in laying the foundations of your baby's healthy development, although there are few visible signs of your baby's phenomenal growth.

YOU
● You'll start to gain weight; any morning sickness will soon disappear.
● The uterus is rising out of the pelvis and can be felt.
● The risk of miscarriage is almost zero now.
● Your heart is working flat out and will continue to do so right up to labor.

YOUR BABY
● She has a fully formed body, complete with fingers, toes, and ears.
● Her eyes move, although her eyelids are closed.
● Her body is covered with fine hair.
● She wriggles if poked – her muscles are growing.

WHAT'S HAPPENED BY SIX MONTHS

The period from about the third to the sixth month (the second trimester) is when pregnancy sickness ends, your baby really grows, and you begin to feel her move. You're brimming with energy, vitality, and well-being.

YOU
● You're putting on about 12oz (0.5kg) weight per week.
● Your uterus is a good 2in (5cm) above the pelvis.
● You may have bouts of indigestion.
● From about 16 weeks, you'll feel the baby move.

YOUR BABY

- Her hearing is acute, she can recognize your voice.
- She's becoming better proportioned – her body is catching up on her head.
- She's well muscled but thin.
- Her lungs are maturing fast.

WHAT'S HAPPENED BY NINE MONTHS (FULL TERM)

The final 12 weeks or so of pregnancy, known as the third trimester, are when the baby puts on fat in preparation for birth and the brain and lungs mature in preparation for independent life.

YOU

- You may feel a "lightening" as your baby's head drops into the pelvis.
- It's more difficult to find a comfortable position for sleep.
- You visit the prenatal clinic every week.
- Your breasts secrete clear-colored nutritious colostrum.

YOUR BABY

- She weighs about 6–8lb (2.7–3.5kg) and she measures 14–15in (35–38cm) from crown to rump.
- Her head is "engaged," lying just on top of your cervix.
- The placenta is 8–10in (20–25cm) across and there is 2 pints (1 liter) of amniotic fluid.
- Her breasts may be swollen due to the action of your hormones.

PREGNANCY AT A GLANCE

It's useful to be able to visualize what is happening by the end of each of the three phases, or trimesters, of pregnancy, so that you understand why certain complaints may occur (see opposite).

FATHER

Although you're experiencing the pregnancy secondhand, following its progress helps you to become emotionally attached to your unborn baby.

THE PROGRESS OF PREGNANCY

- Accompanying your partner to prenatal appointments (see p. 28) lets you find out together how your baby is growing.

- Remember that the baby is part of you as well as your partner. It's amazing to think that a single cell created from your sperm and your partner's ovum (see p. 20) can develop so rapidly.

- Understanding and learning about the impact of the growing baby and uterus on your partner's body helps you be sympathetic when she suffers the inevitable discomforts caused by the pregnancy (see box opposite).

31

AT THREE MONTHS
Your uterus is about the size of a grapefruit and can just be felt above the pubic bone. All your baby's organs are formed and virtually impervious to the potential dangers, such as an infection and medication.

The fetus is recognizably human and all her internal systems are in place

AT SIX MONTHS
Your baby's organs are fully formed, her face is that of a newborn, and she sucks her thumb. Your uterus is poised for labor. You may notice Braxton-Hicks contractions (see p. 40).

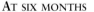

Hearing is developed; she may respond to noise. Skin is red and thin, with little fat beneath it

Below: Size of the baby's hand in relation to your hand at six months.

AT NINE MONTHS (FULL-TERM)
You'll find you get breathless because your baby is now so big. Her eyes are open and she's fat and healthy. If your baby is a boy, his testes have descended.

By full term, the baby is usually positioned head downward

Below: Size of the baby's hand in relation to your hand at full-term.

"SMALL FOR DATES"

After reviewing the date of your last period and your expected date of delivery, both your heights, and scans of the baby, your pregnancy may be pronounced "small for dates." This is no cause for alarm, but for reassurance doctors will keep an eye on you by:

■ Giving you weekly ultrasound scans for a while to ensure all's well and to check the placenta.

■ Checking on the baby's heart rate for any sign of strain.

■ Discussing with you the possibility of delivering your baby by cesarean section (see p. 50), to prevent the baby having to go through a vaginal delivery.

PREECLAMPSIA

Preeclampsia is a potentially serious condition that can affect as many as one in ten women, especially first-time mothers and women carrying more than one baby. It's unique to pregnancy, starting at any time in the second half. It's not known precisely what causes it, but it does tend to run in families.

HOW IT AFFECTS YOU

Preeclampsia is symptomless, but raised blood pressure and protein in the urine detected at a prenatal visit may alert staff to its presence. It arises in the placenta, so the baby may grow more slowly than normal. The pregnancy can't be restored to normal, but delivery of the baby and placenta ends the disease. Admission to the hospital allows close monitoring of mother and baby so that delivery can be arranged before serious complications arise. For almost every mother, delivery of her baby reverses all the effects.

DIFFICULT PREGNANCIES

ALTHOUGH THE MAJORITY OF PREGNANCIES proceed without incident, occasionally things don't go according to plan. When something unexpected happens or there's cause for concern at your prenatal checkup, you're both going to feel extremely concerned about it, especially if all has gone well up to this point. Until now you may have been confident, perhaps had even taken it for granted, that all would be problem-free. Now, suddenly, the pregnancy seems to be in question, and you may feel apprehensive and confused. It helps enormously to face what's ahead together and to get as much information as you can.

CAUSES FOR CONCERN

Some worrying development, like vaginal bleeding, may strike out of the blue; a "small for dates" baby (see above left) or high blood pressure (preeclampsia – see below left) may be diagnosed at routine prenatal tests. Whatever the concern, get a full explanation from your doctor or consultant; it may be necessary for both of you to insist on this to get the answers you need.

VAGINAL BLEEDING

PLACENTA PREVIA
The placenta embeds close to or across the cervix, where pressure from the baby may cause vaginal bleeding.

Never ignore vaginal bleeding at any stage of your pregnancy. Although it's always worrying, close medical supervision can help avoid serious problems.

Bleeding in the first three months Bleeding in early pregnancy doesn't mean you'll lose your baby. You may not yet have high enough hormone levels to subdue your periods. You may have a condition like cervical erosion or polyps, neither of which are likely to interfere with your pregnancy. Contact your doctor or hospital as soon as possible so you can be referred for a scan; if the heart is beating well, bleeding will probably stop and pregnancy continue normally. You'll need to rest and forego sex for a while.

Bleeding in later pregnancy It's rare to bleed late in pregnancy, but it's serious since it may indicate problems with the placenta such as placenta previa or approaching abruptio placentae. In placenta previa, the placenta is positioned in the lower part of the womb, possibly across the cervix (see left). The placenta starts to separate prematurely from the uterine wall in abruptio placentae. Both conditions can be confirmed by ultrasound scanning, and hospital admission for observation and subsequent cesarean delivery (see p. 50) will be necessary.

PREGNANCY AND PREEXISTING MEDICAL CONDITIONS

If you have any existing medical condition, your pregnancy will be carefully monitored to safeguard you and your baby. Medical conditions like asthma, epilepsy, heart disease, or kidney disease don't in themselves make pregnancy and labor difficult. If you take care of yourself, have meticulous prenatal supervision, and prepare yourself for inpatient hospital care in the last ten weeks of pregnancy, the chances are you'll have a normal birth.

DIABETES

Sugar – a sign, but not proof, of diabetes – may appear in your urine at any time in pregnancy. The most common reason for this is a change in the way the kidney handles sugar in pregnancy: no treatment is needed. "Latent" diabetes can do the same thing and can be controlled with diet alone, although you'll be checked more frequently at the prenatal clinic. Preexisting diabetes requires strict supervision because your insulin needs may change and your dose will be adjusted. Babies of diabetic mothers tend to be large so you may be induced early or your baby may be delivered by cesarean section (see p. 50).

MULTIPLE PREGNANCY

You will undoubtedly receive more professional attention and more prenatal appointments during your pregnancy if you are carrying more than one baby. The diagnosis of twins, triplets, or more will be confirmed with an ultrasound scan, and the news may take getting used to, but there's a lot of help and support for you both.

If both twins are head down, it's more likely that both will be delivered vaginally

If one twin is breech, a cesarean is more likely

HOW TWINS LIE
Twins normally lie both head down, or one head down and one breech. How they lie may affect the way your delivery is managed (see p. 49).

HOW YOU MAY FEEL

Nausea Multiple pregnancies often cause severe nausea, even vomiting, in the first three months. Eat little and often, and drink plenty of fluids – drinks containing glucose or glucose tablets may boost energy levels if you feel too nauseous to get calories from food.

Increasing size You get bigger faster than a mother with one baby because, as well as carrying two babies, you produce more amniotic fluid.

Backache Be careful about posture and avoid carrying or lifting heavy weights, because the additional levels of pregnancy hormones make your pelvic ligaments more liable to soften and stretch, and become painful.

Fatigue You'll tire very easily, and this may be made worse by anemia. Rest, eat meat, and take folic acid and iron supplements.

Indigestion This may be worse than in a single pregnancy (see p. 30) because your stomach is squashed against your diaphragm. Have nourishing drinks and soups and eat frequent small meals.

LOSING YOUR BABY

No one can imagine the grief of a couple losing a longed-for baby. For your own sakes, seek counseling so that you can grieve fully and finally come to terms with your loss.

EARLY MISCARRIAGE

A miscarriage in the first few weeks is more common than you might think – in fact one in three of first pregnancies. It usually happens because there was something amiss with the fetus or perhaps it had not implanted correctly. Early miscarriage may not be accompanied by much pain, although you may suffer severe period-like cramps. However, you're both going to feel really let down, and a woman has to deal with sudden hormonal changes that can make her very emotional.

LATE MISCARRIAGE

This occurs between 13 and 24 weeks, usually because of placental problems or a weakened cervix that opens due to the weight of the growing fetus. You have a minilabor to expel the fetus with whatever pain relief you choose.

STILLBIRTH

Losing your baby at or close to full term is very hard to bear, but today you'll be given a chance to hold your baby if you want to, to name him, and to give him a proper funeral.

DEALING WITH YOUR LOSS

Whatever the reason for your loss, your distress needs careful handling: it's a bereavement that may be complicated by feelings of guilt and blame, which could trigger depression or drive a wedge between you as a couple. Discuss your feelings with each other and your doctor; ask her to explain the reasons for your loss, but accept that no one may know exactly why your baby died. Above all, look forward to the future; most couples who have lost a baby go on to become proud parents of healthy babies.

33

BALANCING YOUR DIET

To provide for your baby's needs as well as your own, note the following tips about your diet:

■ Complex carbohydrates such as pasta, potatoes, or pulses (beans and lentils) are needed for energy.

■ Protein is needed for your baby's growth. Eat fish and poultry, dairy produce, wholegrain cereals, seeds, and pulses.

■ Don't cut out fats altogether, but don't eat too much either. You'll get enough from dairy products and normal cooking methods.

■ Get vitamin C daily from raw fresh fruit and vegetables, and the B complex from wholegrains, nuts and pulses, green vegetables, dairy products, eggs, oily fish, and meat.

■ Iron maintains red blood cells; it's found in red meat, fish, egg yolks, apricots, and cereals.

FOOD SAFETY

Scrupulous kitchen hygiene (see p. 97) is essential because some infections transmitted in food are hazardous during pregnancy:

■ Listeria is a rare bacterium found in products made with unpasteurized milk, liver, undercooked meat, and precooked meals. Avoid these products since infection during pregnancy may result in miscarriage or stillbirth.

■ Salmonella is a bacterial infection found in eggs and chicken that causes fever, abdominal pain, and severe diarrhea. It's destroyed by thorough cooking.

■ Toxoplasmosis is caused by a parasite in cat and dog feces, and also in raw meat. It can cause birth defects. Cook meat thoroughly, wash your hands after handling pets, and wear gloves if gardening.

TAKING CARE OF YOURSELF

PREGNANCY IS NOT A DISEASE, it's a natural part of life and women's bodies are designed to accommodate it. But your body does have to work hard to provide for your growing baby, so it's important to pay attention to nutrition and exercises that help you build stamina, maintain your energy levels, and minimize discomfort.

WEIGHT AND DIET

Your body uses up a lot of energy during pregnancy and you need to eat well to fuel your requirements and those of your growing baby. You could reasonably increase your intake of food by 200–300 calories a day and expect to put on 20–30lbs (9–15kg) in weight, much of which is accounted for by the baby, uterus, and amniotic fluid. Pregnancy is not a time to go on a diet, but you should also forget the myth about "eating for two"; the rule is to eat to satisfy your hunger, and no more. Later in pregnancy you may find you simply can't take in much food at any one time, so eat little and often. Keep healthy snacks such as dried and fresh fruit, rice cakes, and crispbreads in your bag, car, or office, and low-fat cheese and yogurt, raw vegetables, fresh fruit, and unsweetened fruit juice in the refrigerator at home.

BODY MAINTENANCE

The pregnancy hormones have profound effects on teeth, hair, nails, and skin, so don't be surprised by some temporary changes.

Teeth Progesterone makes the gums soft so they may bleed more easily. Take care of your teeth and gums, and visit your dentist at the beginning of your pregnancy. Make sure you tell him you are pregnant in case he wants to take X rays, since these are dangerous to a developing embryo.

Hair and nails Straight hair can become curly, and vice versa. Hair grows and falls out in phases – pregnancy often prolongs the growth phase, making thin hair thick and glossy, whereas thick hair may become dry and unmanageable. The downside is that you'll experience hair loss after the birth, although it'll grow back eventually. Your nails grow faster too, but become brittle. Keep them short and use rehydrating creams to keep them moist.

Skin Estrogen gives your skin the legendary bloom of pregnancy, but dry skin becomes drier and greasy skin more oily. Patches of brown pigment (chloasma) may appear on your face and neck but will eventually fade. All skins deepen in color with browning of the nipples and a line down the abdomen. Tiny dilated capillaries (spider nevi) on the face are common but disappear later. Stretch marks on the breasts, thighs, and abdomen are very common; they're related to the breakdown of protein in the skin by the high levels of pregnancy hormones. Because of this, rubbing in oils and creams doesn't help, but most marks will fade after the birth.

DEALING WITH FATIGUE

Fatigue is a periodic problem during pregnancy, especially during the first three months and the last six to eight weeks. Its extent may take you by surprise, especially during the first few weeks – it's the kind of tiredness where you feel you don't even have the energy to blink, but just stare straight ahead. You're sleepy in the early stages of pregnancy because you're sedated by the high levels of progesterone. Your metabolism speeds up to deal with the demands of your baby and the extra work all your organs are called on to do. Later on in pregnancy you're tired because your whole body is working 24 hours a day, and you're having to carry extra weight around that puts a strain on your heart, lungs, and muscles.

WAYS OF COPING

- Never stand when you can sit, never sit when you can lie.
- If possible, put your feet up whenever you sit – if you're in the office, invert a wastebasket or box under the desk.
- Sleep anywhere; put your head down on your desk during the lunchbreak; close your eyes on the bus or train home after work.
- When you're at home, plan specific rest times and let nothing interfere with them; some people like to lie down after lunch, others find they need to rest in the late afternoon or early evening.
- Sleep as late as you like on weekends.
- Go to bed early at least three times a week.
- Find ways to help you drop off, such as watching TV or reading.
- Lie down and listen to music – not too loud since the baby can hear it.
- Find different comfortable resting positions for instant relief of tiredness. Try lying on the floor on cushions with your feet on a bed, sofa, or chair and your knees at right angles, or take the first-aid recovery position with cushions under your knees and upper body (see below).

Relaxation Use whatever technique you can to relax – you're going to need at least 30 minutes a day from now on and it will be so refreshing if you teach yourself to let go in seconds. You'll probably be taught relaxation techniques at your prenatal classes (see p. 26), and there are plenty of books and tapes to guide you. Practice with your partner, if possible; it will be good for both of you and learning to relax is an essential part of most of the techniques used for the natural control of pain during labor (see p. 43).

POSITION FOR RELAXATION
This position takes the weight off your back and allows free blood circulation, increasing the supply of oxygen to your baby.

Support your head with pillows

Pillows between the legs support the upper knee

35

ON YOUR OWN

If you decided at the outset that you wanted to have a baby but not a continuing relationship with the baby's father, fair enough. However, most women facing pregnancy and parenthood on their own did not make that choice voluntarily and, if you find that this is the case, work through your feelings of disappointment and even outrage.

COPING WITH YOUR FEELINGS
At a time when women naturally expect support, comfort, and the shared pleasure of contemplating parenthood, you are experiencing the very opposite. Ideally, explore your feelings with a friend or, even better, a professional counselor, who will help you isolate each issue and deal with it.

BEING POSITIVE
Once you have embarked upon your pregnancy, you must be ruthless about avoiding those people who may not take a positive view of either you or your condition. Since you do not have the most obvious form of support, a partner, the last thing you need is negativity, no matter where it is coming from.

LOOKING AFTER YOURSELF
Try not to neglect your health; when you're on your own, it's only too easy to skip meals or opt for easy snacks because you can't be bothered to cook. Make sure you go to all your prenatal checkups. The health professionals are there to help you and if you need extra support, they will help you find it.

FEELINGS TOWARD YOUR BABY
If you are feeling hostile toward the baby's father, try not to associate this feeling with your unborn baby; it's not her fault. You've taken on a challenge, but you can give her the best start in life: by deciding to have her without the support of a partner, you have already demonstrated how committed you are to her.

KEGEL EXERCISES

The pelvic floor consists of muscles and fibrous tissue suspended like a funnel from the pelvic bones. The layers of muscle are thickest at the perineum, where there are openings for the urethra, vagina, and anus, which the pelvic floor muscles also support. If you don't know where your pelvic floor muscles are, you can locate them by stopping your flow of urine in midstream: the muscles you are using are those of your pelvic floor.

EXERCISING YOUR PELVIC FLOOR

The pelvic floor is put under strain by pregnancy, when certain hormones cause it to soften and relax. You can keep it toned by doing the following simple Kegel exercise routine daily:

■ Pull in your pelvic floor muscles, then let them go quickly; do this five times.

■ Pull the muscles in and hold for a count of five, then let them go slowly; repeat this five times.

■ Finally, do the first, quick exercise five more times.

Restart these exercises after your baby is born to minimize the risk of prolapse.

PRECAUTIONS

Before any exercise session, do some stretches to warm up: keep your back straight, breathe evenly, and flex your feet. Your ligaments are softened through the action of the pregnancy hormones, so take it easy and don't twist suddenly, to protect your back. Stop at once if you become breathless, dizzy, or overheated, or feel pain. Avoid dehydration by drinking plenty of water, and cool down afterward with more gentle stretches.

EXERCISE IN PREGNANCY

Both you and your baby benefit from exercise: your blood starts circulating freely, there's a blast of oxygen to your baby's brain, exercise hormones such as endorphins give you both a wonderful high, and your baby loves the swaying motion. Exercise increases your strength, suppleness, and stamina, which will make pregnancy easier and equip you for the rigors of labor. But exercise in pregnancy is not just about fitness. It helps you understand your body, to believe in its power, and it gives you the key to relaxation so that you can cope with fatigue and prepare yourself for the actual birth.

WHOLE-BODY EXERCISE

Try to incorporate some exercise into your day, beginning gradually at a pace that is comfortable. Always stop if you get out of breath or feel pain. Whole-body exercise is best because it tones your heart and lungs, so walking and swimming are excellent. Dancing is good as long as it's not too energetic. Yoga is ideal because it stretches tight muscles and joints and also relieves tension. Yoga methods can help with labor and pain relief too.

EXERCISE TO AVOID

Pregnancy is not a time to start learning an energetic contact sport; however, you can continue sports activities for a while if you're already fit and play often. Don't engage in sports like skiing, bicycling, or horseback riding after 20 weeks because balance may become a problem from that time. Take it easy on very energetic sports like tennis or squash and don't do heavy workouts at the gym, especially tough abdominal exercises.

PREPARING FOR LABOR

Help yourself prepare for labor and birth by introducing your body to some exercises and postures that will help when the baby is coming. You'll be taught different techniques at your prenatal classes (see p. 26), but it's a great help if both of you can learn the exercises so that your partner can help and encourage you to practice at home.

POSTURES TO PREPARE FOR BIRTH

If you're hoping to have an active birth, it's a good idea to begin learning the postures as early as possible. There are different techniques you can follow, which may be taught in locally run active birth classes. An active birth entails keeping mobile rather than being confined to the bed, and using breathing and relaxation techniques to help control the pain of labor.

Tailor sitting Sit up with your back straight (lean against a wall if necessary), with the soles of your feet together. This opens up the hip joints.

Squatting Squat down on your haunches as low as possible, supporting your back against a wall or sofa – or lean against your partner when he is sitting in a chair. Squatting stretches and relaxes the birth canal, and when it comes to the delivery you may well find that this is the position that you adopt naturally, since it will help you bear down (see p. 44).

All fours Getting down onto all fours is very helpful during pregnancy when you have a bad back, especially if you combine it with a few gentle pelvic tilts (see above left). Put a pile of cushions in front of you so you can rest on them with your head on your arms, and ask your partner to massage your back. Many women also find this a comfortable position for backache during labor, and for the actual delivery of the baby (see p. 44).

LOOKING AFTER YOUR BACK

The hormones of pregnancy soften your ligaments in preparation for the birth; the problem is that this also makes them more susceptible to strain during pregnancy, and your back is the most vulnerable.

Shoulders straight and relaxed

Buttocks tucked in keeps back straight

STANDING POSTURE

As pregnancy progresses, good posture becomes increasingly important, otherwise you'll have a tendency to bend your spine to balance the bump in front, leading to an arched back and slumped shoulders. Try to avoid this by keeping a straight back, tucking your buttocks under, and tilting your pelvis forward.

CARRYING AND LIFTING

Avoid carrying a heavy bag for long periods; this can put a strain on your shoulders and neck. If you need to lift something from floor level, always bend your knees and keep a straight back, lifting the object high against your chest. Never bend down or twist from the waist; you could damage your lower back. After lying down, always get up by pushing yourself up onto your hands first and then move into a kneeling position if you're on the floor, or swing your legs over the edge of the bed.

SITTING POSTURE

Sitting badly for long periods can be as bad for your back as poor posture when standing. If you have to sit for a long time, such as at the office, make sure you use a firm, straight-backed chair and sit well back with your feet flat on the floor or raised slightly on a footstool. Sitting badly, slumped in your chair, forces your baby up against your diaphragm and stomach, constricting your lungs and causing breathlessness and indigestion.

Shoulders are rounded

Whole back is not supported

INCORRECT SITTING POSTURE

Feet should be flat on the floor

Back is well supported

CORRECT SITTING POSTURE

FATHER

Making sure you look after your partner's well-being during pregnancy is good for your unborn baby, good for your relationship, and essential to your partner's long-term physical and emotional health. Try the suggestions below, but don't treat her like an invalid!

HOW YOU CAN HELP

■ Your partner's hair and skin will look marvelous, especially during the middle trimester, from four to seven months. Tell her how good she looks to boost her self-esteem. Toward the end of the pregnancy she may begin to get very bored and feel uncomfortable and unattractive; encourage her to go out and treat herself at this time.

■ Encourage your partner to eat and drink well. Get involved in the shopping and cooking, if you haven't done so before. The basic advice on diet (see p. 34) doesn't just apply to pregnant women – it will also do you good to adjust your diet in line with it.

■ Give your partner opportunities to rest: bring her breakfast in bed on weekends and make sure visitors aren't invited when she normally likes to rest, whether it's after lunch or early evening. Put the television in the bedroom, if there isn't one there already, so she can watch in bed.

■ Do the heavy lifting so that your partner doesn't strain her back or other muscles softened by pregnancy hormones (see left). If she does lift something, make sure she bends her legs, rather than bending from the waist. Carry the shopping and climb the ladder to paint the ceiling (yes, it's true that pregnant mothers have been known to do this during the burst of energy that often presages birth – see p. 40).

37

THE BIRTH OF YOUR FIRST BABY IS ONE OF THE MOST AMAZING MOMENTS OF YOUR WHOLE LIFE. IT'S THE SORT OF EVENT THAT PARENTS REMEMBER IN MINUTE DETAIL YEARS LATER, EVEN WHEN OTHER MEMORIES HAVE FADED. ALTHOUGH NO BIRTH EXPERIENCE IS EXACTLY LIKE ANY OTHER, YOUR FIRST IS SPECIAL SIMPLY BECAUSE YOU HAVE NEVER DONE IT BEFORE. BUT JUST BECAUSE YOU CAN'T PREDICT EXACTLY WHAT IT WILL FEEL LIKE EITHER PHYSICALLY OR EMOTIONALLY DOESN'T MEAN THAT YOU CAN'T BE PREPARED FOR MOST EVENTUALITIES. KNOWING HOW A NORMAL LABOR PROGRESSES, WHAT YOUR PAIN-RELIEF OPTIONS ARE, AND WHAT CAN BE DONE IF THINGS DON'T GO ACCORDING TO PLAN, ALLOWS YOU TO APPROACH LABOR AND BIRTH POSITIVELY. THE IMPORTANCE OF HOW YOU EXPERIENCE THE BIRTH AND THE FIRST FEW PRECIOUS MOMENTS YOU SPEND TOGETHER WITH YOUR BABY CANNOT BE OVERESTIMATED. AT THIS TIME, THE BONDS OF INTERDEPENDENCE AND LOVE BEGIN TO FORM AND TIE YOU TOGETHER AS A FAMILY. DON'T BE PERTURBED IF IT DOESN'T HAPPEN IMMEDIATELY, HOWEVER, AND REST ASSURED THAT THE BONDS WILL STRENGTHEN GRADUALLY AS YOUR BODY RECOVERS AND YOUR CONFIDENCE BUILDS DURING THE FIRST FEW DAYS AFTER THE BIRTH.

YOUR NEW BABY, YOUR NEW LIFE

COUNTDOWN TO BIRTH

Y OU'VE REACHED THE 38TH WEEK of pregnancy and your due date is fast approaching; if you're the expectant mother, the days may seem to drag by, and you probably feel uncomfortably large and cumbersome. If you're the expectant father, you'll be on edge every time the telephone rings because it could be the call you've been waiting for.

GETTING READY

Although pregnancy is said to last 40 weeks, this is only a convenient method of calculation – it's quite normal for a baby to be born at any time between 38 and 42 weeks. If your baby hasn't been born by the official due date, don't worry. Most doctors aren't in a hurry to induce a baby if the mother is healthy and there are no obvious problems such as raised blood pressure. This is the time for the father to take the initiative in organizing outings and visits for his partner; keeping active occupies her mind and is much better for the whole family – and the baby – instead of hanging around the house feeling apprehensive.

PACKING YOUR HOSPITAL BAG

It's a good idea to have everything ready for the baby's arrival and your bag packed for the hospital a few weeks before the due date, so that you are prepared for any eventuality. Check with your midwife what the hospital supplies for you in the way of toiletries and other items, such as sanitary pads, and diapers, bedding, and clothes for your baby. Your tour of the delivery ward (see p. 26) will help you decide what bulkier items you might need, such as extra pillows or cushions.

GETTING NEAR LABOR

In the few days before labor begins properly, you may notice some signs that indicate you haven't got much longer to wait.

Feeling premenstrual You may experience similar feelings to those before your period, such as a low, nagging backache.

Braxton-Hicks You may become more aware of the painless tightenings of the uterine wall. These are Braxton-Hicks contractions, which can begin at around six months, and occur on and off during the last few weeks.

Mild diarrhea You may have looser bowel movements because your system is affected by the increasing uterine activity.

Abdominal lightening There may be an easing of discomfort under your ribs – a feeling of lightening – as your baby's head engages in your pelvis. This may happen a week or two before the birth with a first baby, but just as often it does not happen until labor.

Burst of energy Many women experience a sudden burst of energy even if they have been very tired and sluggish for several weeks previously. You may find you want to rush around making sure everything is ready for your baby's homecoming; this is known as the "nesting instinct."

Irritability Understandably, you may become short-tempered and impatient, with a definite sense that it's time pregnancy was over!

MOTHER

Your due date is only a guide so be prepared for labor to start any time from 36 weeks. Keep the telephone numbers of your partner, your midwife, and the hospital delivery ward by the telephone at all times. Have your bag packed (see below) or get everything ready for a home delivery (see p. 44).

YOU NEED FOR THE HOSPITAL

■ Your hospital notes; birth plan.

■ A large T-shirt or short, loose nightgown for labor.

■ Socks in case you're chilly immediately after delivery.

■ For labor you may also need a hot water bottle to relieve backache, bottled mineral water and a natural sponge to suck, a water spray bottle to cool your skin, and a hand mirror to see your baby's head as it appears.

■ Two front-opening nightgowns or pajamas, a bathrobe, and a pair of slippers.

■ Two packages of super-strength sanitary pads and several pairs of cotton pants to hold them in place.

■ Properly fitted nursing bras and disposable breast pads.

■ Washbag with toiletries, washcloth or sponge, and a couple of bath towels.

■ For your baby you'll need stretch suits or nightgowns and undershirts (see p. 82), a package of first-size diapers, and diaper-changing equipment (see p. 76).

■ You may also need a blanket or shawl in which to wrap your baby, since most hospitals supply only basic crib bedding.

40

THE STAGES OF LABOR

Labor has three distinct stages. The first stage is when the uterine contractions pull the cervix open; second stage, when the baby is born; and third stage, when the placenta is delivered.

The first stage During the first stage of labor, contractions begin and are established, gradually becoming stronger and lasting longer; this stage can last up to 12 hours, or even longer with a first baby. First stage has three phases: the latent phase is the longest, lasting around eight hours. This is when the cervix is "taken up" and thins. Then there is the active phase, when the cervix is opened up wide; and finally the transitional phase, when the cervix reaches full dilation, before pushing the baby out. You're most likely to need pain relief during the active phase, and you're likely to feel a burst of energy toward the end to take you through the second stage.

The second stage During the second stage of labor the baby leaves the uterus and is pushed through the birth canal into the outside world. This stage can take anything from a few minutes to two hours with a first baby, and can be exhausting.

The third stage The delivery of the placenta is the third and final stage of labor; it is the shortest stage and it's almost painless, although you may feel some cramping like a severe menstrual pain. It happens within half an hour of the baby's birth, sooner if helped by an injection (see p. 46).

(see p. 46)

FATHER

Make sure you can always be contacted easily. If you have a mobile phone, keep it turned on.

WHAT TO TAKE TO HOSPITAL
■ A change of clothes; labor wards are very hot.

■ Food and drink – hospital cafeterias are rarely open at night.

■ Tape player and cassettes.

■ Camera or camcorder.

■ Phone card or change for a payphone, plus important numbers. (Do not use a mobile phone in the hospital.)

41

THINKING ABOUT PAIN RELIEF

It is sensible to consider options for pain relief before labor starts; discuss what is available a few weeks in advance with your midwife and put your wishes in a birth plan (see p. 27). Most people like the idea of a birth without the need for medication, but it's as well to be prepared. When it comes to the reality of labor, you can't predict how you'll react, since everyone's pain threshold is different.

(see p. 27)

GAS AND OXYGEN (ENTONOX)
A mixture of oxygen and nitrous oxide is breathed in through a mask or mouthpiece during a contraction so that it deadens the pain at its height. You start using it as soon as you feel a contraction starting because it takes about 20 seconds to be effective. The baby is not affected.

PETHIDINE
A form of pain relief given by injection. Pethidine is quite strong, so you may feel sick or woozy afterward. It can affect a baby's breathing at delivery (although this can be treated), and makes the baby drowsy, so it isn't given late in labor.

EPIDURAL

Canula is between vertebrae

Site of injection for epidural

EPIDURAL ANESTHETIC
An anesthetist injects anesthetic into the spinal column through a catheter via a hollow needle (a canula); it numbs your uterus, vagina, and vulva completely. A tube is attached to the needle and taped to your back so that the anesthetic can be supplemented.

TENS

Pulsar connects with stimulator

Electrodes are taped to back

TENS
Transcutaneous electrical nerve stimulation (TENS) involves electrodes taped to your back that are connected to a stimulator. You give yourself small, safe amounts of electric current to stimulate the production of endorphins, which are natural painkillers.

BIRTH POOL

Warm water is soothing

Water supports mother

BIRTH POOL
Many hospitals now have pools available for use during labor to help relieve the pain. Buoyancy helps reduce the pressure on the abdomen, making your contractions more efficient, and being in water makes it easy to move into different positions.

HOW LABOR STARTS

Labor can start in a variety of ways, but once it's really underway, you will know about it. If you're unsure, you probably aren't quite in labor. There are various signs that labor is starting.

THE "SHOW"
This is a brownish-pink discharge. It indicates that the mucus plug that has sealed the cervix during pregnancy has now come away in readiness for labor.

YOUR WATERS BREAK
Sometimes the amniotic sac ruptures before labor starts, causing fluid to leak slowly or in a gush from your vagina. This is painless. If your waters break, put on a clean sanitary pad and call your midwife or hospital delivery ward immediately for advice. Most doctors would prefer labor to start within 24 hours because of the risk of infection to the baby.

CONTRACTIONS START
The muscular tightenings of the uterus – contractions – gradually start to pull open the cervix. They last a few seconds to start with, and you may feel them as sharp cramping pains in the lower abdomen or as backache. If they're coming regularly about every 10–15 minutes, you're in labor.

WHAT HAPPENS IN LABOR

WHEN YOU GO INTO LABOR for the first time, it's natural to feel both excited and apprehensive. In spite of all the preparations you've made, for first-time parents labor is a journey into the unknown. Experiencing it together is something that you will always be able to share, regardless of what kind of labor it turns out to be.

KEEPING ACTIVE

When you realize you're in labor your first reaction may be to rush off to the hospital. Try to resist this because the most important thing for a mother in early labor is to keep active. Moving around is a great help in getting and keeping labor established, and most people find it easier to cope with contractions if they're upright. If your partner isn't with you, telephone him so he can join you as soon as possible. While you're waiting, telephone a friend or relative, or see if someone can come around to keep you company until your partner arrives. The best thing is to putter around at home for as long as possible, trying to be normal; if you have a contraction just stop and breathe through it. You might like to have a shower or bath to relax yourself. However, it's best to avoid having a bath if your waters have already broken (see left) unless your midwife advises it.

EATING AND DRINKING

While you're still at home, try to eat and drink quite frequently in small quantities. Having high-energy snacks and warm drinks will help keep your strength up. Once you're in the hospital this may be discouraged, and you probably won't feel like it anyway, but you'll need plenty of energy later.

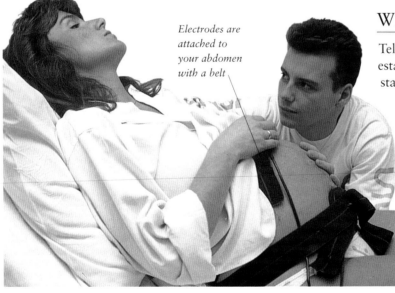

Electrodes are attached to your abdomen with a belt

WHEN TO GO TO THE HOSPITAL

Telephone the hospital when you think labor is established, but unless the hospital is far away, stay at home until contractions are coming every 5–10 minutes and lasting about a minute. However, bear in mind that you have a journey ahead of you: don't wait until the idea of getting into a car is beginning to sound like agony. If your partner can't get home in time, don't try to drive yourself; call an ambulance or a taxi.

ELECTRONIC FETAL MONITORING
When you arrive at hospital, your baby's heartbeat will be measured during contractions through electrodes attached to your abdomen.

WHEN YOU'RE IN THE HOSPITAL

It's now accepted that childbirth is not a disease and most delivery rooms are designed to be as homely as possible. You'll be assigned a nurse or midwife when you arrive, and she'll check how far the cervix has dilated, and measure your baby's heart rate, repeating these checks throughout your labor. You'll need to be near the equipment while your baby's heartrate is being monitored, then you can move around. Some medical interventions require constant monitoring so you'll have to stay on the bed.

MANAGING CONTRACTIONS

There are several ways of managing labor pains. Discuss the options with your midwife, including deciding when and if you want to use any pain relief (see p. 41). She'll try to accommodate your wishes and she'll support you both in finding ways of coping with contractions.

POSITIONS FOR LABOR
Keeping upright as much as possible helps labor to progress so the contractions work with, not against, gravity. Standing or squatting supported by your partner allows you to control the pain and provides warmth and loving reassurance.

Squat between your partner's knees while he sits on a chair, taking your weight on his legs

Stand with knees bent, if necessary, letting your partner take your weight

STANDING UPRIGHT

SQUATTING SUPPORTED

COPING WITHOUT PAIN RELIEF
● Relax as much as possible, especially between contractions: concentrate on the out-breath as you exhale, and drop your shoulders.
● Keep moving around between contractions, then get into the position that feels right for you. These may include a supported squat, leaning against your partner, on all fours, or kneeling down and leaning forward on a pillow placed on a chair.
● Try counting backward from 100 through a contraction – the concentration needed to do this takes your mind off the pain. Keep your eyes open to externalize the pain; focus on something in the room such as a picture.
● Take sips of still mineral water from a sponge if your mouth is dry and ask your partner to massage or knead your back during a contraction.
● Don't be afraid to say – or shout – anything you like; no one's going to hold it against you afterward.

FATHER

You may feel that there's not much you can do, but just being there is a huge comfort to your partner. Trust your intuition and judgment as to what's needed, but ask for feedback too.

HOW YOU CAN HELP
■ Be loving and intimate with your partner: slow and gentle, quiet and reassuring.

■ Be there for her when she wants you, and give her space when she doesn't.

■ Be positive and never criticize; she needs lots of praise, encouragement, and sympathy.

■ Offer practical help, such as a warm hot-water bottle if she's got backache, sprays of water or a cool washcloth if she's too hot, and sips of water if her mouth is dry.

■ If your partner wants to go without pain relief, encourage her while it seems reasonable, but if she asks for it, don't put her off. She's the one who is in pain.

■ Talk to the midwife or doctor if you don't understand what's happening, or if you're worried. She's there to help both of you, but remember that she is a professional who has your partner's and your baby's best interests at heart. At the same time, don't let the hospital staff and their machines become your focus.

■ Keep your sense of humor; if your partner shouts or swears at you, seems to get angry or overwrought, take it in stride. It's her way of coping with a very stressful situation. This is particularly likely to happen at the transition phase of the first stage of labor (see p. 41), so treat it as a positive step toward the birth – it's a sign that the second stage isn't far off.

43

WHO'S WHO AT THE BIRTH

For a normal vaginal delivery, you'll probably have just one midwife and an assistant, and possibly a pediatric nurse to look after the baby immediately after the birth. Sometimes, however, the delivery room may seem to be almost crowded with other people, and you should be ready for this. Personnel present may include:

■ Your assigned midwife.

■ An assistant midwife and/or a pediatric nurse.

■ Your obstetrician.

■ An anesthetist, if you have an epidural (see p. 41).

■ A pediatrician to check your baby's health if you have an epidural or any form of assisted birth (see p. 49).

■ Student doctors, midwives, or nurses, if it's a teaching hospital. You'll be asked about this first, and you can refuse permission.

■ A pediatrician and midwife assigned to each baby if you are having a multiple birth.

THE BIRTH OF YOUR BABY

THE EARLY STAGES OF YOUR JOURNEY to parenthood are now complete: the cervix is open, and the birth canal is clear for your baby's progress to the outside world. Ahead of you is a shorter, but not necessarily easier, stage: that of pushing the baby out. But this is the culmination of all the hard work, and at last you'll meet your new baby.

COPING WITH SECOND STAGE

As your baby is gradually pushed down your birth canal, you should try to use gravity as much as possible to help, so keep as upright as you can. Get into whatever position feels most comfortable – it may be sitting up on the bed, squatting on a mat with the support of your partner, leaning against a chair, being on all fours, or using a birthing stool – your partner and midwife can follow your lead. Between contractions use your breathing techniques; in particular, let your pelvic floor, rectum, and anus relax.

CROWNING

Your midwife will tell you when your baby's head appears at the vaginal opening – this is called crowning. Listen to your midwife; she'll tell you when to push and when to relax. If you take your time and let your vagina stretch slowly, you may avoid a tear. Once the baby's head crowns your partner can show you by holding a mirror – this is very encouraging because you know your baby will soon be born.

BIRTH AT HOME

More and more women are giving birth at home, although birth in the hospital remains the norm because it's difficult to predict how your labor will progress.

PRACTICAL PREPARATIONS
About a month before your due date the midwife will let you know what equipment you need readily available, such as buckets, rubber gloves, and polyethylene sheeting to cover furniture and carpets. She will provide all the medical equipment. Decide where in your home you want to have your baby and try to work out your expectations. You can then discuss these with your midwife and she'll be able to reassure you, dispel any misconceptions, and help you be realistic.

WHEN YOU'RE IN LABOR
● Call the midwife, who will come as soon as possible. She will probably have an assistant with her.
● For pain relief, your midwife will only be able to provide gas and oxygen and pethidine (obtained by prescription beforehand), so you're likely to try drug-free ways of managing the pain first (see p. 43). You'll probably be better able to cope at home, anyway.
● You're more likely to feel in control of events because the medical staff are on your territory, and that's an important psychological difference for everyone.

IF THERE'S A PROBLEM
Talk through with your midwife beforehand when and why she'd recommend a move to the hospital. If that were to happen, you'd go in an ambulance – and in most instances, the same midwives who'd attended you at home would continue looking after you once you arrived.

AFTER THE BIRTH
The midwife will stay for a couple of hours to make sure that you and your baby are comfortable and healthy, and will return later. You, your partner, and your new baby can spend your first few hours as a family together in the comforting surroundings of your own home.

EPISIOTOMY

An episiotomy is a surgical cut in the perineal floor that helps to allow the baby's head to pass through. Given time, you may not need one, but if it's felt you should have one, the midwife or doctor will ask your permission to do this procedure when your baby's head crowns (see opposite). It's more common to have an episiotomy with a first baby because the vaginal opening may be less elastic and you are more likely to tear. Episiotomies are also performed if your baby is very large, or is in the breech position, or you need assistance with forceps or a vacuum extractor (see p. 49). If you haven't had an epidural, the pelvic floor muscles will be numbed first with an injection of local anesthetic. Then the vaginal tissues, plus underlying muscle, are cut at the height of a contraction to extend the opening. The incision is stitched after the placenta has been delivered (see p. 47).

THE DELIVERY

The head is the widest part of your baby – it will emerge slowly, and the midwife will check that the cord isn't around the neck and will clear fluid from your baby's mouth and throat. The midwife will ask you to pant, not push at this stage, then with the next contractions she will gently turn the baby so that the shoulders can be born one at a time and the rest of your baby's body will slide out; the pushing contractions stop immediately and you'll feel a wonderful sense of release. Your baby may or may not cry out; some babies whimper, some cry lustily, and some begin breathing without any crying.

MEETING YOUR BABY

This is the moment for which you've waited nine months, when you can take your baby in your arms together for the first time, the moment that will make everything you've just gone through worthwhile. Your midwife will probably lay the baby on your tummy or give him to you to hold while the cord is clamped and cut; let your baby feel your skin, hold him close to your face, and let him look up into yours. Share this moment – you're both his parents – and savor it; this is a meeting that will change both your lives forever. It is also the moment when you claim your new status as parents.

THE MOMENT OF BIRTH
You'll never forget the experience of holding your baby for the first time, immediately after he's emerged. It's so emotional that you may well find yourselves weeping with joy and relief.

FATHER

Helping your partner and watching your baby being born is an overwhelming experience for all fathers. The second stage is hard work for mothers, but there are ways you can help your partner during this stage so that you can feel as involved as possible.

HOW YOU CAN HELP
■ Help your partner get into the position she feels is most appropriate, and support her there.

■ Talk to her and encourage her all the time, and keep in physical contact so she knows you're with her all the way.

■ If you can see your baby's head as it crowns, describe it to your partner or hold a mirror for her to see the head – this will be very encouraging to her. However, don't get in the midwife's way because she will need to be able to monitor the baby's progress second by second, and to check the birth of the head.

■ Announce that you have a son or a daughter, not just "it's a boy" or "it's a girl" – the words "son" and "daughter" express family feelings.

■ If the midwife agrees, clamp and cut your baby's cord yourself. It's a fantastic moment – the moment your baby really becomes an individual being.

■ If you feel like weeping, don't hold back. It's one of the most emotional moments of your life.

■ When the baby is born, share with your partner in the first minutes of your child's life.

■ By all means photograph or video your partner and the new baby, but don't do this to the exclusion of helping them. They are more important than anything else.

45

BONDING

Parent-infant bonding is sometimes misunderstood. Most newborn animals have an instinct to bond; more recently research has shown that human babies have similar instincts.

WHAT HAPPENS AT BIRTH

Your baby can recognize your voice at birth and can focus on your face at 8–10in (20–25cm) away. You will also be hyper-sensitive to your baby in the minutes after birth. You can bond with your baby for life almost instantly, if you can be left alone together without interference – if this private time isn't offered, ask for it. However, don't worry if you don't bond at once – you might both just feel utterly exhausted after the delivery. Falling in love will have to wait.

AFTER THE BIRTH

THE FIRST HOUR OR SO after your baby's birth is a very precious time for all three of you – and it's a moment that most parents will always remember. Although there will be various medical and administrative procedures that still need to be carried out, you'll still have time to enjoy your baby and begin to get to know her together.

YOUR BABY AFTER DELIVERY

The midwife or doctor will check your baby's condition immediately after the birth by assessing her "Apgar score" (see opposite). Providing she is breathing without difficulty from the start, your baby will probably remain in your arms for the first minutes after birth. If she needs help to start breathing, she'll be put on the delivery room resuscitation table, which has an oxygen mask and a heater to keep the baby warm. Usually she'll soon be pink enough to be handed back to you, but in a few cases she may need to be taken to the neonatal intensive care unit for a while (see p. 58). Some time in the first couple of hours your baby will be weighed and measured, and every part of her thoroughly examined by a midwife or pediatrician.

DELIVERY OF THE PLACENTA

The placenta is usually delivered with the help of an injection of ergonovine and oxytocin given as the baby's body emerges. The cord is cut and the midwife will then press gently on your abdomen and pull the cord slowly to draw out the placenta. Once the placenta is delivered the midwife will check to make sure that none has remained inside you where it could cause bleeding and infection. If you'd prefer the placenta to be delivered naturally – without medication – it will take about half an hour; putting your baby to your breast will help the process.

HOW YOU WILL FEEL

Immediately after the birth, your body temperature drops a few degrees and you may shiver and shake quite violently as your internal thermostat resets. You'll need to be wrapped in a blanket, and putting on a pair of socks may help warm you up quickly. If you are famished after labor, ask your midwife or partner for whatever food sounds good to you at that point and drink plenty if you are thirsty. This will also help you to maintain the calories and fluids you need for breast-feeding.

GETTING TO KNOW YOUR BABY
Hold your baby close to your breast so that she can suckle if she wants to. This helps the bonding process and the breast-feeding hormones also encourage the uterus to contract.

IF YOU NEED STITCHES

The midwife will examine your perineum and assess whether or not you need stitches. Research shows that minor tears heal better on their own, so it's not necessarily true that any tear will inevitably mean stitches; however, an episiotomy (see p. 45) must be stitched. If you do need stitches, you'll probably have your feet placed in stirrups, and you'll usually be given a local anesthetic to deaden the pain. Depending on the length of the cut or tear, stitching will be done either by a senior midwife or the doctor on duty. You may be able to cuddle your baby while you're being stitched if you want to, but this is also a good chance for your partner to have time with his baby so that you both get a chance to bond individually with your new member of the family as early as possible after the birth.

THE FIRST BREAST-FEEDING

Putting your baby to the breast within an hour of the delivery increases your chances of breast-feeding successfully; many women feel able to put their babies to the breast immediately after the birth, although not all babies want to suck then. Ask your midwife to help you get your baby to latch on, but don't worry if she doesn't want to suck immediately. It doesn't mean she isn't able to breast-feed, just that at this point she doesn't feel like sucking, or she may be tired. She may also be affected by pain medication used during labor, such as pethidine, which leave her rather drowsy and may take a few hours to wear off (see p. 41).

THE IMPORTANCE OF COLOSTRUM

You won't produce milk for three or four days after the birth (see p. 61), but it is very beneficial for your baby to have the high protein "pre-milk" called colostrum that is produced in your breasts at this time. It contains important antibodies from your body that protect a newborn baby from infections, plus a substance called lactoferrin, which acts like a natural antibody. Putting your baby to the breast also helps the uterus contract, and if you've opted to deliver the placenta naturally (see opposite), suckling your baby will aid this because the same hormone that triggers the "let down" of milk in your breasts also acts on the uterine muscle.

THE APGAR SCORE

The Apgar score is a standard method of assessing the condition of a newborn baby immediately. At one minute and five minutes after the birth, the midwife or doctor checks the heartbeat, breathing, muscle tone, reflexes, and skin color, and gives them a score of 0, 1, or 2, with a possible total of 10. A score of 7 or over is normal, and a low first score that improves to a normal second score is fine. This may occur if you had a long second stage, or your baby was affected by pethidine given during labor (see p. 41).

HOW THE SCORE WORKS
- Heart rate over 100 scores 2; below 100, 1; no heartbeat, 0.
- Regular breathing or crying scores 2; slow or irregular breathing scores 1; absence of breathing scores 0.
- If the baby is active (good muscle tone), the score is 2; if only the hands and feet are moving the score is 1; if the baby is limp, the score is 0.
- Strong reflexes score 2; weak reflexes score 1; no reflexes score 0.
- Pink coloring scores 2; body pink but extremities blue scores 1; blue or pale coloring scores 0.

FATHER

After the birth, you may feel as emotionally exhausted as your partner, but it's important not to underestimate the physical effort of labor and birth on a woman.

HOW YOU CAN HELP
■ You will probably experience a wave of euphoria now that your baby is born, but if labor has been long and arduous your partner may be too exhausted to experience this same "buzz" immediately. It doesn't mean she isn't as excited and delighted as you are, but after a lengthy labor, it's not surprising if she finds it difficult to express immediate enthusiasm. Just hold her close and let her know how proud you are of her and of your new son or daughter. Stay with them both for as long as possible after the birth, including settling them into the postnatal ward.

■ Congratulate your partner on her achievement and let her know how much you appreciate her. But don't underestimate your own contribution and the support you've been able to give. You may think you haven't really been much help – this is a common reaction for fathers who have seen their partners struggling through labor, particularly if it was long. However, most mothers will say how beneficial it was to have the emotional support and encouragement from their partner throughout labor and at the birth.

■ Hold your baby while your partner is being stitched or checked; go into a quiet corner of the room and get to know your baby. Let your baby look into your eyes; if you hold her close so she's just 8–10in (20–25cm) from your face, she can see you and smell you, and she'll learn to recognize you from the very beginning (see p. 134).

47

MOTHER

It's understandable for you to feel disheartened if something happens that necessitates an assisted delivery, or even an emergency cesarean section (see p. 50) so that you're unable to experience the natural vaginal delivery that you'd been hoping for. Being prepared for the fact that intervention may be required can help avoid too much soul-searching and disappointment after the birth.

COPING WITH A SPECIAL LABOR

■ The medical staff will always tell you why a particular course of action is recommended, whether it's before labor or when labor is in progress. Don't think you're making a fuss by asking questions, or by asking that an explanation be repeated: you have a right to know.

■ If you're in labor, it may be difficult to concentrate; ask your partner to make sure that all the reasons for certain procedures are clarified so that he can relay the information to you. Unless you're actually unconscious, staff must specifically seek your permission to proceed; they won't accept your partner's opinion.

■ In the final analysis, the most important thing will be that your baby has been born safely. But that doesn't mean your feelings don't matter, and many women can't shake the idea – however illogical – that they were in some way to blame that things didn't go according to plan. If you find yourself in this position, talk it through afterward: with your partner, and with your midwives, other health professionals, or your family doctor. Having a baby can unleash deep emotions and you may need to work through them before you can move on to enjoy new motherhood fully.

SPECIAL LABORS

IN THE PAST, WOMEN HAD TO RELY on nature alone to see their baby's birth through, and in many cases this unfortunately led to tragedy. Today, however, modern obstetrics has given doctors many ways to intervene if labor proves difficult. Although some interventions may bring a small risk of complication, and one intervention may build on another, the risk is usually far outweighed by the benefit. If a particular procedure is suggested, ask the midwife or doctor to explain exactly why it's necessary, what the risks are, and what would happen if you waited a while before it was started.

WHEN LABOR IS INDUCED

Sometimes labor may need to be induced (started artificially). If you haven't gone into labor spontaneously by 42–43 weeks, or if there are worries about your own or your baby's health in the last few weeks of pregnancy, induction may be suggested. Similar procedures will be needed if your labor is not proceeding as it should.

HOW LABOR MAY BE INDUCED

Induction is often introduced gradually, first with pessaries; then, if necessary, ARM (see below); finally, an oxytocin drip if things are going too slowly.
● You may be given vaginal pessaries containing prostaglandin, a hormone that should trigger labor.
● Your membranes may be ruptured artificially (ARM), which can either start or strengthen contractions.
● You may be given an artificial hormone (oxytocin) into a vein to induce contractions. Oxytocin contractions will probably be more immediately intense and painful than if labor had started naturally. An oxytocin drip is also used to speed up labor.

BREECH BIRTH

Instead of being born head first, in a breech birth your baby is born buttocks first, usually followed by the legs and lastly the head. Breech babies frequently end up having to be delivered with the help of forceps or by cesarean section for the baby's safety, although a natural breech delivery is occasionally possible with the help of an experienced midwife and obstetrician. A breech baby is almost always delivered in the hospital; because of the likelihood of intervention you'll probably be offered an epidural, so that you're already anesthetized if your doctor needs to apply forceps or do a cesarean (see p. 50). You're more likely to have an episiotomy (see p. 45), because your baby's buttocks may not stretch the vagina enough to let the head out safely, or to allow forceps to be inserted to help lift the head out.

ASSISTANCE WITH FORCEPS OR VACUUM EXTRACTOR

Even if you have a normal vaginal delivery, there may be times when you need help, particularly in pushing the baby out during second stage. Depending on the circumstances, your hospital will provide assistance with forceps or vacuum extraction. You'll need to have an episiotomy for either of these procedures.

Forceps The two blades of forceps cradle your baby's head, allowing it to be pulled safely through the birth canal without too much compression. However, forceps can normally only be used once the baby's head is engaged in the pelvic bones.

Vacuum extraction This is a gentler procedure than using forceps and is used in similar circumstances. Your cervix has to be fully dilated but the head does not have to be in the birth canal. The vacuum plate leaves a bruise on your baby's head where the suction was applied, but this will fade within the first 2–3 weeks.

Blades of forceps cradle the baby's head

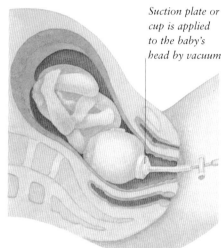

Suction plate or cup is applied to the baby's head by vacuum

FORCEPS DELIVERY
Forceps are instruments that look like the two halves of very large sugar-tongs. The blades are inserted one at a time and the baby is drawn out with a few gentle pulls during contractions.

VACUUM EXTRACTION
With this method, a small suction plate or cup is applied by vacuum to the lowest part of your baby's head. The doctor will help your baby to be born by gradually applying gentle traction.

IF YOU'RE HAVING TWINS

Twins or higher multiples are exciting for everyone, although you're bound to be apprehensive about their arrival. Medical interest in the birth will be much greater if you're expecting more than one baby, and some intervention is more likely to be recommended. Often this becomes necessary, but there's no need to think it's inevitable: many twins, and even triplets, are born vaginally after a normal labor. But continuous electronic fetal monitoring is much more common and, as with breech birth, you'll probably be offered an epidural because of the likelihood of intervention. It will therefore be in place just in case there are problems with the delivery of the second twin and you need to have assistance with forceps or even a cesarean. If one twin is known to be breech, you will probably be advised to have both delivered by elective cesarean.

FATHER

A labor that doesn't go according to plan can be scary both for you and your partner. Be prepared for the fact that unexpected interventions may be necessary.

HOW YOU CAN HELP

■ Well before your baby is due, talk to your partner about what she feels about any special situation that may arise. Make sure you know her views and preferences for any eventuality. Bear in mind, however, that she may change her mind during labor and delivery.

■ Unless it's an absolute emergency, make sure that any interventions suggested are talked through properly with your partner, and either or both of you ask questions if it isn't clear. But remember that the final decision is your partner's – the health professionals must have her consent for any intervention.

■ If something is suggested that you know your partner is trying to avoid, try to buy time. For instance, if labor has slowed, suggest a change of position before procedures to accelerate labor are introduced.

■ If the medical team decide the labor needs monitoring with high tech equipment, try not to be distracted by it. Concentrate on your partner, not the technology.

■ Remember that if something unexpected occurs and the medical team has to intervene, it's never your partner's fault. These things happen, and everyone will be working in the best interests of your partner and baby.

■ Whatever happens, talk about it afterward, especially with your partner, but also with friends and, if necessary, health professionals. You'll have a lot of feelings to work through.

MOTHER

You're bound to feel apprehensive about the outcome if you have a cesarean, and you may feel let down if you have an emergency cesarean after going into labor spontaneously.

CONCERNS ABOUT CESAREANS

■ You may worry that you won't be able to deliver a subsequent baby vaginally. However, about 75 percent of women who have a cesarean have a normal delivery the next time.

■ If you have a general anesthetic, you'll need a longer period of recovery, so it may be a little while before you feel close to your baby. You'll bond with your baby eventually, especially when you start breast-feeding, so don't worry if you feel a little distant to start with (see p. 46).

■ You'll only be left with a tiny scar on your "bikini line," usually hidden by your pubic hair.

WHY YOU MIGHT NEED A CESAREAN

There are several reasons why you may require a cesarean delivery, whether elective or emergency:

■ The baby's head is too large for your pelvis (disproportion).

■ Your baby is breech (bottom first).

■ Your baby takes up a crosswise position (persistent horizontal lie).

■ You have a medical condition, such as preeclampsia or diabetes.

■ Any problems with the placenta.

■ Your labor is progressing too slowly or has stopped, which might cause fetal distress.

■ There is fetal distress, even if labor hasn't slowed or stopped.

CESAREAN SECTION

Nowadays, a significant number of babies are born surgically by cesarean section. In many countries, cesarean section is currently on the increase, partly because this procedure in expert hands may be safer than, say, a difficult forceps delivery. Sometimes, however, interventions earlier in labor, such as induction or epidural anesthetic, may lead to a situation in which cesarean section becomes more likely. If a cesarean delivery of your baby is recommended – either before or during labor – your doctor is obliged to give you clear reasons why, even in an emergency. If you had wanted to avoid a cesarean, ask your obstetrician whether you could wait or if there is anything else you could try first.

ELECTIVE CESAREAN

If a cesarean operation is planned in advance it is known as "elective." This means the reason for it has become apparent before labor started – for example, your blood pressure may have shot up, or your pelvis is so small that delivery is likely to be difficult, or your baby is breech (see p. 48). Your obstetrician will probably discuss this with you 2–3 weeks before your due date and a date will be booked for you to come in, so you'll know well in advance exactly when your baby is going to be born.

EMERGENCY CESAREAN

An emergency (unplanned) cesarean happens when events during labor make it preferable to vaginal delivery. For example, your baby may show distress (measured by heartrate and movements); the labor may not progress despite the use of drugs to speed things up; or your own condition may deteriorate. If you have not already had an epidural anesthetic, the cesarean will take place under general anesthetic.

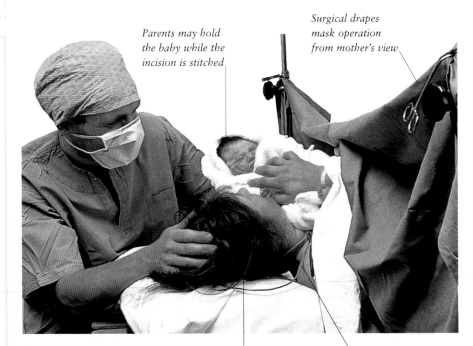

Parents may hold the baby while the incision is stitched

Surgical drapes mask operation from mother's view

DELIVERY OF THE BABY
If you have a cesarean under epidural anesthesia, you'll both be able to share your baby's first moments after delivery.

Mother is awake during operation

Catheter for continuous epidural anesthesia

WHAT HAPPENS DURING THE OPERATION

Before a cesarean, your pubic hair will be shaved and a catheter inserted into your bladder. You'll probably be given glucose via an intravenous drip.

The anesthetic Most elective, and some emergency, cesareans are performed under epidural anesthesia because women recover more quickly afterward. If you have an epidural anesthetic, you'll be awake during the operation, but you won't feel anything, and your partner can be with you throughout. You won't be able to see anything because the operating team will be masked by a surgical sheet draped across your chest. However, an epidural takes about half an hour to take effect, so if there's an emergency and you haven't had an epidural set up already, you'll be given a general anesthetic instead. In this case, your partner won't usually be allowed into the operating room, but will be able to hold the baby afterward while you recover.

The operation Your abdomen is opened through a small, low, horizontal incision along the line of the top of your pubic hair, and your baby delivered through a similar cut in the uterus. The amniotic fluid is drained off by suction before the baby is gently lifted out. You may feel some rather odd tugs and rummaging around in your insides as the operation proceeds. Your surgeon will tell you when the moment approaches that she can lift your baby from your uterus.

After the birth It takes about ten minutes to deliver the baby: you or your partner can then hold your baby while the placenta is removed and you are stitched. A baby born by cesarean is likely to need help in starting to breathe, but a pediatrician will be available to help with this. Closing the wound can take as much as 45 minutes; depending on the hospital, the stitches may be self-absorbing or they may need to be removed a few days later.

SUDDEN BIRTH – THE FATHER'S ROLE

Far from needing a cesarean, occasionally it happens that labor comes on with such speed that your partner could be overwhelmed by your desire to push before you have access to professional help, let alone getting to the hospital! Although second stage can take a couple of hours, it may not, and babies have been known to be born after a couple of pushes. If this happens, neither of you need to panic – babies who come quickly are almost always strong and vigorous and most emergency births are perfectly straightforward.

WHAT TO DO

• Do not leave your partner alone for more than a minute or two. Help her position herself wherever she feels most comfortable.
• Telephone the doctor or midwife and explain the situation. If it's difficult to reach them, call the emergency services and ask for an ambulance as soon as possible.

• Wash your hands well and have a pile of clean towels ready. Fold one and put it to one side for the baby. If you have time, find some old sheets or plastic sheeting to cover the floor or furniture.
• Watch for the top of the baby's head at the vaginal opening. When it's visible, ask your partner to stop pushing and just pant. This will give the vagina a chance to stretch fully without tearing.
• Feel around the baby's neck to see if the cord is looped around it. If it is, hook your finger under the cord and draw it over the baby's head.
• Hold the baby firmly as she emerges – she'll be slippery – and give her straight to her mother to hold. Wrap her immediately in the spare towel so she doesn't get cold.
• Don't touch the cord. If the placenta is delivered before medical help arrives, put it in a dish or plastic bowl so it can be checked by the midwife or doctor.

FATHER

Even an elective cesarean delivery can be worrying, because it is quite a major operation. If it's an emergency, your partner may be feeling distressed, bewildered, and helpless, but there's much you can do to smooth the way for her.

HOW YOU CAN HELP

■ If an emergency cesarean is recommended, and your partner is finding it difficult to talk to the doctors, make sure you ask any questions for her. Although she has to give her permission for a cesarean, your partner may still not be quite clear afterward why the operation was necessary, and it is important that you are able to help her understand the reasons for the operation.

■ Unless your partner wants a general anesthetic or the operation is too urgent, see if it can be done under epidural anesthesia. This means you can share the experience and meet your new baby together.

■ During the operation, sit by your partner's head and reassure her that all is well.

■ You don't have to watch what is going on; you'll both be shielded by the surgical drapes. But if you find the operation distressing or you feel faint – and many people do, even nurses – leave the room quickly. Don't hang on; you may cause further difficulties for the medical staff.

■ If the cesarean is being done under general anesthetic, your partner may not regain consciousness for an hour or more, and you'll probably be given your baby to hold. Cherish this time with your baby: father-child bonding can be at its best after a cesarean section birth, because the early time you have together is so precious.

51

HOSPITAL ROUTINE

Some aspects of hospital routine can be tiresome, although you may enjoy talking to other mothers.

KEEPING YOUR BABY CLOSE
Almost all hospitals expect babies to remain in their cribs beside their mothers' beds at all times.

FOOD AND DRINK
The food may be bland, so ask your partner to bring fresh fruit to help prevent constipation. Drink plenty of water.

VISITS FROM STAFF
The midwives will check your stitches, lochia, and uterus (see p. 60). They'll also give advice on cleaning your baby's umbilicus and breast-feeding. At some point an obstetrician and pediatrician will check you and your baby, and a physical therapist may visit to advise you on postpartum exercise.

FIRST DISCOMFORTS

You'll feel a little shaky in the first 24 hours, and there may be some specific discomforts, although these pass quite quickly:

■ Your perineum will feel bruised and tender, especially if you had stitches. Have frequent salt baths, but don't stay in the bath too long because water can harm scar tissue and soften stitches.

■ You may find it difficult or even painful to pass urine. Take a pitcher of tepid water to the toilet to pour over your vulva as you pass urine.

■ A sore perineum plus stitches may deter you from opening your bowels. Support your vulva with a pad of tissues as you bear down.

■ Sitting upright can be awkward when your abdominal muscles are weak and your vulva and perineum are sore. Prop yourself with plenty of pillows and half sit and half lie on your side to reduce pressure.

THE FIRST DAY

YOU HAVE BOTH been looking forward to this moment for the best part of a year; your baby is safely delivered and you've experienced a heady brew of strong emotion: relief, pride, elation, excitement, and triumph. Now your baby is lying quietly in his crib by your bed and you both have a chance to take stock.

YOUR REACTIONS TO THE BIRTH

Unlikely as it may seem, this could be an awkward moment for you both. It could be passing through either or both of your minds that there is something missing. Where is the rush of love for your baby? It isn't a subject that gets much attention, but it is, nevertheless, a fact that large numbers of parents, quite possibly the majority, don't feel an overpowering attachment to their baby right after the birth. Most highs, because of their intensity, are followed, not necessarily by a low, but by a reduction of emotion that leaves you feeling somewhat flat in comparison. Having a baby is no exception. It may have been a momentous event for you, but the hospital routine has to proceed as normal and, anyway, a hospital ward isn't conducive to the kind of closeness that you would like to feel for each other on this shared birthday, especially if you're both exhausted.

LOOKING FORWARD

When you go to the postnatal ward – and this may be two or three hours after the birth – the father goes back to an empty home and the mother is left wondering what her first night as the mother of a baby is going to be like. If it isn't quite what either of you envisaged, be philosophical. In a real sense, life with your baby will actually begin on the day you take him home.

IF YOU'VE HAD A CESAREAN

A cesarean section is major abdominal surgery and you'll feel quite sore once the anesthetic wears off. In addition to asking for pain relief, there are other ways of coping:

● Holding and feeding your baby may be difficult since pressure on your scar may be painful. Try laying him next to you on the bed (see p. 71) or supporting him on pillows – the so-called "football position" (see right).
● Mobility helps you recover so you'll be encouraged to get up as soon as possible. Support your wound as you walk.

Baby's body is raised and supported on a pillow

COMFORTABLE FEEDING
Put your baby on a pillow and tuck his body under your arm.

HANDLING YOUR NEW BABY

It's natural to be nervous about holding and handling your baby for the first time; although he may seem vulnerable, remember that he is really very robust. The main problem is that he has no neck control so his head is very floppy, and his joints are very soft so you need to be gentle when putting on his clothes (see p. 82). Support your baby's head at all times and pick him up as shown here.

Hold baby firmly as you lift him gently

1 To lift your baby, slide one hand under his rump and cradle his head with the other. Talk to him all the time.

Slide hands under rump and head

2 Lift him gently but firmly toward you, using a smooth upward movement so that he isn't startled.

Support baby's back along length of your arm

3 Swing his body around so that he's resting against your chest and his head and back are cradled by your arms.

YOUR BABY'S FIRST DAY

There's a lot to learn on your baby's first day, and you may feel awkward and anxious about looking after him. On top of trying to get him to feed, you'll have to come to grips with changing a diaper, washing his face, hands, and feet (see p. 78), and dressing him. (Most hospitals and midwives leave the first bath for three or four days after birth.) A midwife will show you both what to do; if you're uncertain about anything, don't be afraid to ask.

RELUCTANCE TO FEED

You may be concerned if your baby is reluctant to feed for the whole of the first day, but this is no cause for worry. Express colostrum (see p. 72) if your breasts feel uncomfortable, so that you will find it easier to feed him as soon as he is ready. Once he feels the need to feed, you may find you are putting him to the breast as often as every two hours.

THE SLEEPY BABY

Your baby will probably have been wide awake and alert for the first hour or two after the birth, but then he may well sleep on and off for much of the first day. Take turns holding him rather than simply leaving him in his crib.

YOUR BABY'S CRIES

Unless he is very sleepy, you will probably experience your baby crying several times during this first day and you may be astonished both by its force and the fact that you'll recognize it immediately. Neither of these things is accidental. Babies are programmed to signal their needs vociferously and adults are programmed to respond with a feeling of urgency. Always pick him up when he cries; cuddle him in bed with you unless you want to sleep.

FATHER

When you go home after the birth you are likely to feel a bit lonely. Use that time to telephone everyone since you'll probably have an urge to talk about all that's happened, and your relatives will want all the details.

GET SOME SLEEP

Although you may feel too excited at first, make sure you catch up on your sleep. You've had an exhausting time during the labor and you can't support your partner when she comes home if you're tired as well.

PREPARE YOUR HOME

Use your time at home alone to do the washing and cleaning and stock up on groceries and other household items. Fit the straps for the baby seat in the car, if you haven't already done this, so that everything is ready when your new baby comes home.

53

GOING HOME EARLY

Some hospitals now encourage mothers to return home as soon as four or five hours after a normal delivery – an intermediate approach between full hospital treatment and a home delivery. It may seem very soon after the birth, but you are likely to relax better in your own environment, and recovery will probably be easier at home, where you'll be checked twice on the first day by a visiting midwife. However, remember that going home early doesn't mean you're back to normal. Childbirth leaves you exhausted and it's a good idea to keep the first day or two visitor-free because you won't have the professional back-up that you had in the hospital.

MOTHER

Even though you're longing to be home, try to take advantage of your time in the hospital to regain your strength and to lean on the professional staff for advice. If you're back at home within a couple of days of the birth, get as much help as you can. Friends and relatives are usually only too happy to help, but need to know that it's going to be accepted when offered.

HOW YOU CAN ADJUST

■ When your partner visits you both in the hospital, share any aspect of your baby's care with him that you've been shown by the midwives. If you learn how to care for your baby together, you'll start out on an equal footing and he'll be more likely to take the initiative to help you once you're home.

■ Use these first few days to build on the network of support systems which you will hopefully have set up through prenatal classes before the baby was born. Within a week or two of the birth, your partner may have gone back to work, and friends and family will have withdrawn back to their own lives, so prepare for time on your own.

■ Be ready for mood swings. At some point during the first few days you may experience tearful moments – it often happens just as your milk comes in, three or four days after the birth. The so-called "baby blues" (see p. 112) are your normal reaction to the sudden withdrawal of pregnancy hormones and to the enormity of your new situation; they usually subside in a week to ten days. You'll probably be very tired too, especially if you had a fairly long labor. Don't try to hide your feelings from your partner – be open about them and share them with him.

54

ADJUSTING TO PARENTHOOD

THE FIRST FEW DAYS of parenthood can be bewildering, as you seesaw between intense periods of close attention by many different health professionals and moments of isolation, when you are expected just to get on with it by yourselves. Although you may feel that learning about the very basic day-to-day care of your new baby leaves little room for your own relationship as a couple, it will help to draw you together if you concentrate initially on sharing the simple practicalities of first diaper changes or cleaning your baby's umbilicus and acknowledging rather than hiding your natural nervousness and apprehension.

TAKING CARE OF EACH OTHER

When a baby comes to first-time parents, three new relationships begin: mother-baby, father-baby, mother-father. This last is the most complex. Of course a relationship has existed between the parents that predates the baby, but you will not have related to each other before in the roles of mother and father. You have to start thinking of each other in an entirely new way. You have to "redesign" your relationship in the light of your new roles – being more understanding, more patient, more flexible, more long-suffering than you were before. Most of all, you have to be more generous and less self-centered. This can put a strain on your relationship, so you need to be ready to respond to each other (see p. 108).

HELP AND ADVICE

Use your time in the hospital or when you are in the daily care of a midwife or doctor to get the advice you need. Don't feel shy about asking, even if it seems trivial; most health professionals recognize that it is vital to provide reassurance. However, in the hospital they may not have enough time to advise you exactly when you need it, particularly with breast-feeding problems, so it may be helpful to contact a breast-feeding counselor when you get home. Most counselors are themselves mothers who have been trained to provide support in a nonmedical way and will continue their support for some months. This helps alleviate the nervousness many mothers feel when they are finally discharged by the midwife, ending a close relationship with the midwifery service that's built up over months.

ADVICE FROM FAMILY AND FRIENDS

In the early days of parenthood, your friends and relatives may be eager to offer advice. Although it can be irritating if delivered in an overbearing way, the advice that other parents give you reflects their own experience and can be very reassuring. However, if the advice goes against your own beliefs, simply ignore it and do things the way you know is best.

FEELING ISOLATED

After the intense activity of labor and birth, when you were fully involved and couldn't think about anything else, you may both feel quite isolated, disoriented, and lonely for a few days; this could affect how you relate to each other when you do have time together. The new mother may feel bewildered in the hospital. Even though she's surrounded by other people, she suddenly finds herself in sole charge of the needs of her tiny new dependent when she's feeling exhausted and possibly in pain. The new father, too, may feel very odd and detached from his new situation when he has to come and go from an empty home.

TALK TO EACH OTHER

When you're together try hard to talk about how you feel, and make sure you tell each other what you have been doing while you're apart. Most hospitals now have unrestricted day and evening visiting for new fathers, so it should be possible to spend a lot of time together supporting each other through this short but significant period of separation. It may be difficult to articulate your feelings, but the charts below set out some of the needs of both partners at this difficult time.

WHAT A NEW MOTHER WANTS FROM HER PARTNER

RECOGNIZE HER VULNERABILITY	A father needs to recognize how vulnerable a new mother feels, both physically and emotionally, in the days after the birth.
APPRECIATE THE DEPTH OF HER FEELINGS	A father needs to accept the strength of his partner's overwhelming involvement in the baby and not to construe this as a rejection of him.
PROTECT HER PRIVACY	One of the most important duties for a new father is to make sure that his partner is not overwhelmed by visitors and to give her time and space to establish breast-feeding and recover from the physical stresses of labor and birth.

WHAT A NEW FATHER WANTS FROM HIS PARTNER

RECOGNIZE HIS DIFFICULTIES	She should be ready to accept that this is also a confusing and emotional time for her partner.
GIVE HIM SOME OF YOUR TIME	The baby may be time-consuming but it is good – for your relationship as a couple and as new parents – for a mother to reserve some of her time and attention for her partner.
ALLOW HIM TO MAKE MISTAKES	After a hospital birth, a new mother necessarily has more time to get used to the baby, but she needs to allow her partner to handle and care for the baby, and not criticize him if he is awkward.

FATHER

As a new father you may feel rather cut off from your partner, particularly during her time in the hospital. At the same time, you may feel an intense elation that you want to share with your partner, but she may seem a bit distant as her body recovers from the birth and she tries to establish breast-feeding.

WHAT YOU CAN DO TO HELP

■ Take the initiative: don't wait to be asked to share your baby's care. Give yourself the opportunity to learn how to do all the practical things your baby needs while your partner is still in the hospital.

■ Get to know your baby. Use these early days to establish a close relationship if you are going back to work in a week or two. Even if your partner is in the hospital, change the baby, learn to handle her, talk to her, hold her close so that she can focus on your face if she's awake, or simply hold her if she's asleep. Bring her to your partner when she needs to be fed, carry her around, try to be there for the first bath.

■ Be ready for your partner's mood swings. At some point during the first week your partner will probably experience the so-called "baby blues" that come as a reaction to the sudden withdrawal of the pregnancy hormones as well as to new responsibilities; she may also be very tired as well if the labor was prolonged. These "baby blues" are temporary; they subside after a week to ten days. Your partner may try to hide her feelings from you so as not to worry you or because she fears that you won't take her seriously. Never trivialize or make light of her feelings: she has a lot to cope with. Be sensitive to her needs and talk to her about them (see p. 108).

55

YOUR NEWBORN BABY

MOST PARENTS THINK THEIR NEWBORN is the most beautiful baby in the world, but in truth, few newborn babies are conventionally pretty. And even though everything is perfectly normal, your baby's appearance may make you slightly apprehensive, so you'll find it hard to resist going over him with a fine-toothed comb, just to make sure.

WHAT YOUR BABY LOOKS LIKE

The size of newborn babies varies enormously – a perfectly normal birth weight could be anything from 5lb 8oz–9lb 12oz (2.5–4.5kg). But even a 9–10lb (4–5kg) baby will seem tiny and vulnerable when newborn. Your baby may look slightly battered and bruised after the birth, and his head may be rather elongated because of molding in the birth canal, but it will return to a normal rounded shape in a week or so. There may be the odd bruise here and there on his head, especially if your birth was assisted (see p. 49), or there may be a small scar if a fetal monitor was attached to his scalp. Until he has his first bath, his hair may be a bit matted with dried blood and fluid from the birth.

A NEWBORN'S REFLEXES

A newborn baby has a whole set of built-in reflexes that help him survive. These will disappear within a few weeks as he grows and develops (see p. 134).

GRASP
He grasps anything put into his fist; the reflex is so strong he can take his own weight. The reflex is lost in a couple of weeks.

STEP
Let his feet touch a firm surface and your newborn baby takes a step – this has nothing to do with real walking.

"MORO" RESPONSE
If startled, he throws out his arms and legs in a star shape to stop himself from falling.

ROOTING
If you stroke his cheek, he automatically turns his head ("root") to find the nipple.

56

Your baby's head is large compared to the rest of him. The head may have a bump on one side where the skull bones have been compressed during birth – the skull bones are soft and can overlap one another to protect the brain. The skull bones don't fuse completely for a few months, leaving a diamond-shaped soft spot on the top of the head, covered by a tough membrane, called the fontanelle. You may notice a pulse beating there. If the birth was assisted with forceps or vacuum delivery, there may be bruising that will fade in a few days.

Your baby's eyelids may be puffy from the pressure of uterine contractions. A baby's eyes are almost always a deep blue; true eye color develops during the first year. Sometimes there may be a burst blood vessel in the white of the eye, due to pressure during the birth. This will disperse in time.

Your newborn's hair will usually fall out by three months and grow in a different color later. A preterm baby may have downy body hair, known as lanugo.

A preterm baby's skin may be covered with a protective white substance called vernix. The skin is smooth, but may appear blotchy during the first days. Overdue babies may have dry, flaky skin.

Your baby's hands will be curled into fists most of the time. Nails may be long and sometimes stained with meconium (see opposite).

The stump of the umbilical cord usually dries and shrivels within 2–3 days, and your midwife will remove the clamp at the fourth or fifth day. The remains of the stump usually drop off within ten days.

Your baby's legs may be so tightly flexed that you can't straighten them easily, but don't apply force.

Your baby's genitals will be proportionately large because of the action of pregnancy hormones. For the same reason both girls and boys may have pronounced breasts, which will shrink, and girls may produce a slight vaginal discharge for a day or two.

A newborn baby's feet are rounded like his hands and the toes tend to be curled. They may be slightly bluish because of his immature circulation.

CONCERNS ABOUT YOUR NEWBORN BABY

YOUR CONCERN	WHAT IT IS AND HOW IT IS TREATED
BIRTHMARKS	Many babies have birthmarks, most of which fade within a few months, although some, such as the so-called strawberry mark, which is raised, may take much longer. The Mongolian blue spot, a bluish birthmark on the lower back of babies with dark skin tones, is sometimes mistaken for bruising.
MILIA	Tiny white spots on the bridge of the nose; they disappear after a few weeks.
URTICARIO NEONATORUM	A blotchy rash, a bit like hives. It only lasts a couple of days.
MECONIUM	At birth your baby's bowel contains a dark green sticky substance called meconium, which is usually passed into the diaper during the first 2–3 days.
JAUNDICE	Neonatal jaundice is quite common due to a baby's immature liver; it makes the skin yellowish and the urine dark. Your baby may be sleepy so he'll need to be wakened for feedings to ensure he has enough fluid. Persistent cases may be treated with ultraviolet light.
BREATHING	Babies snuffle and sneeze a lot, and get hiccups. They may even stop breathing for a second or two, but breathing soon becomes strong and regular.
SUCKING BLISTERS	Some babies develop a white sucking blister on the lips. It doesn't cause discomfort and will fade in a few days.
SCALP SWELLING	Some babies develop a swelling on the scalp due to bleeding under the skin during the birth. This is quite normal, but it does take a few weeks to disperse.

NEWBORN BABY CHECK

Your baby is given a top-to-toe check before you leave the hospital.

VISION AND HEARING
The doctor will shine a light into your baby's eyes and note if they move on hearing her voice.

HEART AND LUNGS
She'll listen to your baby's heart and check his lungs and breathing.

ABILITY TO SUCK
She'll put her finger into your baby's mouth to check that he can suck properly.

INTERNAL ORGANS
She'll gently feel his abdomen and check his anus.

SPINE
She'll pick him up and feel his spinal column to make sure the vertebrae are in place.

HIP MANIPULATION
She'll remove his diaper and maneuver his legs and hips to rule out the possibility of any congenital hip dislocation.

THE GUTHRIE TEST
On about the sixth day, your baby will have a tiny drop of blood taken from his heel to test thyroid function, and for a rare disorder called phenylketonuria, which may cause mental retardation if it is undetected.

57

WHAT YOUR NEWBORN BABY CAN DO

SKILL	HOW TO STIMULATE YOUR BABY
SIGHT	He can see you clearly if your face is 8–10in (20–25cm) from his. He's wired to respond – his heart rate rises when he focuses on your face, so talk and smile. He'll react with body jerks and fish-feeding movements of his mouth – that's his first attempt at a conversation.
HEARING	His hearing is acute – he knows both your voices from having heard them while in the womb and he'll respond instantly to pleasure in your voice. Start talking, singing, saying rhymes from the moment of birth and never stop – he wants to communicate with you.
MOVEMENT	He loves physical movement – after all he's been jogging and swaying in the womb for nine months – so carry him around as much as possible. Move his limbs gently while changing him, clap his hands gently, do gentle knee bends. But avoid sudden movements that startle him.

HOW A PRETERM BABY MAY LOOK

If your baby is born prematurely, she may not conform to the idealized picture you've had in your mind during your pregnancy:

■ Her skin will be loose, wrinkled, and red because she hasn't had time to fill out with fat.

■ She'll be covered in downy hair called lanugo hair.

■ Her head will seem very large.

■ She's very thin and bony, especially her ribs and buttocks, with sticklike limbs.

■ Her breathing seems labored and uneven.

■ Her movements may be jerky.

FEEDING SPECIAL CARE BABIES

In the early days your baby may need to be fed glucose intravenously, or have milk fed through a tube in her nose, but hopefully will soon be well enough to try sucking. Breast milk is especially good for a premature baby because your body will make milk that is suited to your baby's gestation, and you may need to express your milk in the early days and weeks so your baby can be tube-fed. Expressing can be time-consuming and difficult (see p. 72), but stick with it, it gets easier – and you'll know you're doing the very best for your baby by providing her with nourishment.

INTRODUCING BREAST-FEEDING
When your baby is ready to try breast-feeding, don't expect her to suck immediately – it may take time and patience to get her used to it. Avoid bottles as much as possible if you intend eventually to breast-feed fully, since weaker babies can quickly get used to bottles and may then reject your nipple.

THE SPECIAL CARE BABY

IF YOUR BABY NEEDS specialist care, you'll be understandably anxious, especially if it entails her spending some time away from the neonatal ward in the intensive care unit. However, it will only be done for the best of reasons – to increase your baby's chances of thriving as a normal, healthy baby.

WHY DO BABIES NEED SPECIAL CARE?

Although many people think special care applies only to premature births, in fact about one in ten babies need some sort of specialist attention, and by no means are all of these born before term. There are several possible reasons.

Prematurity A baby born before 37 weeks is preterm or premature and may need close monitoring, as well as help with breathing and feeding.

Low birth weight Any baby who weighs 5lb 8oz (2.5kg) or less at birth is considered to have a low birth weight. Low birth weight babies may be either preterm, or full term but "small for dates" (see p. 32), and may need to spend a short time in a special care unit.

A health risk A baby who may have had difficulties with breathing during the birth, or have picked up an infection, may need special attention for a while. Alternatively, there may be birth defects such as a "hole in the heart" that may have been diagnosed before or at the birth.

WHAT SPECIAL CARE MEANS

If your baby needs special care, her needs can be catered for in a special care baby unit (SCBU) or a special section of the unit called a neonatal intensive care unit (NICU). This may mean she has to be moved to a different hospital. If she was premature or of low birth weight, she could have difficulty with breathing, be prone to infections, or be unable to regulate temperature or feed properly. Without support, low blood sugar levels can cause brain damage and she may lack iron and calcium. For these reasons she may need the protection and constant monitoring of incubator care, with intravenous or tubal feeding (see left), until she catches up in growth and learns to feed and breathe without help.

GETTING THROUGH IT

Having a baby in special care is a bit like feeling you've lost a leg: something is missing; your baby is born, but isn't yet able to be where she should be – in your arms. If she was born early, you may feel cheated on having missed out on the end of your pregnancy. Another common reaction is to feel that your baby isn't really yours – while she's in the SCBU it may seem as though she belongs to the medical staff. Try to remind yourself that this is your child, and that soon she will be home where she belongs. Be as involved as possible in discussions about her condition and in her care, and try to look forward to the day when she'll truly be yours, and you can take her home.

HELPING TO CARE FOR YOUR BABY

All special care baby units welcome parents and actively encourage them to help with feeding, washing, and diaper changing. There may be rooms where you can stay overnight from time to time, and many units provide space for a day or two before your baby is discharged so you can get used to the normal care routine of a small baby – this is particularly important if you had a multiple birth.

MAKING CONTACT

Just because your baby is in an incubator doesn't mean you can't touch, kiss, and cuddle her. This sort of contact is vitally important because it actually helps your baby develop and become strong. If it's a closed incubator, you can reach her through hand-holes to play and fondle, and you should talk and sing to her as much as you can so that she hears your voice. Open special care cribs enable you to stroke and fondle directly. All this will keep her contented and help her to thrive – love is an essential vitamin for premature babies. If it's practical, give your baby as much skin-to-skin contact as you can: when you hold your baby to your skin, her body temperature rises if she is cold, and then falls once she has warmed up. A successful experiment has also revealed that babies who are born prematurely thrive if they are nursed continuously between their mother's breasts – ask if you can try it. Skin-to-skin contact is essential for your baby, but it's essential for you, too, in fostering the bonding process. It will especially help if you're nervous; you may feel this way because your baby is so small and you're finding it difficult to relate to her because she's in a special care unit.

SPENDING TIME WITH YOUR BABY
It's important to spend as much time as possible in the special care baby unit with your baby. It will help to demystify the technology and help you bond with your baby.

COPING WITH THE TECHNOLOGY

Many parents are intimidated and frightened by special care technology with its many tubes, computerized monitors, electronic displays, and alarms. But the staff in the unit will be sympathetic to your concerns so share your feelings with them and ask if it's possible for you to see the ward psychologist together and get your feelings out in the open. It also helps to have some understanding of the functions of the equipment. These are some of the items that may be in use:

■ An incubator provides a warm, humid environment for the baby.

■ A ventilator takes over the baby's breathing, getting air into and out of the lungs.

■ A humidifier ensures that air in the ventilator is warm and moist before it goes into the baby's lungs.

■ The apnea alarm alerts the staff if a baby stops breathing.

■ The saturation monitor and blood gas analyzer measure levels of oxygen and carbon dioxide in the baby's blood.

■ The blood pressure gauge measures a baby's blood pressure.

■ A perspex head box may be used to provide extra oxygen when the baby is breathing without assistance.

■ The glucose monitor records the baby's glucose levels.

■ The ECG (electrocardiogram) monitor measures heart rate.

■ The bilirubinometer measures the risk of jaundice.

■ A phototherapy lamp is used to treat neonatal jaundice with ultraviolet light.

■ An eye shield would be used to cover a baby's eyes during phototherapy.

■ A heat shield keeps the baby warm in an open crib.

You and your body

Postnatal check

Your family doctor or hospital obstetrician will examine you about six weeks after the birth. Your baby will also be checked at about this time, and it may happen at the same appointment (see p. 133). The purpose of checking you at six weeks is to make sure that your body has fully returned to its prepregnant state. Your doctor will assess your progress by examining your uterus, heart, and blood pressure, your breasts, and any scarring if you had to be stitched after the birth. Your postnatal check is an ideal time to discuss contraception and an opportunity to air anything that concerns you. At the checkup your doctor will:

■ Test your blood pressure.

■ Listen to your heart to check your heart rate.

■ Check your weight.

■ Examine your abdomen to make sure the uterus has contracted.

■ Look at your breasts and nipples.

■ Do an internal examination to assess the size and position of your uterus and the state of your vaginal muscles.

■ Check the site of perineal stitches. Let your doctor know if the area is still sore, especially during sex.

■ Carefully check your scar and abdomen if you had a cesarean.

■ Offer you a cervical smear test if you have not had one recently or if you had one just before you became pregnant, which necessitated the treatment to be postponed.

■ Give you advice about contraception; during the internal examination an IUD can be inserted or a diaphragm fitted.

It takes a woman's body more than nine months to recover completely from pregnancy and childbirth, so go easy on yours. For the first week or so, you'll be as weak as water and unable to walk any distance or carry anything heavy. Even if you feel quite well, don't make the mistake of overdoing it, or you'll prolong your recovery period.

Getting back to normal

The medical term for the immediate period of recovery after the birth of your baby is the puerperium. It's defined as the first four weeks, but most women are physically back to normal well before that, even if their emotional adjustment takes much longer. However, you may well be concerned about what is happening to your body during the first week or two after the birth, when changes are rapid but often accompanied by a certain amount of discomfort. If this is your first experience of childbirth, it's important to realize that vaginal discharge, painfully engorged breasts, and unexpected abdominal cramps are quite normal!

How your body recovers

Where	What you can do to help
Cervix and vagina	Because both were stretched during delivery, they will take at least 7–10 days to regain their former elasticity and close up. Doing your Kegel exercises (see p. 36) will help your vagina to tighten again. Start immediately after the birth.
Placental site (lochis)	As the placental site heals, it bleeds for at least two weeks. This discharge (lochia) has three color phases: red (4–5 days), pink to brown (6–8 days), yellow to white (7–10 days). If you overexert yourself, you may start to bleed, making the lochia red and copious again, so let your doctor know and rest with your feet up.
Uterus	Immediately after the birth, your uterus shrinks down to the size it was at about the fourth month of pregnancy. By about the tenth day it can no longer be felt in your abdomen – your midwife will check daily to make sure that it is shrinking normally. It takes about six weeks to revert to its normal prepregnant size.
Ovulation	If you're not breast-feeding, you may begin to ovulate within 6–14 weeks of the birth; menstruation will follow in anything between 8 and 16 weeks. Breast-feeding hormones can suppress menstruation so you may not have a period for months, but don't rely on breast-feeding as a contraceptive. Use contraception as soon as you resume penetrative sex (see p. 117).

POSTNATAL DISCOMFORTS

DISCOMFORT	HOW TO RELIEVE IT
COPING WITH STITCHES	Discomfort from stitches can last up to a couple of weeks. Don't stand for long periods and have daily salt baths to prevent infection. Dry stitches with a hairdryer rather than a towel. Keep a bottle of witch hazel in the refrigerator and apply cold on a sterile pad to soothe the stitches. Occasionally stitches may not dissolve and need to be removed by your midwife or doctor.
STRESS INCONTINENCE	Leaking urine when coughing, sneezing, taking exercise, or even laughing is a common though embarrassing problem for many women after childbirth. It's the result of stretched and weakened perineal muscles, so once again it is important to concentrate on doing your Kegel exercises (see p. 36).
BREAST ENGORGEMENT	Three or four days after birth lactation begins; your breasts become engorged with milk, making them uncomfortably large, hard, and tender. Relieve this by expressing, putting your baby to the breast as often as he wants, and taking warm baths or laying hot washcloths on your breasts. Always wear a supporting nursing bra.
AFTERPAINS	As your uterus shrinks back you may continue to experience quite severe cramps, similar to menstrual pain, especially during breast-feeding. This is due to the action of the hormone oxytocin, which controls the "let down" of milk in your breasts (see p. 70), and also causes the uterine muscles to contract (see p. 47).
HEADACHES	In a very few cases (less than 1 percent), some women experience a severe headache after an epidural anesthetic. It's caused by a minute puncture in the membrane of the spinal column, made when the needle was inserted. If you experience this sort of headache, you'll be advised to lie down flat and drink plenty of fluids, and you'll be given painkillers such as acetaminophen until the tiny hole has healed and the headache lifts. This usually takes a couple of days.

POSTNATAL SEX

You can have nonpenetrative sex whenever you both want to after the birth, but you'd be wise to abstain from penetrative sex until after the lochia has stopped (see p. 116). However, neither of you will probably want it for a while. Nature has seen to it that most men have a low sex drive for some time after the delivery of their baby, especially if they are present at the birth. Not surprisingly, low libido lasts longer in women who have just had babies. No one who has vaginal bruises, painful stitches, and enlarged, tender breasts finds it easy to feel sexy; your need for rest and recuperation is much more important. If you've had stitches, make sure your partner feels your scar when it's healed – he'll be more understanding and compassionate about sex after he's felt the extent of it (see p. 45).

AFTER A CESAREAN

If you have a cesarean delivery, you'll be monitored more closely while you're in the postnatal ward, and your stay in the hospital will be longer than with a normal delivery. The doctors will want to be sure that both you and your baby are progressing well before you go home. Even so, your stay in the hospital is likely only to be about five days.

REMOVAL OF STITCHES
Your stitches will be removed on the sixth or seventh day at home by your midwife or doctor. This may be uncomfortable, so practice your breathing techniques to help you through it.

TIME FOR RECOVERY
You may find that it's only when you get home that you realize how much you have been knocked back by a cesarean. This won't last long – most women are amazed at how quickly they bounce back – but don't expect to feel completely back to normal for at least a month after the cesarean.

HELP IN THE HOME
You need to avoid exertion while the wound is healing so it's a good idea if your partner can arrange to take a little extra time off work to help, or to see if a friend or relative can stay for a while. You won't be able to do any heavy lifting, and will probably be warned not to drive a car for several weeks.

YOUR HEALING SCAR
At first your scar just needs to be kept dry and well ventilated, and you'll be able to bathe once the dressing is removed. If the wound becomes red or inflamed, consult your doctor, since there may be a slight infection that can be treated with antibiotics. Your scar will feel less sore as the weeks go by, but may begin to itch as the pubic hair grows back. Since the scar is on your "bikini line," it's a good idea to wear briefs that come up to your waistline to avoid irritation.

61

BEFORE YOU EXERCISE

You can start the gentle program of exercises given here at any time, but you should avoid vigorous exercise until the lochia has stopped (see p. 60).

WARMING UP
Professional athletes and dancers never start an exercise routine, competition, or performance without warming up first – they know the damage they could do to their bodies without it. It's equally important for you when doing postnatal exercises. Warming up helps relieve tension and warms up muscles and joints so that they don't overstretch when you begin more demanding exercises. It also helps to avoid cramp and stiffness afterward.

IF YOU'VE HAD A CESAREAN
You can do Kegel exercises right away, but don't attempt any other exercises until you've had your postnatal check.

TAKING CARE
Don't exercise if you feel exhausted or sick, and be careful if you've had back trouble. Avoid sit-ups or straight leg lifts.

RESUMING SPORTS

Even if you were taking part in a regular sport to a high level before you were pregnant, you should avoid strenuous aerobic exercise for at least nine months after the birth. Avoid anything that involves putting a strain on your abdominal muscles, and don't resume working out in the gym until your doctor advises it. Ask a qualified fitness trainer or sports instructor to give you a graded program, take it very easy, and don't expect to be back to your previous level of fitness or stamina for at least a year.

LOOKING AFTER YOUR BODY

Pregnancy and childbirth aren't illnesses, and your body is designed to recover naturally. However, this doesn't mean it couldn't do with a little help. Gone are the days when women were literally "confined" for several weeks, but you will need to conserve your energy during the first two or three weeks to help the healing process and to enable you to get breast-feeding successfully established (see p. 70). The fat laid down in your body during pregnancy specifically to provide the calories for breast-feeding will take a few weeks to be used up, but many women are surprised by how quickly they regain their prepregnancy shape and weight when they breast-feed.

POSTNATAL EXERCISES

Losing weight isn't the same as regaining muscle tone; you'll need to exercise the muscles in your abdomen and perineum to bring them back to normal. But finding the time and energy to do postnatal exercises may seem an impossible dream to you immediately after the birth. While you're in the postnatal ward you'll probably be visited by a physical therapist within a day of the birth. She will explain exactly what has happened to your body and will show you the best way to start exercising. Your abdominal muscles will have stretched and parted to accommodate your growing baby; this muscle tone can be regained if you find ten minutes a day to do the simple exercises given here. Make sure you warm up properly first (see left).

GETTING STARTED
Start gently – your muscles and ligaments are still soft from the action of progesterone – and don't forget your pelvic floor muscles (see p. 36); just because you can't see them doesn't mean they aren't important.

HOW TO EXERCISE
Little and often is best; start with one or two repetitions of each, every day, then progress to ten. Remember to exhale on the effort, and inhale as you relax. Always stop if any exercise hurts.

Feet are slightly apart

Hands are flat on floor

CAT ARCHING

1 Kneel on all fours with knees and hands slightly apart. Make sure your back, head, and neck are straight.

Arch lower back upward

2 Tighten your buttocks and slowly arch your back upward. Keep your arms straight but don't lock your elbows. This exercise is wonderful for relieving lower backache.

Head remains in line

Push up on arms without locking elbows

62

STOMACH TONER

Lift head forward from pillow

1 Lie on the floor, with knees bent and arms straight by your sides. Pull in your tummy muscles and press the small of your back down. Hold for four seconds, then relax.

Knees are bent and feet flat on the floor

2 Keeping your feet flat, tilt your pelvis up and lift your head off the pillow as far as you can. Don't try to sit up, it's sufficient just to lift your head and perhaps your shoulders.

Keep feet flat and curl up pelvis

CURL UPS (AFTER TWO WEEKS)

Lift head to reach forward

1 Try this more advanced abdominal exercise at least two weeks after the birth. Lie down with legs bent as before. Try to reach your knees by sliding your hands up your thighs.

Hands are flat on front of thighs

2 With your hands as close to your knees as possible, as you exhale, pull in your tummy muscles and lift your head for a count of four, then relax.

Slide hands up toward knees, keeping feet flat

63

LEG LIFTS

Legs are in line, one on top of the other, facing forward

1 Strengthen your thighs and abdominal muscles with these simple lifts. Lie on your side comfortably supporting your head with one hand, and balancing your body by resting the other hand in front of you. Make sure your legs are in line with your hip and shoulder.

Lift leg to shoulder height or higher

Keep foot facing forward as you lift

Leg should remain straight without locking knee

2 Keeping your knee and foot facing to the front, lift your whole leg straight upward to shoulder height, hold for a count of two and then lower. Do this a few times, then turn over and repeat with the other leg.

Keep lower leg flat on floor as other leg is lifted

Turn lower foot for balance if necessary

SIDE BENDS

Keep head straight as you bend to the side

Slide hand down to knee as leg is stretched

Stand with feet about 18in (45cm) apart

Stand with your feet apart and arms by your sides. Slowly bend sideways at the waist, stretching your leg outward at the same time. Return to upright, and repeat with the other side.

Tᴴᴱ ᴇxᴄɪᴛᴇᴍᴇɴᴛ ᴏғ ᴛʜᴇ ʙɪʀᴛʜ ɪs ᴏᴠᴇʀ ᴀɴᴅ ɴᴏᴡ ʏᴏᴜ'ʀᴇ ʙᴀᴄᴋ ʜᴏᴍᴇ. Bᴜᴛ ᴀs ɴᴇᴡ ᴘᴀʀᴇɴᴛs, ᴛʜᴇ ᴄʜᴀɴᴄᴇs ᴀʀᴇ ʏᴏᴜ'ʟʟ ғᴇᴇʟ ᴅᴀᴜɴᴛᴇᴅ ʙʏ ᴛʜᴇ sʜᴇᴇʀ ᴡᴏʀᴋ ɪɴᴠᴏʟᴠᴇᴅ ɪɴ ᴛʜᴇ ᴅᴀʏ-ᴛᴏ-ᴅᴀʏ ᴄᴀʀᴇ ᴏғ ʏᴏᴜʀ ʙᴀʙʏ. Tʜᴇʀᴇ ᴀʀᴇ ᴘʀᴀᴄᴛɪᴄᴀʟ ᴅᴇᴛᴀɪʟs ᴛᴏ ᴛʜɪɴᴋ ᴀʙᴏᴜᴛ, sᴜᴄʜ ᴀs ᴍᴀᴋɪɴɢ sᴜʀᴇ ʏᴏᴜ ʜᴀᴠᴇ ᴀʟʟ ᴛʜᴇ ᴇQᴜɪᴘᴍᴇɴᴛ ᴀɴᴅ ᴄʟᴏᴛʜᴇs ʏᴏᴜ ɴᴇᴇᴅ, ᴡʜᴀᴛ ᴅɪᴀᴘᴇʀs ᴛᴏ ᴜsᴇ, ᴀɴᴅ ʜᴏᴡ ᴛᴏ ᴋᴇᴇᴘ ʏᴏᴜʀ ʙᴀʙʏ ᴄʟᴇᴀɴ. Aɴᴅ ᴛʜᴇɴ ᴛʜᴇʀᴇ ᴀʀᴇ ᴛʜᴇ ᴍᴏʀᴇ sᴇʀɪᴏᴜs Qᴜᴇsᴛɪᴏɴs ʟɪᴋᴇ ʜᴏᴡ ᴛᴏ ɢᴇᴛ ʙʀᴇᴀsᴛ-ғᴇᴇᴅɪɴɢ ᴇsᴛᴀʙʟɪsʜᴇᴅ, ʜᴏᴡ ᴛᴏ ᴘᴀᴄɪғʏ ʏᴏᴜʀ ᴄʀʏɪɴɢ ʙᴀʙʏ, ᴀɴᴅ ʜᴏᴡ ᴛᴏ ᴄᴏᴘᴇ ᴡɪᴛʜ ɪɴᴛᴇʀʀᴜᴘᴛᴇᴅ ɴɪɢʜᴛs. As ᴛɪᴍᴇ ᴘᴀssᴇs, ʏᴏᴜ'ʟʟ ɢᴇᴛ ᴛᴏ ᴋɴᴏᴡ ʏᴏᴜʀ ʙᴀʙʏ ᴀɴᴅ ʜɪs ɴᴇᴇᴅs ᴡɪʟʟ ʙᴇᴄᴏᴍᴇ ᴇᴀsɪᴇʀ ᴛᴏ ᴘʀᴇᴅɪᴄᴛ ᴀɴᴅ ᴛᴏ ᴄᴀᴛᴇʀ ᴛᴏ. Iᴛ ᴡɪʟʟ sᴛɪʟʟ ʙᴇ ʜᴀʀᴅ ᴡᴏʀᴋ, ʙᴜᴛ ɪғ ʏᴏᴜ sʜᴀʀᴇ ᴛʜᴇ ᴊᴏʏs ᴀɴᴅ ʙᴜʀᴅᴇɴs ᴇQᴜᴀʟʟʏ ʏᴏᴜ'ʟʟ ғɪɴᴅ ᴛʜᴇ ᴊᴏʏ ᴏғ ᴡᴀᴛᴄʜɪɴɢ ʏᴏᴜʀ ʙᴀʙʏ ɢʀᴏᴡ ᴀɴᴅ ᴅᴇᴠᴇʟᴏᴘ ᴍᴀᴋᴇs ɪᴛ ᴀʟʟ ᴡᴏʀᴛʜᴡʜɪʟᴇ.

CARING FOR YOUR BABY

MOTHER

Your baby's first few months of life would be tiring for you even if you hadn't been through the rigors of labor and birth. Spoil yourself and make sure your own needs are satisfied: if you're happy and fulfilled you'll be better able to enjoy your baby.

HOW TO BE KIND TO YOURSELF

■ Rest with your baby. Use the time when your baby is asleep to catch up on your own sleep. It doesn't matter if you're still in your bathrobe at lunchtime. If she has her longest unbroken sleep period in the morning, take advantage of it, or rest in the afternoon when she does.

■ Share with your partner. If things are getting on top of you, he needs to know, for your sake and for your baby's – especially if he's at work during the day. Equally, encourage him to look after the baby when he's at home; don't be overprotective and try to do everything yourself.

■ Ask for help. If you're feeling isolated, don't struggle alone. Early offers of help may dwindle because friends and family don't want to impose, but they will be glad to be asked, and their help and experience may prove invaluable to you.

■ Get out of the house (see p. 114). Being tied down can make you feel cooped up and depressed, so try to get out as much as possible. It's helpful if you have friends locally who are also at home with young babies; you will probably have met like-minded parents at prenatal classes. Building a network of new parents enables you to share the good times as well as your concerns and, as your baby grows and becomes more sociable, she will have an instant circle of available playmates.

THE FIRST WEEKS

AFTER THE MONTHS OF PREPARATION, the excitement of the birth, and following the many postpartum medical routines, you find yourselves back at home in a completely new situation – at last you are a family. Now you can get down to the serious business of learning how to care for your child as she grows and develops from a small and vulnerable baby who depends on you to meet her every need, into a social and communicative one-year-old who is very mobile and might even be walking. It's immensely rewarding but there's a lot to do, with no "trial period" to ease you in – it's a full-time commitment from the start.

FINDING A PATTERN

When you become a new parent, perhaps the most difficult thing to adjust to is the fluidity and unpredictability of your new lifestyle. Most people's lives have very distinct patterns, based on doing roughly the same things at roughly the same times, and they feel uncomfortable if this structure dissolves. Alternatively, you might be used to doing what you want exactly when you want to do it. But trying to impose this sort of orderliness on a young baby is futile. If you can both relax and follow your baby's lead, a pattern of some sort will eventually emerge.

FOLLOWING YOUR BABY'S LEAD

Ignore anyone who tells you that you shouldn't pick up your crying baby because "she's only exercising her lungs" or "she'll cry herself back to sleep in a minute"; very young babies shouldn't have to wait. If a baby learns that she has to scream for ten minutes to receive attention, she is laying down a pattern of behavior that you will not appreciate in the future. So-called "good" babies are either those who are contented because all their needs are met promptly, or those who have been taught by experience that their needs won't be met at once and have become apathetic. You cannot "spoil" a young baby except by imposing a regime that is governed by the clock – and by placing your needs before hers. This will lead to her becoming discontented and hard to pacify. Helping her separate her needs from others' needs will come much later on in her development.

CHANGING YOUR PRIORITIES

If you're both following your baby's lead, you'll have to learn to be as relaxed as possible about things like mealtimes and housework, even if you normally have a set routine and are proud of your household. It's much more important for both of you to concentrate on becoming skilled and confident in the practical care of your baby. Initially, there may seem to be a lot to learn and you'll feel clumsy and nervous (everybody does), but you'll soon find that it becomes second nature, and you'll gradually develop a routine that allows you time to do chores at some point in your day.

COPING WITH THE NIGHT SHIFT

WHAT TO DO	HOW IT HELPS
PREPARE YOURSELVES FOR INTERRUPTED NIGHTS	Many babies continue to wake up once or twice during the night well beyond 12 months of age. If you're both prepared for this, you'll find it much easier to adjust.
SHARE THE BURDEN	Taking turns to get up is important. You may have followed the traditional pattern of father going to work while mother stays at home, but remember that looking after a baby is also a full-time job.
CHANGE YOUR SLEEP PATTERN	Interrupted nights are not necessarily sleepless nights. By developing a new sleep pattern, you'll find that you're able to wake, attend to your baby, and then go back to sleep immediately.
KEEP YOUR BABY CLOSE	If your baby's crib is by the side of your bed, you don't have to disturb yourselves too much when she wakes for a feeding. Put her back in her crib when you're ready to go back to sleep (see p. 86).
STAY TOGETHER	Sleeping separately could undermine your relationship as a couple and with your baby. Only sleep in separate rooms as a last resort, because of illness or extreme fatigue, for example.
AVOID SLEEP DEPRIVATION	Long-term sleep deprivation can have serious consequences, so it's better that you both lose some sleep than for one parent alone to take all the burden and become completely exhausted.

IF YOU FEEL LOW

If either or both of you feels disillusioned or dissatisfied with what you imagined you would be experiencing at this time, you're not necessarily depressed, you're probably just out of sorts. This is natural: you're both tired. If the baby is fractious, the mother may feel that somehow it is her fault and she may also be suffering from the "baby blues" (see p. 112), while a new father may feel inadequate if he's unable to help as much as he'd like, because he's at work. Don't worry: you'll both soon begin to adjust to the new situation, but if negative feelings persist, talk to your doctor or visiting nurse. They'll help you realize that lots of people feel the same way, but will also be able to tell if you're suffering from the signs of actual postpartum depression, which is easy to treat if recognized early (see p. 113).

REASSURE EACH OTHER

If you both start out with the knowledge that these first few months can seem like hard work, you'll be able to reassure each other that you're coping extremely well. If you accept the validity of each other's feelings, and hold onto the fact that any difficulties are temporary, you'll discover that parenthood really is as pleasurable as you expected.

FATHER

The first few weeks with your baby are important in helping you establish your new role as a father. The contribution you make while your baby is still small and vulnerable is important for the whole family.

HOW YOU CAN HELP

■ Support your partner. She will be very tired to start with as a result of going through labor and delivery, and from the physical and emotional responsibility of breast-feeding. Provide her with the time and space to meet your baby's nutritional needs, and reassure her constantly that she's doing a difficult job well. Your support can make all the difference.

■ Find time to help. If you're back at work, your time will be limited during working hours, but relish the opportunity to do as much as you can for your partner and your baby when you're at home.

■ Give your baby love. Babies need as much love as they can get, and there's no difference between the love of a father and a mother. If your baby is being breast-fed, then obviously she'll need her mother when she's hungry, but at all other times she'll benefit just as much from your closeness and attention. This closeness from you will mean that your baby learns to be secure with both of you, which will help her to settle and take the pressure off your partner.

■ Concentrate on building a relationship with your baby from the start. Your own feelings as a parent will be enormously enriched if you spend as much time as possible with her. Don't isolate yourself or just see yourself as the breadwinner. Being an equal partner in your baby's care will be rewarding and beneficial to you and to your family as a whole.

67

SAFETY MEASURES

You'll need to have a major overhaul of general safety equipment throughout your home. Before the birth of your baby you should install smoke alarms, if you don't have them already, and before your baby becomes mobile you will need:

- Covers for all electric sockets.
- Corner protectors for furniture.
- Locks and catches for video recorders, doors, cabinets, and drawers (especially in the kitchen and bathroom), as well as the refrigerator.
- Retractable cords for electrical goods such as the teapot, iron, and toaster.
- A stair gate at the top and bottom of stairs and across the kitchen door or opening.

EQUIPMENT

PROVIDING FOR YOUR NEW BABY is exciting and rewarding, and you naturally want the best. However, as you set out to plan the nursery, do bear in mind that to start with your new arrival will need very little in the way of essentials.

THE BASICS

Manufacturers of nursery "hardware" have recognized that couples expecting their first child are among the biggest spenders around, but you don't need to break the bank to provide for your newborn baby if you stick to the basics shown here.

Lining should be washable

MOSES BASKET
Simple and lightweight for a newborn. You could make linings and trimmings yourself – use cotton fabric.

BABY CHAIR
A rigid or bouncing baby chair with back support is useful for young babies before they can sit. Always place it on the floor.

CHANGING MAT
Comfortable and practical to avoid mess when diaper-changing and at bathtime.

Plastic cover can be sponged clean

BABY BATH
Head rest   *Flat base can be rested on a stand or firm surface*

A flat-based bath comes with a stand or can be rested on a firm surface; others fit over the big bath. For use in the first 3–4 months.

FULL-SIZE CRIB
When your baby outgrows his Moses basket, you'll need a crib. Choose one with two mattress positions and a drop-side to protect your back when lifting him.

Check that crib bar gaps conform with safety standards

Check that drop-side catches are secure in case your baby pulls them

Removable tray so chair can be pushed to table for family meals

Safety harness

Chair can be used separately

Base converts into toddler table

HIGH CHAIR
Foldaway designs take up less space, but rigid chairs may be more stable. The one shown is expensive, but it's a good investment because it can be taken apart to form a toddler's table and chair when your baby is older.

Choose a firm, stable base

Look for adjustable mattress heights

OUT AND AROUND

Your baby won't be walking until she's at least a year old, and even then she'll need transporting in a stroller or car seat for safety. It's worth looking ahead to future needs when you're thinking about buying any of these larger, more expensive items.

INFANT CAR SEAT
All babies under 22lb (10kg) should be put in a rear-facing seat in the car. Make sure it conforms to safety standards.

Car seat may be used as a carrier and seat outside the car

Changing bag holds all baby equipment

CHANGING BAG
Choose a bag to hold diapers, changing equipment, and clothes, with space for bottles, baby food, and toys when necessary.

SLING
There are several types of carrying sling suitable for young babies; try them on to see which is most comfortable A backpack may be more comfortable once your baby can sit up.

CARRIAGE AND STROLLER
A carriage/stroller combination can be used until your child is about three years old. Check ease of folding, and that the height of the handle doesn't make you stoop. A smaller, umbrella-type folding stroller may be preferable if you use the car a lot, although it's not suitable until your baby is six months old.

Bassinet can be removed

CARRIAGE

STROLLER

Detachable sunshade

Seat should adjust to face forward or backward

Fixed wheelbase is firmer and easier to push

Integral shopping tray

Make sure foot brake is easy to use and secure

BUYING SECONDHAND

If there's a secondhand baby shop in your area, it's well worth a visit. Many nursery items get relatively light use, so there may be good bargains. You can also try shopping at charity shops and tailgate sales. However you should check all equipment carefully, and certain items should be avoided (see below).

GOOD SECONDHAND BUYS
■ Clothes, especially newborn baby clothes and outerwear.

■ Bedclothes (except quilts), but always wash before use.

■ Moses basket, but always buy a new mattress.

■ Plastic or wood toys only, but check carefully for cracks or splinters. Avoid anything that has metal or moving parts; even soft toys or dolls may contain hidden metal parts, for example, eyes, swiveling heads and arms.

■ Large plastic items, such as sterilizing equipment.

POSSIBLE SECONDHAND BUYS
■ Carriage or stroller – check brakes, folding mechanism, and accessories before committing yourself.

■ Crib, but always buy a new mattress and check drop-side mechanism is safe.

■ Travel crib. Always check the folding mechanism and carrying case. Buy a new mattress if necessary.

■ High chair. Check that all screws are really secure and check crevices for food deposited by the previous user.

■ Safety items such as baby monitors or stair gates, but check that they work properly.

BAD SECONDHAND BUY
■ Never buy a secondhand car seat for your baby. It's too risky because the seat may have been weakened in an accident.

69

ADVANTAGES OF BREAST-FEEDING

There are many advantages to breast-feeding, both for your baby and for you. Here are some of them:

■ Bonds baby and mother closely.

■ Readily available, sterile, and always at the correct temperature.

■ Easy for your baby to digest.

■ A perfect balance of protein, carbohydrate, fat, salt and other minerals, vitamins, and iron.

■ Protects against infection.

■ May protect against allergies.

■ Breast-fed babies have fewer diaper rashes and their stools are softer and less offensive.

■ Helps burn off fat laid down in a mother's body during pregnancy.

YOU WILL NEED

2–3 NURSING BRAS
BREAST PADS
disposable or reusable

THE "LET-DOWN" REFLEX
When a baby suckles, nerves in the areola stimulate the pituitary gland in the brain to secrete oxytocin, which causes the breast to release ("let down") milk.

Pituitary gland secretes the hormone oxytocin

Nerves in areola signal to pituitary when baby sucks, so milk is released

BREAST-FEEDING

THERE ARE NO DRAWBACKS to breast-feeding, only advantages. Breast milk is, by definition, the most suitable food for your baby, providing all her nutritional needs during her first six months. Although as a father you can't actually breast-feed, you can be involved in supporting your partner, knowing that this is beneficial to your baby.

GETTING STARTED

Some people have no difficulty with breast-feeding; but for many others it doesn't go smoothly in the beginning. Don't feel demoralized; follow the step-by-step guide opposite and discuss any problems with a midwife or breast-feeding counselor, who will be happy to give advice at any time. Don't give up without consulting one of them first. Remember that your baby is learning too, so you have to be patient for her sake.

ENSURING A GOOD MILK SUPPLY

When you put your baby to the breast, the milk she drinks first – the foremilk – is thin, watery, and thirst-quenching; the hindmilk that follows is richer in fat and protein, so your baby gets all her nutritional needs at one feeding. To make sure that you provide a good milk supply, eat a good diet and drink lots of fluids, especially in hot weather, when your baby will be thirsty too. Feed on demand, when your baby is hungry; your body will automatically produce enough. If your baby feeds slowly in the first few days, you may have to express milk (see p. 72) in order for more to be produced. If your baby feeds often and hungrily, you will always keep pace, no matter how small your breasts are; don't believe old-wives' tales about small breasts not making enough milk – breast size is irrelevant. However, it is important for you to get plenty of rest between feedings, so your own metabolism can catch up. Many women find the mid-evening feed the most difficult since the milk supply is often lower because you are tired, and your baby may be fretful at this time of day. Plan ahead by resting in the afternoon if possible, preparing an evening meal earlier in the day, or better still, leaving the cooking to your partner.

FREQUENCY OF FEEDS

Be prepared to feed often at the beginning – your newborn baby could feed ten or eleven times in 24 hours for the first few weeks. Feeding will take over your life to start with, but you'll find that your baby is contented, goes to sleep easily, and by the time she's six to eight weeks, she'll be feeding more efficiently and less often. Don't try to impose a rigid routine – your baby will be upset and the stress will affect your ability to feed. During the first few weeks, use alternate breasts for feedings, with ten to fifteen minutes per feeding. This helps balance the milk supply and prevents either breast from becoming sore as a result of over-sucking. Many babies find one side easier than the other; if this happens with your baby, put her to the less favored breast first.

SUCCESSFUL BREAST-FEEDING

To establish successful breast-feeding, it's important to understand how your baby sucks. "Sucking" is really the wrong word; in fact she "smacks" the nipple between her tongue and the roof of her mouth. To do this properly she has to latch on correctly (see below) with her gums firmly gripping the areola (this stimulates the let-down of milk – see opposite) and the nipple is so far into her mouth that the milk is then squeezed right into her throat for her to swallow.

BREAST-FEEDING POSITIONS
It's important to be in a comfortable position before you start feeding since you're likely to be there for 10–20 minutes. Whether sitting or lying, make sure your baby's whole body is angled toward you; she's more likely to latch on first time.

Support your head with your hand or lie on a pillow

Lie the baby facing you and feed from the lower breast

SITTING IN A CHAIR
Sit with both feet firmly on the ground. Support your back and arms with pillows and place a pillow on your lap to raise and support your baby if necessary.

Use both hands to bring your baby to the breast

71

FEEDING WHILE LYING DOWN
This is a good position when you're tired or if you need to keep your baby's weight off a cesarean wound. Lie on your side and lay your baby alongside you so she can reach your lower breast.

LATCHING ON AND RELEASING

1 Cradle your baby in the crook of your arm and use your other hand to bring her up to your breast. Line up your nipple with your baby's nose. As soon as she smells your milk, she'll open her mouth. While your baby is very young, you can gently stroke her cheek; when you do this, she'll turn toward your breast as a reflex action.

2 Your baby should "latch on" to your nipple at once. If not, support your breast with your hand and guide her onto it so that she has a mouthful of nipple.

Baby's gums should encircle the areola

3 A breast-feeding baby creates a strong vacuum on the breast, so when she has finished, you may need to release her grip on the nipple by gently easing your little finger into the corner of her mouth. Never pull your nipple away from your baby; this is a sure way to make it sore, and sore nipples (see p. 73) may deter you from breast-feeding.

EXPRESSING MILK WITH A BREAST PUMP

Electric pumps apply a rhythmical suction to the breast and are quite efficient at obtaining substantial amounts of milk. You can buy one or rent or borrow it from the hospital or one of the organizations that promote breast-feeding. Smaller hand or battery-operated pumps work by holding the funnel over the breast and drawing the plunger in and out, or switching it on, using an intermittent suction rhythm that avoids bruising the tender breast.

HAND PUMP
Many hand pumps incorporate a container that doubles as a feeding bottle.

72

EXPRESSING MILK

When you're breast-feeding you can express milk so your partner can feed your baby; it also helps relieve overfull breasts in the first days. If your baby is in a neonatal baby unit (see p. 58), you can express milk to feed him. Few women find it easy to express milk, so don't be disheartened – it's a knack that takes a bit of learning. If you "leak" milk while feeding, place a breast shell against the other breast. Keep the expressed milk in a sterile container.

EXPRESSING MILK BY HAND

1 Massage your breasts with flat hands, beginning at your ribs and working toward your areola, gradually going over the whole breast.

2 Then roll your fingers and thumb together below and above your areola so that you press on the wider milk ducts behind the nipple.

3 Collect the milk in a sterile bowl, transfer it to a sterile container, and keep it in the refrigerator for a few hours. Freeze it for longer storage.

WHAT IF IT'S TWINS?

Don't be put off by people who say you can't breast-feed twins. Lots of mothers prove otherwise and, like all babies, twins benefit enormously from breast milk. Human breasts are quite capable of nourishing two babies, each of whom has the same need to bond with his parents, and you can feed them at the same time once breast-feeding is established.

GET ADVICE
Confidence is a crucial factor in breast-feeding twins. Try to talk to other mothers who've done it successfully – there are support groups to help you (see p. 163).

FEEDING TOGETHER
To feed your babies at the same time, lay them on their backs one under each arm with their heads forward, supported on pillows.

ONE AT A TIME TO START WITH
Concentrate on latching on with one baby at a time at first. Feeding singly may be easier in the early days, and gives you a chance to get to know each baby individually. However, this does take much longer than feeding together.

THERE'S PLENTY OF MILK
Breast-feeding is always controlled by demand, so your breasts will produce as much milk as your babies need. If one feeds more readily than the other, put the slower baby to the breast first; the stronger baby will stimulate more milk.

LOOK AFTER YOURSELF
Eat well, have plenty to drink, and rest whenever you have the opportunity. Although twins' practical needs are the same, there are two of them to look after, and you'll find that you tire easily; make sure you get as much help as you can.

BEING DETERMINED

Few women breast-feed without encountering problems at least once, and sometimes several times. So while you shouldn't necessarily expect to find it difficult, neither should you be surprised if you seem to have a series of problems. The important thing to bear in mind is that most breast-feeding difficulties can be corrected – provided you have support and the commitment and confidence to continue.

SORE NIPPLES

Painful nipples are the most common reason for giving up breast-feeding. However, there are ways to avoid them. Make sure your baby is properly latched on and never pull your baby off the nipple (see p. 71). Keep your nipples dry with disposable or cotton washable breast pads or clean cotton hankerchiefs. Don't use tissues since they will fall apart. Let your nipples dry naturally at the end of each feeding whenever possible. If they become cracked, calendula or camomile cream may help. If your nipples become very sore, feed your baby before he is desperate since he will be calmer and more gentle. Try to get the milk flowing before the feeding starts by expressing a little first.

BLOCKED DUCTS AND MASTITIS

A red, tender patch on your breast may be a sign of a blocked milk duct. You may even feel feverish. Take immediate action by feeding as frequently as possible, or express milk, particularly from the affected side. Massage any lumps gently as your baby feeds. See your doctor if there's no improvement within 24 hours, since you may need a mild antibiotic to clear any infection.

FATHER

Your support is essential when your partner begins breast-feeding, especially if she has any difficulties.

WHAT YOU CAN DO TO HELP
■ Be gently encouraging. This is not the time for a hint of criticism.

■ Don't leave your partner to feed the baby alone unless she asks you to – she could feel isolated and you'll feel neglected.

■ Your partner may like to express milk that you can give in a bottle at night. Undo your shirt and hold your baby against your skin to mimic breast-feeding (see p. 74).

■ Be aware that your partner's breasts may be tense, sore, and very sensitive for the first few weeks of breast-feeding.

73

CONCERNS ABOUT BREAST-FEEDING

YOUR CONCERN	WHAT YOU CAN DO
HOW LONG ON EACH BREAST	Your baby takes 80 percent of the feeding in the first five minutes; five minutes more and he's sucked out the creamy aftermilk, so as a rough guide, expect him to spend about 10 minutes per breast. Breast-fed babies are rarely underfed although they may only feed for a short time.
SLOW FEEDING	Many babies take a few days to get the hang of latching on and may be slow to feed. If this becomes a problem, seek advice. A baby who sucks a long time isn't necessarily feeding. He may just love sucking. If your baby has a tendency to fall asleep at the breast, let him take all he wants from one side, then offer the other breast first next time.
BABY'S WEIGHT GAIN	Don't weigh your baby before and after feeding. Weight gain in breast-fed babies should always be calculated over a two- to three-week period, since they often gain unevenly. The very rare instances of underfeeding usually occur because the baby isn't properly latched on.
IF YOU'RE SICK	Common infections such as colds needn't interrupt breast-feeding. Stay in bed and let your partner bring the baby to you just to feed. You could also express milk so your partner can feed your baby instead. If you need medication of any sort, make sure your doctor knows you are breast-feeding since some medicines are not recommended for breast-feeding mothers. If you go to the hospital, breast-feeding is usually still possible if you take your baby in with you.
BREAST-FEEDING IN PUBLIC	Breast-feeding is the most convenient way to feed your baby, and you should be able to breast-feed anytime, anywhere. It's possible to feed discreetly if you use a nursing bra that undoes easily in front with one hand, and a big shawl or cardigan to screen yourself. A baggy T-shirt or sweatshirt also works – you can tuck your baby up underneath it.

CLEANING AND PREPARING BOTTLES

Hygiene and correct formulation of feedings are important if you are bottle-feeding because the lack of either one could lead to health problems with your baby. To make sure your baby thrives and to avoid infection:

■ Buy equipment well in advance and practice cleaning bottles and placing them correctly in the sterilizing unit (see opposite), if the doctor has recommended that you use one.

■ Always wash your hands thoroughly before handling bottles and feeding your baby.

■ With 6–7 feedings in 24 hours for the first few weeks, you may need to sterilize bottles twice a day. Later you can reduce this to once a day.

■ Make up batches of six bottles at a time and store them in the refrigerator. When all but two bottles have been used, make up some more.

■ Never add extra scoops of formula or sugar.

■ When a feeding is over, pour out leftover formula, clean and rinse the bottle, and cover and place it to one side.

■ Never give a baby leftover formula from a bottle because it may be contaminated. Always use or make up a fresh bottle and keep a couple of cartons of commercially prepared formula for emergencies.

■ You can avoid the cleaning and sterilization process by using disposable bottles. These are plastic bags that are fitted into a dispenser and filled as you would a normal bottle. When your baby has finished a feeding, the "bottle" is thrown away, the dispenser can be reused, and only the nipple needs to be cleaned.

BOTTLE-FEEDING

I'M NOT GOING TO PRETEND that bottle-feeding is as good for your baby as breast-feeding, but I don't want you to feel guilty, either. If you're undecided, look back to the sections on breast-feeding so that you're aware of its positive advantages. Bottle-feeding does, however, mean that both of you can share all of your baby's care equally.

FEEDING YOUR BABY

Either of you can bottle-feed your baby, but bottle-feeding really allows a father to come into his own. When you are giving your baby a bottle, you can mimic the closeness of breast-feeding by cradling her close in the crook of your arm. Hold her so her face is 8–10in (20–25cm) away from yours, in a position where she can make eye contact with you (see p. 57). If possible, open your shirt and hold her against your bare skin.

GIVING YOUR BABY A BOTTLE

Before you start, check also that the flow from the nipple is neither too fast nor too slow – before giving the bottle, tip it to make sure the nipple produces a flow of several drops a second. Your baby may break naturally for a burp halfway through the feeding, but it isn't necessary to force her to burp by rubbing her back; if she's still hungry she'll just get upset. If she seems comfortable, let her feed without a break until she's had enough.

If possible, hold your baby as close as possible to your bare skin

BOTTLE-FEEDING YOUR BABY
Cradle your baby close enough to keep eye contact throughout, and talk to her while you feed. If necessary, put a pillow on your lap to raise her. She'll soon learn to associate the pleasure of feeding with the sight of your face.

Your baby will look at you while feeding if held close enough

MAKING UP A FEEDING

*Level off
formula with
back of knife*

*Use powdered
infant formula*

*Add
formula
a scoop
at a time*

*Measure
boiled water
in measuring
cup*

1 Fill the scoop provided and level off the formula with the back of a knife. Do not pack the formula down.

2 Pour the required amount of boiled water into a measuring cup and add the formula one scoop at a time.

3 Stir the formula with a clean spoon to make sure it is completely dissolved. Never add extra scoops of formula, which could be dangerous to your baby. Pour the formula into bottles through a funnel.

*Formula
dissolved
in hot water*

*Fill bottles
through
funnel*

*Put enough for
one feeding in
each bottle*

*Cover bottles
until needed*

*Invert nipple
in bottle*

4 Cover bottle immediately, keeping clean nipples inside the bottles ready for use. Allow to cool and store in the refrigerator until ready for use. Don't keep formula more than 24 hours.

YOU WILL NEED

MEASURING CUP AND
FUNNEL

HOT, BOILED WATER

POWDERED FORMULA
with measuring scoop

STRAIGHT-BACKED KNIFE
*for leveling scoopfuls of
powdered formula*

STERILE SPOON
for stirring formula

6 BOTTLES, NIPPLES,
AND COVERS

*Place bottle in bowl of
hot water to reheat*

75

5 When you are ready to feed, take the bottle from the refrigerator and warm the formula by placing it in a bowl of hot water. You can also cool hot formula by placing it in cold water.

TESTING THE FORMULA
Always check that the formula is not too hot or too cold before offering it to your baby by shaking a few drops onto your wrist. The formula should be blood temperature, which means it should feel neither hot nor cold against your skin.

*Shake
drops
from
bottle*

*Formula should
not feel hot or
cold on your wrist*

KEEPING BOTTLES CLEAN

Scrupulous hygiene is essential if you are bottle-feeding. Formula can be a rich breeding ground for the bacteria that cause diseases such as gastroenteritis, so you need to sterilize bottles, nipples, and all other equipment used for feeding if your doctor recommends it. Clean bottles and nipples thoroughly using the method shown (right) before sterilizing.

*Use bottle brush
to clean inside
bottle*

*Inside of
nipple is
rubbed
with salt*

*Use hot,
soapy water*

1 Scrub each bottle with a bottle brush and hot, soapy water to remove all traces of formula, then rinse thoroughly in cold water.

2 Rub the nipple inside and out with salt, paying attention to the inside rim. Make sure that the holes are also clear. Then rinse in cold water.

CLEANING YOUR BABY

CLEANING GIRLS

Always clean your baby's vulva and anus from front to back to avoid spreading bacteria from the anus to your baby's vagina. Don't clean inside the labia; just rinse away feces gently with damp cotton.

Lift your baby's legs by holding her ankles

Wipe labia on the outside only

Use cotton or baby wipes to clean

Wipe vulva from front to back

CLEANING BOYS

Cover a boy's penis with a tissue as you take off his diaper. Clean around the penis and scrotum with damp cotton; always wipe the anus from front to back. Don't try to pull back the foreskin because this remains fixed until your son is much older.

Clean around genital area with lotion

Clean anus from front to back

Make sure you remove soiling from creases

DIAPERS

Y OU'LL HAVE TO USE DIAPERS for at least two and a half years, until your baby gains full bladder and bowel control, so it's worth familiarizing yourself with the most efficient way to change your baby. Give some thought, too, to which type of diaper best suits your circumstances – there's certainly plenty of choice.

WHICH DIAPERS TO USE

There's a wide variety of disposable diapers available and you may be bewildered by the choice. If you want to use reusable diapers, there are several more modern alternatives to the traditional terry toweling square that requires safety pins (see opposite). Neither type is better than the other: unless you use a diaper laundry service, reusable diapers are a lot more trouble as they have to be washed and dried, while disposable diapers are more expensive, even taking into account the hidden costs of washing and drying reusables. There's been discussion about the adverse impact on the environment of disposable diapers both in their manufacturing and disposal; reusable diapers are probably more ecologically sound in the long run.

DIAPERS FOR BOYS OR GIRLS

The most important feature when choosing diapers is to make sure they accommodate your baby boy and are comfortable for your baby girl. Some manufacturers of disposables have taken this into account: boys tend to wet the front of diapers so boys' disposables have extra padding in the front. Girls tend to wet the back of diapers more, and this is also accounted for in the design of girls' disposables.

DIAPERS, LINERS, AND FASTENERS

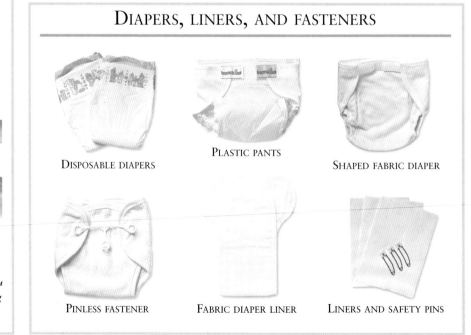

DISPOSABLE DIAPERS

PLASTIC PANTS

SHAPED FABRIC DIAPER

PINLESS FASTENER

FABRIC DIAPER LINER

LINERS AND SAFETY PINS

CHANGING YOUR BABY'S DIAPER

Always change your baby on a firm flat surface, covered with a changing mat or towel. Protect your back by using a changing table of the correct height, or kneel beside the bed. Never leave your baby alone on the changing mat if it's on a surface above floor level. Even a newborn baby can wriggle off a mat, particularly if she's upset or angry. Collect together all the equipment you need before you start. Dispose of feces in the toilet if possible; don't flush disposable diapers or diaper liners down the toilet. Dispose of used diapers in diaper bags, preferably placing them in a covered can.

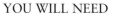

YOU WILL NEED
CHANGING MAT
TISSUES
DIAPER
BOWL OF WARM WATER OR BABY LOTION
COTTON OR BABY WIPES
BARRIER CREAM
CAN WITH LID OR DIAPER BAGS

1 Remove the soiled diaper and clean carefully as shown opposite. Make sure all creases are clean and dry if you used water to clean. Slide the clean diaper under your baby, lifting her buttocks gently into position.

USING SHAPED FABRIC DIAPERS
Modern reusable diapers are compact and easy to use.

2 Using both hands, bring the front of the diaper up between your baby's legs, as high as it will go. Tuck in the corners securely around her waist, ready for fastening.

Modern fabric diaper with velcro fastening

3 Holding the diaper in place with one hand, fix the adhesive tabs firmly onto the front flap of the diaper.

77

DIAPER RASH

Diaper rash is preventable if you change your baby promptly, particularly after a bowel movement; bacteria in feces break down the urine to release ammonia, which ulcerates the skin. Use barrier cream only as a preventive measure. If your baby does become sore, leave his diaper off when possible, and apply diaper cream at every change. Check with your doctor if the rash persists for more than two to three days.

FABRIC DIAPERS

Traditional terry toweling squares are bulky, and can be uncomfortable for your baby when he's mobile. Modern reusables are usually shaped, and many types have strong velcro fastenings or you could use pinless fasteners, so you don't have to worry about using safety pins. If you're using these, it's a good idea to also use disposable or reusable liners (see box opposite) to avoid heavy soiling with feces.

BATHING TIPS

To bathe your baby as quickly and as safely as possible:

■ Wash or bathe him in a room that is warm and draft-free; it does not have to be the bathroom. Use a bucket to carry the water and to fill and empty the tub.

■ If you use a sponge and washcloth, make sure they are reserved strictly for your baby's use and wash them frequently.

■ Never poke about inside your baby's ears with a cotton swab, which could easily damage her delicate eardrum. Only remove ear wax that is visible at the opening.

YOU WILL NEED

COTTON
for face, eyes, and diaper area
COOLED, BOILED WATER
for washing the eyes
BOWL OF WARM WATER
for washing face and body
SOFT TOWEL
for wrapping and drying
DIAPER CHANGING EQUIPMENT
(SEE P. 76)
CLEAN CLOTHES

KEEPING YOUR BABY CLEAN

VERY YOUNG BABIES don't get dirty, so they don't need frequent bathing – but bathtime does provide a perfect opportunity for cuddling and playing that infants come to relish. It also gives fathers a chance to spend time with their babies. Later, bathtime will be part of your baby's bedtime routine, a signal that it's time to wind down.

WHILE YOUR BABY IS YOUNG

Many parents are understandably nervous about bathing their newborn baby while she is still tiny and seems so vulnerable. It is, however, worth remembering that a baby is quite resilient provided she's handled gently but firmly, so try to be as confident as possible. You'll be shown the safest and easiest methods for bathing your baby a few days after the birth by a midwife at the hospital or when she visits you at home. As with all aspects of caring for your baby, bathing her will soon become second nature once you have given yourselves time to get used to it. The first few times, your baby may get upset when she is being bathed, so don't feel you have to bathe her every day. Thorough cleaning of the hands, face, and diaper area is quite sufficient.

GIVING YOUR BABY A SPONGE BATH
You can clean your baby thoroughly by washing her face, hands, and diaper area, without undressing her completely. You can do this most days as part of your baby's diaper changing and dressing routine and then just give her a bath every two or three days instead. This will save you time and be less upsetting for your baby.

1 Undress your baby on a changing mat or towel. Leave her undershirt on or wrap her in a towel. Gently wipe her face, ears, and neck folds with cotton moistened in warm water. Pat her dry, making sure that you have dried thoroughly between her neck folds.

Use separate pieces of cotton for each eye to avoid cross-infection

3 Take off her diaper and clean the diaper area (see p. 76), then wipe with cotton moistened in warm water, especially around the folds in your baby's thighs. Wash the genital area front to back. Pat dry, put on a fresh diaper, then dress her in clean clothes.

Clean from front to back

Wash face with small pieces of damp cotton

2 Take two more clean pieces of cotton and moisten them with cooled boiled water. Using separate pieces of cotton for each stroke, to avoid the risk of cross-infection, carefully wipe your baby's eyes from the inner corner outward.

BATHING YOUR BABY

Choose a bathtime that suits you and your baby; it doesn't always have to be in the evening, especially if your baby tends to be fretful at that time of day. However, if you're working parents, bathing your baby in the evening is often a good way for you to spend time with her; you can even have a bath with her when she's older (see p. 81) to make it more fun! Make sure you've got all of the items you need within easy reach to make the task quicker and easier.

Look at your baby and talk to him

1 Fill the tub 2–3in (5–8cm) deep, putting cold in first. Test the temperature with your elbow or wrist; it should only feel warm.

Support your baby's head and shoulders

Wrap him in a warm, dry towel

Add baby bath solution to bath water

Gently wash his hair and scalp

4 Holding your baby in the tub and supporting his head with one arm, gently wash his body with your free hand, and encourage him to kick and splash in the water.

Make sure his head is dry since most heat is lost through the head

Place the tub on a flat, secure surface

2 Undress your baby down to his undershirt and wash his face and neck (see opposite). Wrap him firmly in a towel, then, holding him under your arm and supporting his head over the bath, gently wash and rinse his hair with water from the bath. Pat his hair dry with a towel.

79

5 To get your baby out of the bathtub, raise his head and shoulders with one hand and slide your free hand under his bottom as before, then lift him onto the dry towel. Wrap him up immediately so he doesn't get cold. Pat him dry all over, paying particular attention to the folds of his neck, bottom, thighs, and under his arms, then put on his diaper and dress him.

Support your baby's head and shoulders with your right hand

3 Leave a dry towel ready for after the bath. Unwrap the first towel, remove the diaper, and lift your baby into the bath, supporting his head and shoulders firmly with one hand, and his bottom and legs with your other hand.

Support your baby's legs and buttocks with your left hand and arm as you lower him into the tub

BATHING AN OLDER BABY

SAFETY FIRST

When you use the big bathtub, bear in mind that your baby could drown in just a few inches of water (see p. 103). Take the following precautions to avoid accidents:

■ Have all equipment on the floor beside the tub and change your baby there. It is safer than carrying a wet slippery baby to a chair.

■ Put a nonslip mat in the bath.

■ Kneel on the floor to support your baby, and to prevent straining your back.

■ Never leave your baby alone in the tub, even when he can sit up.

YOU WILL NEED

NONSLIP BATH MAT
SPONGE OR WASHCLOTH
BABY BATH SOLUTION
SHAMPOO
FACE SHIELD
to protect his eyes from shampoo
TOWEL
DIAPER AND CLEAN CLOTHES

ONCE YOUR BABY is three to four months old and has good head control, you could start using the big bathtub. Once he is used to it, he will appreciate the extra room to play in the water. The same principles apply – keep your baby warm before and after his bath, do not overfill the tub, and check that the water is not too hot.

USING THE BIG BATHTUB

Making the transition from the baby bath to the big bathtub can distress some babies, while others love it. It's a good idea to begin by putting the baby bath into the big tub the first few times so that the change is gradual and less frightening. Once your baby is used to it and can sit up in the tub by himself, he'll begin to look forward to it as part of his routine, and enjoy bathtime games and water play (see opposite). You'll find bathtime can become a riotous affair with lots of shouts and splashing, but the problems may come when you want to get him out! It's advisable to make bathtime a part of your baby's overall bedtime routine (see p. 87) so that it acts as a clear signal to him that the day is over.

Pouring games will amuse your baby

THE BIG BATHTUB
Kneel or sit beside the tub so that you're at your baby's level; wear an apron to protect yourself from splashes.

Sit your baby on a nonslip tub mat

GIVING YOUR BABY A TOWEL BATH

Cleaning your baby by towel-bathing him is halfway between sponge-bathing him (see p. 78) and giving him a real bath. It is a useful method if your baby isn't feeling well or if he gets upset when he's having a bath. It is also much quicker and more convenient for you, for those times when he needs a thorough washing but you're short on time; for example, after an enthusiastic self-feeding session (see p. 95).

TOP HALF FIRST
● Collect the same equipment as for sponge-bathing (see p. 78).
● Undress him to his diaper and wrap his lower half in a towel. Wash his face, neck, and upper body and pat dry.

Wash top half with lower body wrapped in towel

LOWER HALF
● Put a clean undershirt on your baby or wrap him in the towel. Remove the diaper, then wash his legs and feet, followed by his diaper area.
● Dry your baby thoroughly all over, then put on a clean diaper and dress him in clean clothes.

Cover top half with undershirt or towel while sponging lower body

MAKING BATHTIME FUN

Older babies really enjoy bathtime and it's an excellent time to catch up on your baby's developing personality and skills if you aren't able to be with him during the day. Bathtime is a wonderful opportunity for creative play and you can use it to help stimulate his development in a variety of ways. Babies love the freedom to sit in the warm water and you'll find that your baby will be endlessly fascinated by filling, pouring, and splashing water. This really is learning through play – your baby is finding out about the properties of water and other liquids. Help him to do this by:

● Using simple household items like plastic cups and pitchers or spoons and sieves to show your baby what holds water and what doesn't, and how water can be poured and stirred.

● Introducing floating toys such as boats or traditional bath ducks that your baby will enjoy handling.

● Having fun with your baby by taking him into the bathtub with you; have a lovely skin-to-skin soak together. Keep the water at an even temperature with a slow trickle from the tap – you should be lying with your head at the opposite end from the taps.

HAIRWASHING

Even though your baby may love his bath, hairwashing may continue to be a problem if he hates having water poured on to his head or over his face, especially if it goes in his eyes. Don't worry; this is very common. Take your time getting your baby used to water on his head and face; make a game of it by dripping tiny amounts over his head from time to time. Until he's more confident, you can simply sponge his hair clean or wipe it with a washcloth.

Some babies love having water on their faces and don't even mind it in their eyes. If your baby likes water, you can use the bath-shower attachment or a cup to rinse his hair and make a game of it. But even the mildest baby shampoo will sting your baby's eyes a little, so it is advisable to use a face shield to keep the soap and water out of his eyes until he's old enough to keep them shut or to hold his head back for you. Dry his hair with a towel and brush it with a soft brush.

TROUBLE-FREE HAIRWASHING
Use a simple face shield to keep water and shampoo away from your baby's face and eyes. Pour water gently so there's no danger of it splashing back.

FATHER

Your baby will grow to love bathtime, particularly if it is his special time with you. Encourage this bonding by handling him with confidence; the more often you do it, the less nervous he (and you) will be. Giving a bath is a positive way of contributing to your baby's care, and he'll know you're an equal partner in his life with his mother.

MAKE THE MOST OF BATHTIME
■ When you have a bath with your baby, lay him on your chest half in and half out of the water. Smile and talk to him all the time as you wash him.

■ Splash water gently over his body, carefully avoiding his face. This way your baby will learn to enjoy, and be unafraid of, water.

■ Allow plenty of time; a bath is not much fun for either of you if you have to rush. Remember, sharing a bath with your baby is also a good and enjoyable way for you to wind down after a stressful day at work.

81

Use a face shield to prevent shampoo from stinging eyes during hairwashing

Your baby will enjoy playing in the bath

DRESSING YOUR BABY

CHOOSING CLOTHES

You could be changing your baby's clothes several times a day to begin with, so choose clothes that are simple to put on and take off, and quick to wash and dry:

■ Choose roomy garments, with loose elastic at the cuffs.

■ Make sure fastenings are easy – snap are better than buttons. Avoid ribbons, which may be difficult to undo.

■ Avoid pure wool, which may irritate skin. Choose nonirritating fabrics, such as cotton.

■ Only get machine-washable, colorfast clothing.

■ Always look for labels that indicate clothes are inflammable.

■ Your baby's fingers and nails may get caught on openweaves.

■ Clothes can safely be bought second-hand, but check for inflammability, shrinkage, and condition of fastenings.

■ Nightgowns are useful for newborns; they're quick to put on and allow easy access to the diaper.

■ Buy adequate protective clothing to avoid sun damage (see p. 98).

YOU WILL NEED

BASICS FOR A NEW BABY
6–8 UNDERSHIRTS OR BODY SUITS
6–8 STRETCH SUITS
2–3 CARDIGANS
2–3 PAIRS OF SOCKS
PROTECTIVE CLOTHING AND SUNHAT FOR SUN PROTECTION
1 BLANKET OR SHAWL

USEFUL EXTRAS
2 PAIRS OF SCRATCH MITTENS
2 NIGHTGOWNS
ONE-PIECE SNOWSUIT

BABIES GROW OUT OF CLOTHES very quickly in the early months so don't spend a lot of money on size-0 babywear. Many of the presents you will be given for your baby will be tiny outfits that will only fit your child for the first few weeks, so you should concentrate on buying a few practical, simple items for the first four months.

HOW TO DRESS AND UNDRESS YOUR BABY

Many parents are nervous about dressing their very young baby, particularly when it involves handling her "wobbly" head with its soft fontanelle (see p. 53). Always lay her down on her back on a changing mat or towel to dress and undress her; it's safer and you will both feel more secure. Although your baby doesn't know day from night, nightgowns may be easier to use when she's tiny. By the time she's three or four months old, she will have developed some head control, and you can safely dress and undress her on your lap, if you haven't had the confidence to do so previously.

PUTTING ON YOUR BABY'S UNDERSHIRT

Undershirts are probably the most awkward items of clothing to put on a tiny baby, because they have to be put on over her head, which is the biggest yet least manageable part of the body. Most undershirts are now designed with wide, "envelope" necks or shoulder fastenings to make it easier for you to slide the undershirt over her head.

Slide over your baby's head gently but quickly

Stretch the neck of the undershirt wide open with both hands

2 Slide the undershirt over your baby's head, gently lifting her head up to bring it over to the back of her neck.

1 Lay your baby on a flat, firm surface on her back. Stretch the neck opening of the undershirt or stretchie as wide open as you can with both hands.

3 Widen each sleeve or armhole with your fingers and bring your baby's arms through, fist first, one at a time. Draw the undershirt over her body.

PUTTING ON A STRETCH SUIT

Stretch suits are a very practical and economical item of clothing for you to buy for your baby. They're particularly useful at first because they allow freedom of movement, easy access to the diaper area, keep your baby warm but not too hot, and they are simple to put on even the tiniest baby. They are ideal for all-day use for the first 3–4 months and can also be used as sleepwear when your baby is older. To put on a stretch suit, follow the steps illustrated here; to take it off, reverse all the steps, beginning by undoing all the fastenings.

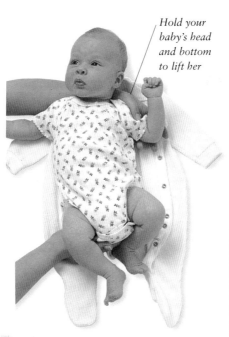

Hold your baby's head and bottom to lift her

Baby is secure on a flat surface

Pull leg up with both hands

1 Undo all the fastenings of the stretch suit and lay it on a flat surface. Then, lay your baby on top of the suit so that her neck lines up with the neck of the suit.

2 Put your baby's legs one at a time into the legs of the suit feet first. Fasten the suit under the diaper area so she can't kick her way out again.

Hold baby's wrist with one hand to guide it into sleeve

3 To put her arms in, roll back one arm of the stretch suit, holding it open with one hand. Then guide your baby's arm, fist first, into the arm of the suit and roll the sleeve up into place. Repeat with the other arm.

Fold back sleeve if too long

PRACTICAL CLOTHES FOR OLDER BABIES

Once your baby is sitting up, and especially when she becomes mobile, clothes have to be sturdy and comfortable, as well as machine-washable. Look for:

■ Bigger sizes, especially with outdoor clothes, so movement isn't restricted and she doesn't grow out of them too quickly.

■ Clothes that have easy access to the diaper area, such as overalls or all-in-one suits with snap fasteners, or tights.

■ Lightweight clothing to protect your baby's skin from the sun. Use a wide-brimmed sunhat and shirts with sleeves and collars.

■ Soft boots or socks with nonslip soles when she starts to pull herself up to stand.

83

DRESSING OLDER BABIES

Once your baby can sit up, you'll find he's a lot easier to dress. But he may also wriggle and protest when you want to put on his clothes, so hold him firmly while you dress him. You could make a game of it to keep him occupied.

Name parts of clothing (sleeve, sock, zipper) as you put them on

For safety, hold your baby firmly on your lap while you dress him

MOTHER

If you find you are trying to encourage your baby to sleep as much as possible, ask yourself for whose benefit you're doing it.

DOES YOUR BABY NEED TO SLEEP?
Trying to get your baby to sleep when he doesn't need to is pointless; even if you would like a break, you're going to feel more frustrated when your baby doesn't drop off. He's longing for your company, so talk and play with him instead; put him in a baby chair so that he can watch what you're doing. Research has shown that even young babies are very receptive to interaction with their parents, and with increased stimulation overall, your baby is much more likely to sleep more soundly and for longer.

YOU NEED REST TOO
You may find you're becoming overwrought if you're suffering from lack of sleep. Being over-tired builds resentment and makes you irritable and liable to get things out of proportion. If you're exhausted, express breast milk (see p. 72) and ask your partner to take on the nighttime feedings for a couple of days so that you can get some rest. If you're really desperate, ask a relative or friend to come and help for a day or two. That way you can catch up on sleep during the daytime.

84

YOU WILL NEED

FOR THE FIRST 3 MONTHS

4 THERMAL CRIB BLANKETS
(cotton is better than wool)

6 FLAT COTTON TOP SHEETS

6 FITTED COTTON
MATTRESS SHEETS

SPARE MATTRESS (OPTIONAL)

PORTABLE MOSES BASKET OR
BASSINET (SEE P. 68)

WHEN YOUR BABY SLEEPS

SLEEP IS IMPORTANT to babies, and to parents. Young babies spend a large proportion – up to 14 hours – of any 24-hour period asleep but, unfortunately, this doesn't often coincide with their parents' sleeping pattern, because it takes a few months for babies to learn the difference between night and day. However, if your baby is tired, he will sleep, no matter where he is or whether it's light, dark, noisy, or quiet.

HOW BABIES SLEEP

The way babies fall asleep differs from adults; adults can crash suddenly, whereas babies sleep lightly for about 20 minutes, then go through a transitional stage before reaching deep sleep. Nothing will wake them until they've had enough sleep. This means that babies who are simply "put down" will not necessarily go to sleep peacefully. You may need to nurse your baby to sleep for quite a while, so try to be patient, particularly if you are trying to get him back to sleep at night, when you are longing to go back to bed.

USE A MOSES BASKET
While your baby is small, put him to bed in a Moses basket or bassinet. You can then keep him in the room where you are most of the time, while he sleeps.

WHERE SHOULD A BABY SLEEP?
Where a baby sleeps isn't important to him to start with. He won't automatically fall asleep when put into a darkened bedroom; light doesn't bother him at all. He's much more likely to be disturbed by being too hot or too cold. Your baby will be happiest going to sleep hearing your voices and the household noises that he is used to in the background so, from the start, be kind to yourselves and the baby by letting him sleep in a Moses basket or bassinet placed in whichever room you happen to be.

USING A BABY MONITOR
If you leave your baby in another room, set up a baby monitor so you can hear him as soon as he wakes. Bear in mind that your baby may feel disturbed by the silence when you leave the room, and this could make him more fretful; leave the door open so he can hear you moving around the house – unless you have a cat that may climb into the crib. Avoid going back into the room once your baby is asleep; your smell could wake him, so resist the temptation to check him too frequently.

ENCOURAGING LONGER SLEEP PERIODS AT NIGHT

A young baby requires nourishment and calories at regular intervals, so he'll wake for a feeding when his body tells him he needs it. The way to encourage your baby to sleep for a stretch (four, then rising to five or six, hours) during the night is to make sure he's taken in sufficient calories to last that long. This entails feeding him whenever he shows he's hungry during the day. As he gains weight, he can go longer between feedings and by about six weeks he could be sleeping for at least one period of about six hours – hopefully during the night. When he wakes for a night feeding, make as little fuss as possible: feed him in bed; if he needs changing, do it gently and quickly in a dim light. Don't make this a time for chatting and games and he'll begin to learn that waking at night doesn't bring any special privileges.

RESCUE PACKAGE FOR A SLEEPLESS BABY

Night after night of interrupted sleep is wearing for parents, and a young baby who perhaps only "catnaps" during the day makes it hard to catch up. Use this checklist of strategies to reduce unnecessary fatigue.

Be aware of background noise Don't shield your baby from the sounds of your home, such as the telephone, vacuum cleaner, and washing machine. They won't disturb his sleep; in fact, some babies are soothed by the rhythmic noise of household appliances!

Keep him close to you At night, put your baby's crib next to your bed so that you can take him into your bed to feed him. Then put him back in his crib afterward with minimum disturbance.

Play music Babies respond well to soothing music (classical is best). Keep certain pieces for when your baby shows signs of fatigue.

Carry him in a sling Rhythmic movement can hasten sleep, but your baby may wake up when you stop moving. Carry him around in a sling when you are in the house, whenever possible. In addition to being relaxed by the constant movement, your baby will be comforted by your body and your smell if he is this close to you.

Give him plenty of fresh air Fresh air is said to tire babies out. In fact, it's likely to be the stimulation they receive from the sounds and sights that bombard them when they're outside, or simply the movement of trees or branches, that makes them sleepy. Getting out of the house will also benefit you, particularly in the first months.

PUTTING YOUR BABY TO BED
Lay your baby down to sleep on his back, supporting his head and body with both hands. Make sure you don't let him become too hot (see p. 86).

FATHER

Understanding the way your baby's sleep patterns work will help you tune into his and your partner's needs, particularly during the night.

BEING REALISTIC
You need to be realistic about how much time your new baby will sleep – I'm afraid it's probably less than you think. He spends 50–80 percent of the time in light sleep, when he wakes very easily. Your baby's sleep cycle – light, deep, light – is shorter than an adult's sleep cycle, so he's vulnerable to waking each time he passes from one sleep state to another. Your baby isn't waking to spite you; he's programmed to wake up for all kinds of reasons – when he's wet, hot, cold, sick – because his survival depends on it. It may be a comfort to realize that light sleep is likely to make your baby more intelligent because the brain remains active and it enhances brain development.

HAVING A SLEEP ROUTINE
Your baby has to be deeply asleep before he'll settle so try a tranquilizing sleep routine – gentle rocking, quiet songs, and talking. He's deeply asleep when his eyelids don't twitch and his limbs feel limp. Lay him down and gently pat his shoulder at about 60 beats a minute for a few minutes.

GETTING HOME LATE
If you find you're getting home from work and your baby is asleep, ask your partner if it's possible for your baby to nap in the afternoon so that he's awake when you arrive. Be patient if this isn't possible to bring about; it's not your partner's fault. Try getting up earlier and spending time with your baby before work.

85

SAFE SLEEPING

The way babies are put to bed has been shown to have a bearing on Sudden Infant Death Syndrome – or what is more commonly known as "crib death." Recently the number of babies dying has halved thanks to a campaign to inform parents about safe sleeping:

■ Stop smoking – and NEVER let anyone else smoke in the same room as your baby. Preferably, don't allow anyone to smoke in your home at all.

■ Always lay your baby on her back to sleep so that her breathing is unimpeded and so she can lose heat from her front, face, and head.

■ Don't let your baby get too hot, since she isn't very efficient at controlling her temperature. If the air temperature feels hot to you, it's very hot for her.

■ Don't increase the amount of bedding when your baby is sick.

■ Never overcover your baby. Use a cotton sheet and thermal blankets according to room temperature (see right).

■ If your crib is a big one, lay her in the "feet-to-foot" position at the end of the crib so that she cannot wriggle down under the blankets and become too hot (see below).

FEET TO FOOT
Lay a baby under six months with her feet touching the foot of a full-size crib, even if it means her head is halfway down the mattress.

Feet touch the foot of the crib

Head is halfway down bed

WAKEFUL BABIES

Most babies develop a routine of sleeping perhaps for two hours in the morning and again in the afternoon, but there are always exceptions. While wakeful babies can be trying, they reward you in the end – they're usually very bright and affectionate – so don't be downhearted. Your baby is wakeful because she loves you and craves your friendship; she doesn't mean to starve you of sleep, she just wants to learn and be sociable. Every minute spent awake with you, she'll be forging new links with the world and developing many skills. Think about this, too, when she's awake during the day; if she isn't tired, why should she sleep? From her point of view, it's much better for her to stay with you, so don't be surprised if she cries when you leave her.

WHAT YOU CAN TRY
● Keep her temperature even; touch her skin to check that she isn't too cold or hot, add or remove blankets if necessary (see below). Check the room temperature; a temperature of about 65°F (18°C) is comfortable.
● Change her diaper if it's wet or soiled and soothe the diaper area with a bland diaper cream (zinc oxide), if necessary.
● Use a rocking cradle or push her rhythmically in her stroller.
● Play her a tape of the human heartbeat, the sound she heard in the womb.
● Play her music you listened to during pregnancy; an old-fashioned musical box with a simple repetitive melody also can be really effective.
● Play her a tape of you and your partner quietly talking.
● Put the crib on alternate sides of the bed each night so that you can take it in turns seeing to her. Talk to her and rock her; you don't need to pick her up.
● If she's obviously reluctant to sleep, get her up and put her in her baby chair where she can see you.
● Hang a mobile over her crib so she has something interesting to watch when she wakes up. A mobile that plays music is ideal.
● Fix a "baby gym," with different noises and textures, across her crib or attach it to the bars so she can reach for it when she's bored.

BLANKETS AND BEDDING

The traditional practice of swaddling – wrapping infants fairly tightly with a sheet or blanket in their cribs – is tied to a mythological notion of reproducing the conditions they had in the womb. In fact, they were free to move their limbs then and they should now. Swaddling can be harmful if it makes your baby too hot (see left), so simply use enough bedding to keep her comfortably warm (see below). When your baby is under 12 months, don't give her a pillow, and avoid quilts or comforters, baby nests, sheepskins, or crib bumpers because they also prevent loss of heat.

WHAT BEDDING TO USE ACCORDING TO THE TEMPERATURE

TEMPERATURE	WHAT TO USE
60°F (15°C)	A sheet and four blankets.
65°F (18°C)	A sheet and three blankets.
70°F (21°C)	A sheet and two blankets.
75°F (24°C)	A sheet and one blanket.
80°F (27°C)	A sheet only.

86

SLEEP AND YOUR OLDER BABY

As your baby grows, her sleep pattern will gradually change; she will begin to stay awake and alert for longer periods during the day, even after feedings. When she's being stimulated with play and talk from you, she'll start needing longer periods of sleep to recharge her energy levels. The introduction of solid food may also make her settle better. The trick is to persuade her that these longer sleep periods should be at night, to align with your own.

ESTABLISHING A BEDTIME ROUTINE

Your baby may well get upset at bedtime – she could be anxious about being separated from you (see p. 140), or she may simply want to continue playing, so establishing a bedtime routine is essential to build her confidence and to help her learn that there is a time when playing has to stop. Set up your own routine at a time to suit all of you – if you're working you may want it to be a little later than other parents, so that you can have time with your baby when you get home – but try not to vary the routine, whatever time you do it. A suggested routine might be as follows:

- Give her the final meal of the day – preferably not her main meal (see p. 95).
- Give her a bath without too much romping and change her into nightclothes.
- Spend a quiet time together in your baby's room; sing some gentle songs, or read a bedtime story to her (depending on your baby's age and the stage of development).
- Give her the last breast-feeding (unless your baby still wakes at night).
- Lay her in her crib, with any security object she has become attached to, turn the dimmer switch down low, then sit quietly with her for a minute or two.
- Go out of the room quietly, saying good night, and leaving the door open.

THE BEDTIME ROUTINE

Allow time for quiet play with your baby, with books and toys. Remove hard objects when you lay her down.

DAYTIME NAPS FOR YOUR OLDER BABY

As babies grow older they sleep less and less, but up to the age of 12 months your baby may continue to nap during the morning and afternoon; right up to the age of three many toddlers still like to rest sometime during the day:

■ To help your baby relax and drop off, always put her in her favorite place, which may not necessarily be her room, and make sure she has with her any special security object. Play calming music, let her have toys and books in the crib, and stay within earshot so she can hear you bustling about. If she calls out to you, it's probably only for reassurance, so calmly call back.

■ If your baby doesn't want to sleep, that's all right; just make it a quiet time when she can sit in her crib and play happily alone. But never let your baby cry for longer than a few minutes without going to see her or picking her up. If your baby is unhappy, that defeats the purpose of a nap.

■ If your baby falls asleep in the car, or her carriage, never wake her suddenly from her sleep; like you, she'll need time to adjust.

■ Never leave your baby asleep alone in the car or in her carriage outside a store; this could be dangerous.

87

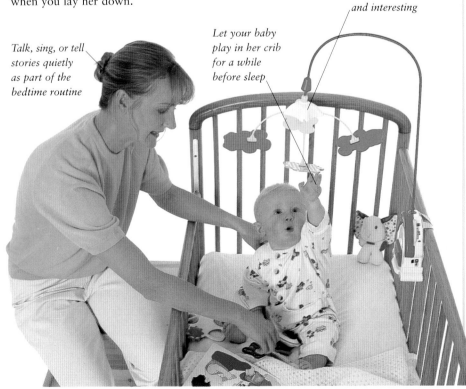

Talk, sing, or tell stories quietly as part of the bedtime routine

Let your baby play in her crib for a while before sleep

Musical mobile is both soothing and interesting

WHAT MAKES A NEWBORN CRY

The circumstances of your baby's birth may affect the amount he cries. It helps if you understand the possible underlying causes of a fretful baby's behavior. Try not to become impatient with him because it is out of his control, but he will begin to settle as he gets older. Your baby may cry more:

■ If you had a general anesthetic during labor.

■ If you had a forceps delivery.

■ If he was born after a long labor, after which babies tend to sleep in short bursts.

■ If he is a boy. Boys may cry more than girls in new situations. Try not to make the mistake of some boys' parents who have been known to attend to them less, in the mistaken belief that it will "toughen them up."

GIVING YOUR BABY ATTENTION
All babies thrive on the company of their parents, and will cry because they miss the comfort of your presence. Try to give your baby as much contact as you can.

Picking up your baby and distracting him will often stop him from crying

WHEN YOUR BABY CRIES

ALL YOUNG BABIES CRY at some time during the day. Whether it's a subdued whine or a full-throated roar, a baby's cries are his only means of communicating his needs. Sometimes his cry will signal some obvious discomfort – hunger, a dirty diaper, boredom, tiredness – and at other times it will be difficult to pinpoint the reasons, but over the weeks you will learn the best way to respond to him. Having said that, there is no doubt that a persistently fretful baby can be a strain for parents, so it's worth thinking about the underlying causes. Look upon crying as conversation rather than an irritant designed to upset you.

RESPONDING TO YOUR BABY'S CRIES

Research shows definitively that babies do better if you respond promptly when they cry. It's a mistake to think of a baby as "good" if he doesn't cry much and one who does as "naughty," because a baby's cries have nothing to do with good or bad behavior. Although constant crying can be difficult to cope with, it is necessary because responding to your baby's cries is a crucial part of bonding – your attitude to your baby in the first few weeks forms the blueprint for your future relationship with him, and for all the relationships he goes on to form later in life. He'll learn kindness and sympathy from you, which is why you should always answer his cry, whatever anyone else tells you. A loved baby will be secure and when the time comes he will be able to take separations in his stride if he's learned that you will answer his needs. A baby who is left to cry is more likely to grow up clingy and attention-seeking because he's learned that he has to work harder to make you respond to him.

WHY YOU SHOULD RESPOND PROMPTLY
● Your baby is longing to communicate with you, but his repertoire is limited to start with. Crying is the only way he can convey his feelings so don't just ignore him.
● Your baby will develop good communication skills and outgoing, friendly behavior.
● It will make him secure and self-confident.
● It will not "spoil" your baby or teach him "bad habits"; you cannot spoil a baby this way.

WHAT HAPPENS IF YOU DON'T RESPOND
● Not responding to your baby's cries is a form of rejection, and your baby will soon sense this.
● If you don't respond, he will cry for longer, continuing until he gets the attention that he needs.
● He will be driven to create a pattern of frequent crying.

WHAT TO DO WHEN YOUR BABY CRIES

PROBLEM	DESCRIPTION	WHAT YOU SHOULD DO
HUNGER	If your baby has been asleep for two or three hours and begins to cry insistently, he is probably ready for a feeding.	Give him a feeding. If he cries afterward, he may not have had enough so offer more. If it's very hot, offer him a drink of water.
DISCOMFORT	A cold, wet, and dirty diaper could be uncomfortable enough to cause your baby to cry. Your baby may also be too hot or too cold.	Check and change the diaper if necessary. Treat diaper rash (see p. 77). Check bedding and air temperature (see p. 86).
INSECURITY	A jerky movement, bright light, or sudden noise can startle a young baby. Many babies are also upset by being undressed and bathed.	Cuddle your baby to promote security. Handle your baby as gently and firmly as possible when dressing or bathing.
FATIGUE	Your baby will cry when he is tired, and may become quite upset when overtired, which can make it doubly difficult to soothe him.	Create a soothing bedtime ritual (see p. 87) of rocking or stroking when you lay him in his crib, or push him in his stroller.
BOREDOM	As your baby grows, he is more aware of people and cries because he wants company.	Cuddle him; at 4–6 weeks, sit him in a baby chair where he can see and hear you.
PAIN	Your baby may have earache, abdominal pain, or persistent diaper rash.	Contact your doctor if he's hard to soothe, off his food, or appears sick (see p. 100).

PERSISTENT CRYING

Some young babies have prolonged bouts of crying, which typically occur in the late afternoon and evening, and can last for anything between two and four hours. Babies often begin this pattern of persistent crying at about three weeks of age, and will usually have grown out of it by about three months. This pattern of crying has become known as "colic," because as the baby becomes increasingly upset and difficult to soothe, he may often pull his legs up and arch his back as if experiencing abdominal pain. In fact, it is probably misleading to give it any special name because there doesn't seem to be any known cause for this pattern.

GETTING THROUGH IT
A baby who is persistently fretful may cry readily at other times, not just in the evening. However, the evening pattern of crying can be a particular strain for parents, especially if one or both of you has been working during the day. It may be that your baby senses and reacts to your tiredness at this time. Although this crying pattern may only last three months, this period can seem never-ending to new parents who have to deal with their baby's distress day after day. Trying some of the suggestions for soothing your baby given above and overleaf should help you through this difficult time.

SOOTHING "COLIC"
If your baby cries persistently, you may find that laying him across your lap makes him more comfortable. Support his head and then gently massage his back and legs.

Gently rub your baby's back

A towel supports your baby and protects your clothes from dribble

SOOTHING YOUR CRYING BABY

LAY YOUR BABY ON YOUR CHEST
Lie on the bed or sofa, well supported by cushions. Lay your baby on your chest and gently rub her back. It will relax both of you. You can also provide skin contact by opening your shirt and laying your baby's face against your chest.

Hearing your heartbeat comforts your baby

USE A PACIFIER
Encourage your baby to find her thumb or use a pacifier. There is no stigma attached to a baby sucking a pacifier, but make sure it is clean and never sweeten it with honey or juice. However, it may only be a temporary relief so it's probably better to look for the underlying cause of the crying, keeping the pacifier as a last resort.

Sucking a pacifier or thumb helps a fretful baby

HOLD UPRIGHT
Bring your baby up against your shoulder and gently rub her back. (Put a cloth on your shoulder to protect it from any regurgitated milk.) Walk around, gently singing or talking to your baby.

A cloth protects your clothes

Support your baby firmly when you hold her upright

90

Rocking often helps a baby to sleep

Cover your baby, but make sure she's not too hot or too cold (see p. 86)

CARRY IN A SLING
Put the baby in a sling and carry her around with you. If you're a working father and your partner has been at home with the baby all day, take the initiative: let your partner rest while you prepare the evening meal, carrying your baby in a sling.

A sling keeps your baby close so she feels secure

COMFORT WITH MOVEMENT
Most babies are soothed by regular movement: it was what they were used to in the womb. Put your baby in a rocking cradle (make sure it conforms to safety standards) or in her stroller and gently rock her backward and forward while you sit and watch television or eat a meal.

ACCEPTING HELP FROM OTHERS

Sometimes a crying baby can make parents who are already tired from interrupted nights feel quite desperate: this is the time to seek help. Don't ever feel that you are failing as parents if you accept assistance; countless other parents have felt as frustrated and exhausted as you because their babies have cried a lot and have been difficult to soothe. Jump at the chance if your baby's grandparents or other friends or relatives offer to look after your baby for a while so you can get out on your own for a couple of hours' break, or enjoy some unbroken sleep. If they don't offer any help, don't be afraid to ask them. There's no need to feel guilty – they will be glad to have the chance to relieve you and it will help you get things back into perspective. It's a great help, too, to talk to health or baby care professionals, who are there to support you.

HELPFUL GRANDPARENTS
Grandparents know that you need a break and enjoy developing their own relationship with the baby.

COMFORTING YOUR OLDER BABY

As your baby grows and becomes more aware of her surroundings, her pattern of crying will change because it's not the only way she can communicate with you now. Her reasons for crying will also be easier for you to both predict and interpret. You'll begin to distinguish between frustration, hunger, pain, and loneliness. Even when your baby is becoming more mobile and independent, the best way to comfort her if she's unhappy is with your company and hugs.

COMFORTERS

Toward their first birthday, many babies will have become attached to a particular comforter – a favorite soft toy, a cloth, or blanket – that probably helps them sleep and that they may grab when they're feeling a bit insecure and upset. Other babies become attached to a pacifier or suck their thumbs (see opposite). This is perfectly normal and there's no point in distressing your baby by removing a comforter on the grounds that it is a "bad habit" – it isn't. As your baby's confidence and independence develop after her first birthday, she'll gradually become less dependent on her comforter, although it may take a year or so. It's a good idea to have some spares in case the main one needs to be washed.

TEETHING AND CRYING

Your baby's teeth will normally start to come through from about six months (see p. 132) so she'll dribble a lot and her gums will occasionally be sore. Your baby may become rather whiny when she's teething and it's usually quite obvious if she's uncomfortable; she'll want to chew a lot and may have a hot, red area on her cheek. However, it isn't a good idea always to blame persistent crying on "teething," when in fact your baby may be bored (see right), or even sick (see p. 100).

TROUBLESHOOTING

As your older baby learns to communicate by other means, she'll start to cry to communicate emotions and pain. There are lots of reasons why she may cry.

SHE'S BORED
The older your baby gets, the longer she spends awake, so she can become bored more easily. You baby may cry from boredom if left alone, unable to hear your voice and with nothing to look at or play with. You are her favorite playmate so keep her in the same room as you, where she can see you and you can talk to her, and don't leave her for long periods alone in her crib if she's crying. Some babies do play happily in their cribs for a short while after waking, so leave toys and books within reach.

SHE'S FRUSTRATED
As your baby grows, her desire to do things outstrips her ability; she gets frustrated and often starts to cry as a result. She may also cry if you don't let her have something she wants. Change her toys frequently – her attention span is still short. Find time to play with her (see p. 152).

SHE'S FRIGHTENED
At about six months your baby will cry when she's separated from you and she'll be nervous of other people, even when she knows them well. Right from the start, get her used to seeing you leave the room and come back in again. This way she'll gradually learn that she can trust you always to return to her. Make sure she meets lots of other people before she reaches this stage and learns that, even if you leave her with someone else for a while, you always come back.

SHE'S SICK OR HAS HURT HERSELF
If your baby hurts herself, you'll know at once from her cry, but it may be more difficult to tell when she's sick. See pages 100–103 for what you should do if your baby is sick or has an accident.

91

MASSAGE TIPS

Babies love massage as much as you do; it's a good way to calm an unsettled baby because it feels nice to him. It's also an expression of love and your baby knows it. It has the added advantage of relaxing you as you do it – you have to be calm yourself to communicate physically with your baby. Always prepare yourself carefully for massage:

■ Make sure the room is really warm. Lay your baby on a soft blanket or towel.

■ Play favorite music or a tape recording of a heartbeat. Talk in a low, gentle voice or sing a song quietly.

■ Although massaging your baby's skin directly is best, many younger babies don't like being undressed. If your baby is one of these, dress him in a cotton undershirt or similar garment, through which you can easily feel his body.

■ Work around his body, massaging both sides with slow even strokes simultaneously. Keep your face close to your baby's and look into his eyes as you massage him. This is very effective for both of you.

TOUCH AND MASSAGE

BEING TOUCHED IS IMPORTANT to all young animals – including humans – it's an essential part of the bonding process that helps young creatures to thrive. It's been shown that premature babies gain more weight on lambswool blankets than cotton ones because it feels as if they're being stroked when they move and they're more contented.

THE IMPORTANCE OF TOUCH

Your baby is born sociable and he craves physical affection. This is best communicated through touch, cuddles, being gently held, kissed, and nuzzled. It's important, therefore, that you're both completely free with your physical affection from the start. Your baby longs to be close to you and to be carried, and he will cry less and be more easily comforted if you carry him. Remember also that being carried in a sling close to your body feels to a baby like being cuddled (see p. 90), and allows you to do other things at the same time. Small babies are much stronger than you think, so be firm but avoid sudden jerky movements – your baby may think he's falling and he'll be startled rather than comforted. As your baby gets older you can be more energetic with him; he'll enjoy tickling and rolling about on the floor with you, but don't overdo it if he becomes at all upset – and don't blame him if he pulls your hair or scratches you; under a year he won't know that it hurts.

GIVING A MASSAGE

NECK AND SHOULDERS
Using fingers and thumbs, gently massage your baby's neck from his ears to his shoulders and from his chin to his chest. Then stroke his shoulders from his neck outward.

Use gentle pressure with finger and thumb

ARMS
Lay your baby on his back and hold his arms up one at a time. Stroke down each arm using your fingertips, first from wrist to elbow, then from elbow to shoulder. (You may discover he's ticklish!) Then gently squeeze all along his arm, starting from the top.

CHEST AND ABDOMEN
Gently stroke down your baby's chest following the line of his ribs. You can use one hand and then the other in a continuous stroking movement, but don't press too hard. Massage his abdomen in a circular motion with one hand, working outward from the navel. Talk and sing softly to him all the time.

Your baby will concentrate on your touch

Your hand will make him feel secure

HEAD

Using both hands, lightly massage the crown of your baby's head using a circular motion, then stroke down the sides of his face. With your fingertips, massage his forehead and cheeks, working from the center outward. This is particularly calming for a fretful baby.

Stroke both sides of his head

Talk to your baby and encourage him to look at you

FEET AND TOES

Rub your baby's ankles and feet, stroking from heel to toe, and then concentrate on each toe individually. Your baby may kick his legs and curl his toes while you're doing this. If he's less than three months old, show him his toes – it will help him realize they are part of himself (see p. 137).

LEGS

Massage your baby's legs one at a time. Place your free hand on his tummy, then gently squeeze his leg from the thigh down to the ankle.

93

BACK

Once you've massaged your baby on his front, gently turn him over on to his tummy and massage his back. Using both hands, run your palms down his back from under his arms to his buttocks, pressing gently against his spine with your thumbs. Talk to him all the time, since he can't see your face in this position.

TROUBLE-FREE WEANING

Knowing what food to give and when to give it will help you introduce it with confidence.

WHAT AGE TO START
Don't introduce weaning until at least four months; before that, a baby's digestion can't cope with foods more complicated. However, most babies will need more than milk from six months (see right).

WHAT TO OFFER
At first, offer a simple, semiliquid food once a day and introduce only one taste at a time. Start with a nonwheat cereal mixed with her normal milk or formula because it's closest to what she is used to, then gradually introduce pureed fruit or vegetables. Don't introduce food at a second meal until she happily takes the first. Milk remains the main food source for at least three months after introducing solids. Introduce different textures from about 6–7 months, although she might not chew until 7–8 months. Ready-to-serve foods are convenient, but can be expensive in the long run; dried foods reconstituted in water are cheaper.

HOW MUCH TO GIVE
At first give a teaspoonful of solids at a time – her digestive system needs time to adapt. Once she's used to solids, she may prefer to take them first, then have her milk feeding. Start with a teaspoonful a day for a week, then progress to two, before introducing solids at another meal as well. Use the suggested weaning schedule (see opposite) as a guide.

YOU WILL NEED

TO START WEANING
2–3 FABRIC PLASTIC-BACKED BIBS
2–3 FEEDING SPOONS AND A CUP
FOR THE OLDER BABY
2–3 MOLDED PLASTIC BIBS
2 NONSPILL PLASTIC BOWLS
TWO-HANDLED TRAINING CUP

WEANING

MANY PARENTS VIEW weaning with trepidation; it seems such a huge step and there are so many pressures from outside sources – when to start, what to give, and how much to give. But it needn't feel so daunting if you try to see the introduction of solid foods to your baby's diet as encouraging her independence rather than as an obstacle. Think positively and remember that all babies are longing to do things for themselves. When she starts to feed herself, it will encourage her self-confidence and give her a chance to show off and receive praise from you. In this frame of mind you'll both take early mishaps in your stride.

INTRODUCING SOLIDS

Weaning is rarely a problem from the baby's point of view, but some babies take longer than others to get used to having solid food as well as their normal milk feedings. It really doesn't matter – until six months milk is enough for many babies' complete nutritional needs. However, after that time they will need the extra calories, vitamins, and minerals in solid food, since there won't be enough for them in milk alone (look at the weaning chart opposite for a suggested pattern of feeding).

When you introduce first solids, choose a feeding when you know she's usually alert and awake – for instance, at midday, halfway through her milk feeding. Sit your baby on your lap or in her baby chair and offer tiny amounts at first on the tip of a sterilized plastic spoon. Don't force it into her mouth; brush her upper lip with the spoon and let her suck it off. She might splutter and dribble a bit the first few times, but keep trying.

GIVING THE FIRST SOLID FEEDING
Hold her firmly on your lap and tilt her head back as you offer the spoon.

WATER OR JUICE

Remember milk is a food, it isn't a drink, so when mixed feeding is introduced, your baby will also need another fluid to drink from a bottle or cup. Offer cooled boiled water alone or with a few drops of pure unsweetened fruit juice added. Look carefully at labels to make sure there isn't hidden added sugar (such as fructose) listed. Start with ½ fl. oz (15ml) of fluids between feedings, increasing gradually according to your baby's needs.

SUGGESTED WEANING SCHEDULE FROM FOUR MONTHS

FEEDINGS	DAYS 1–4	DAYS 5–8	DAYS 9–12
1ST FEEDING	Milk feeding.	Milk feeding.	No early milk feeding.
2ND FEEDING	Half milk feeding. 1–2 tsps cereal. Finish milk feeding.	Half milk feeding. 1–2 tsps cereal. Finish milk feeding.	3–4 tsps cereal. Milk feeding.
3RD FEEDING	Milk feeding.	Half milk feeding. 1–2 tsps pureed fruit or veg. Finish milk feeding.	2–3 tsps pureed chicken and veg. 2–3 tsps pureed fruit. Water or dilute juice.
4TH FEEDING	Milk feeding.	Milk feeding.	2–3 tsps pureed fruit or veg. Milk feeding.
5TH FEEDING	Milk feeding.	Milk feeding.	Milk feeding.

TROUBLE-FREE MEALTIMES

Just as it was important not to get hung up about how much milk your baby drank when you were establishing breast-feeding, try not to worry now about how much she is eating, or indeed about how much is going on the floor! It's going to be messy – until the age of five or six all children are messy eaters – so be philosophical and clean up afterward. As long as mealtimes are happy and relaxed, don't worry and don't allow them to become battlefields. You can never win – your baby simply refuses to eat (you can't force her) and the battle is lost. She's smart enough to learn that it's a weapon she can use to manipulate you, so don't join in the struggle.

ENOUGH TO EAT?
Even if you think your baby isn't taking enough food, she is. Don't make the mistake of forcing adult standards on her. Think of a balanced diet in terms of what you offer your baby over a period of time, such as a week, and make sure it has variety; accept that there's bound to be a certain amount of waste. Don't worry about fads either; she's eating what her body needs.

STARTING SELF-FEEDING

Self-feeding is an important step to your baby's independence, so be patient with her:

■ Use shaped plastic bibs that catch a lot of the spilled food, and put a large plastic sheet under the high chair so you don't have to wash the entire floor every time.

■ Give your baby her own spoon and offer food that is a stiff consistency, such as mashed potato or other pureed vegetables, in a nonspill bowl. Never mind that she gets very little at first, she'll have a lot of fun, which is how mealtimes should be. While you're eating, have a spare spoon handy so that you can feed her, if needed.

■ Even if she finds a spoon difficult, she'll love feeding herself with finger foods (see p. 97). Finger foods are very useful in keeping your baby occupied when the meal isn't quite ready.

■ Above all, be flexible; if one food doesn't suit just try another – no single food is essential. Don't spend ages on preparation; you'll only be resentful if your baby throws it on the floor.

■ Introduce a trainer cup with a spout for drinks as soon as your baby can manage it. Some breast-fed babies never accept a bottle at all, going straight to a cup for juice and continuing to get all their milk from the breast. Others prefer a bottle for juice and may take time to get used to a cup.

RELAXED SELF-FEEDING
While your baby feeds himself, have your own spoon to feed him at the same time.

Use a nonslip plastic bowl to avoid any mishaps

95

FOODS TO GIVE

In addition to making sure your baby has a balanced diet, vary it so that he learns to like different tastes and textures. You should include:

■ Fruit and vegetables: wash them thoroughly in cold running water, and peel potatoes, carrots, apples, and peaches to avoid the risk of pesticide residues. Aim to give some vitamin C at each meal, whether as fruit, vegetables, or juice, because it helps your baby's body to absorb iron.

■ Milk: from six months you can use whole cow's milk in cooking and to mix foods such as mashed potato. From one year, it can be used as a drink.

■ Meat and fish: try to offer at least one serving every day of lean meat or boneless fish.

■ Plenty of protein in the form of low-fiber foods such as cheese or tofu, if you're giving your baby a vegetarian diet.

FOODS TO AVOID

Don't worry too much, but do take some sensible precautions:

■ Don't give foods containing wheat flour or gluten before your baby is six months old since he may find them difficult to digest.

■ Don't add sugar or salt – the former encourages bad habits and bad teeth, and the latter is too much for your young baby's kidneys to cope with.

■ Avoid giving your baby soft-boiled eggs until he is about one year old.

■ Avoid very high-fiber breakfast cereals because they are too difficult to digest.

■ Avoid cheese made with unpasteurized milk until your baby is at least two years old.

BEST FOOD FOR YOUR BABY

TO GROW AND DEVELOP WELL, babies need as varied a diet as your income will allow; research shows that babies who are offered a wide menu to choose from invariably choose a healthy diet and accept varied tastes. On the other hand, if they're given only fast foods and sweet things, they'll inevitably want french fries and ketchup with everything.

WHAT YOUR BABY NEEDS

To provide for your baby's healthy nutrition, he needs complex carbohydrates from such things as sugar-free cereal, whole-wheat bread, potatoes and other vegetables, rice, and pasta; protein from lean white meat, fish, and legumes such as beans, and, after he's about six months, eggs and cheese; and the vitamins and minerals contained in fresh fruit and vegetables. He needs some fat, but he should be able to get enough for his nutritional needs from the other foods you give him, especially milk. Avoid the "empty" calories of sweet foods like cookies and sugary cereal: look at the food pyramid chart below to see the proportions of each type of food your baby needs for healthy growth and development.

THE FOOD PYRAMID

Once your baby is used to a variety of tastes, you can plan his diet to include a combination of foods from each group. The "pyramid" of foods shown illustrates the rough proportions of each type that you should try to give your baby.

Too much sugar is bad for teeth and may lead to obesity

Low-fiber foods provide protein for vegetarians

Fresh fruit is an important source of vitamins and minerals

Give least of fats, oils, and sugars.

Give a little more of proteins: meat, fish, eggs, cheese, and legumes.

Give your baby fresh fruit and vegetables as part of his daily diet.

Give most of complex carbohydrates: bread, rice, pasta, oatmeal, potatoes (not fried or roasted).

JOINING FAMILY MEALS

As soon as your baby is sitting in his high chair he can join you at the table for meals. The sooner you can include your baby in this, the sooner your baby will learn by example what is and is not acceptable behavior at the table. Some suggested menus are given in the chart below.

SUGGESTED MENUS FOR AN OLDER BABY

TIME	DAY 1	DAY 2	DAY 3
BREAKFAST	Rice cakes Chopped hard-boiled egg Milk	Mashed banana Whole-wheat toast fingers Milk	Cottage cheese or yogurt Whole-wheat toast Milk
LUNCH	Vegetable or chicken casserole Stewed apple Diluted fruit juice	Mashed potato and cheese Pear slices Diluted fruit juice	Strained lentils and mixed vegetables Banana and yogurt Diluted fruit juice
SNACK	Toast fingers Peeled peach slices Milk	Rice cakes Peeled apple pieces Milk	Hard biscuits Peeled seedless grapes Milk
DINNER	Cauliflower/cheese Semolina and fruit puree Diluted fruit juice	Pasta with sauce Yogurt and fruit puree Diluted fruit juice	Tuna, mashed potato, zucchini Rice pudding Diluted fruit juice

MAKE MEALTIMES FUN

It's frustrating to find that good food is being thrown on the floor or wiped on the high chair, but remember that your baby will eat if he's hungry. If he starts to throw food around, he's probably bored with eating because he's had enough so he's moving on to experiment with the textures instead. Try tempting your older baby to try new tastes with fun food such as the examples given here, and he'll learn to see mealtimes as enjoyable occasions.

Omelette

Small pieces of potato are easy to eat

Buy pastry shells and decorate them with fruit

Celery "whiskers" can be eaten as finger foods

FUN FOODS
Try decorating foods with vegetables and fruit to encourage healthy eating.

FOOD HYGIENE

Bacterial infections picked up from badly prepared food can be dangerous for babies and children so be careful with hygiene.

■ Always wash your hands thoroughly before handling any food and after you have handled raw meat.

■ Store raw meat away from other foods in the refrigerator and keep fish in the coldest part.

■ Clean the spout holes of your baby's feeding cup regularly.

■ Always throw away leftover baby food. To avoid waste, prepare very small amounts and freeze in individual containers.

■ Don't reheat cooked baby food unless you're able to bring it to the boil, and cook it thoroughly for at least five minutes to kill bacteria.

■ If you're using a microwave, follow the manufacturer's instructions exactly for times. Stir the food thoroughly to make sure the heat is evenly distributed.

FINGER FOODS

Once your baby is about six months old, he'll want to try feeding himself so give him easy-to-hold finger foods. Don't give him very small things and don't leave him alone. Try:

■ Any fresh fruit that's easy to hold, such as a banana or peach; remember to peel and remove seeds.

■ Vegetables, particularly carrots, cut into a shape that's easy to grasp. Don't cut them too small.

■ Pieces of dry, sugar-free cereal.

■ Whole-wheat bread or hard biscuits (without grains), toast fingers, bread sticks, or rice cakes.

■ Cooked pasta shapes.

BABY-FRIENDLY ACTIVITIES

There are lots of activities on offer for new parents and their babies, so there's no need to feel cut off:

■ Coffee mornings and parent and toddler groups (see p. 118).

■ Music groups for babies from six months. Again, the community center may be able to help here.

■ Swimming – once your baby is immunized. Ask at your local pool about parent and baby sessions.

■ Baby movement classes may be run at health centers, for babies from six months of age.

■ Baby massage classes, probably run by a natural health center or local yoga teacher.

PROTECTION FROM THE SUN

Babies have very little skin pigment so they have much less protection than adults from the sun's ultraviolet rays. Being exposed to direct sunlight can lead to skin damage and skin cancer later in life. To protect your baby:

■ Use sunscreen of at least factor 15 in addition to the natural protection of clothes and shade. Twenty minutes before going out, apply the lotion to your baby's face, neck, ears, back of hands, and feet – not all over her body.

■ In very hot weather, avoid taking your baby out in the sun between 11am and 1pm.

■ Dress her in a wide-brimmed hat and protective clothing, such as a shirt with sleeves and a collar.

■ Be aware that your baby is still at risk on cloudy days.

■ Make sure the stroller or buggy has a protective hood or umbrella to shade your baby.

GETTING OUT

Try to get out with your baby as soon as you feel up to it – it helps her get used to travel, new places, and people. It's also good for you – it keeps you in touch with the world outside your home, and gives you a change of scene away from the sometimes claustrophobic world of diapers and baby paraphernalia.

FIRST OUTINGS

The first few outings that involve more than pushing the stroller around to the local stores may seem daunting, and you'll probably be a bit nervous and unsure about how your baby will react. Keep calm and try to relax – your baby will pick up on any anxieties you have. You'll soon become a family of seasoned travelers – the easiest time to be out and about with your baby is while she's small and portable. Make the most of it because when she's a toddler and needing constant supervision, the range of outings will become more limited for a while. Don't be too ambitious on your first outings – go to your local park, perhaps, or for coffee at a friend's house. Make sure you're confident about being away from home with your baby before you opt for something farther afield. Travel at off-peak times when there's less congestion, especially if you're traveling by bus or train.

Hat, especially in hot weather · Changing mat · Diapers · Small toys · Change of clothes · Large bag · Baby wipes · Diaper cream · Bottle, if used · Tissues · Cotton · Toy for amusement · Bib · Bowl and spoon

YOUR TRAVEL BAG
You'll need a bag large enough for everything you need for your baby. Include sunscreen of at least factor 15 to protect your baby against sun damage (see box left).

GOING SHOPPING

There's no need to leave your baby at home when you go shopping because most supermarkets and department stores now provide facilities to help parents with babies (see chart opposite). Shopping malls can be more difficult if they are on more than one level, but most have elevators as well as escalators. When you are in the supermarket:

● Always use a shopping cart that is appropriate to your baby's size and weight and strap her into the seat with a harness. Be aware that she may try to grab items off the shelves.

● Shopping tends to make children hungry and therefore fretful. Avoid this by taking a snack and drink with you. These will provide refreshment for your baby and also keep her occupied.

● Use any nursery facilities that are available.

SHOPPING WITH YOUR BABY

FACILITY	WHAT TO LOOK FOR
PARKING SPACES	Some stores have dedicated parent and baby parking spaces close to the entrance.
WIDER CHECKOUTS	Good supermarkets have at least two wider than average checkouts to accommodate strollers.
SPECIAL DISCOUNTS	Some stores offer discounts for parents with a baby under 12 months.
BABY CARE	Supervised nurseries are available at some stores, as long as you're there to be called if necessary.
CHANGING AND FEEDING	Many stores have a baby changing area in their toilets, and some have a room where you can breast-feed – but if you're happy just to sit out of the way to feed your baby, don't feel you have to do it in private. Just ask an assistant.

TRAVELING BY CAR

Rear-facing car seats (see p. 69) make traveling by car with a young baby relatively trouble-free, but your car seat must be correctly fitted. These seats can be put in the front or back seats; however, don't use a rear-facing seat in the front passenger seat if you have an air-bag. Correct fitting is equally important when your baby graduates to a fixed seat in the back. Most babies are lulled to sleep by the movement of a car, but a hungry baby will wake up and become upset. If you're on your own, find a safe place to park and feed her; it's better than trying to drive on with a screaming baby, which will make you both tense. Keep a few diapers, wipes, and diaper bags in the car for emergencies. The sun can be a problem for babies, so use a detachable blind on your car window to provide shade.

VACATIONS

If you're going away with a very young baby, you may feel more comfortable not going abroad in case you need medical help. Having said this, small babies – especially breast-fed ones – often travel abroad very well, but it's sensible to take out adequate medical insurance. Whatever the age of your baby, before you leave you should:
● Check how far you'll be from a doctor's office, medical center, or hospital.
● Make sure the crib in your vacation accommodation conforms to safety standards – your tour operator, or the travel agent should be able to reassure you on this. Alternatively, take your own travel crib on vacation with you – modern designs are safe and compact.
● Always make sure your baby is adequately protected from the sun (see box opposite): use adequate sunscreen lotion, dress your baby in protective clothing, and keep her in the shade.

PUBLIC TRANSPORTATION TIPS

Planning ahead is the secret to trouble-free travel by any form of public transportation:

■ If you're traveling alone, make sure you can manage everything yourself – although you may hope for offers of help, people are not always as thoughtful to parents with babies as you might wish.

■ Allow plenty of time to reach the station or airport to avoid the extra stress of worrying about missing a train or airplane.

■ On an airplane, feed your baby on takeoff and landing because sucking reduces the risk of earache caused by changing air pressure.

■ If you have a long flight, try to book a seat with a bassinet so your baby can sleep during the flight.

■ A portable car seat is invaluable, although for air travel you may have to pay for an extra seat on busy flights if you want to use one just for your baby.

99

Your baby can see what is going on around him

Choose a backpack with a holdall

USING A BACKPACK
A backpack is more convenient for an older baby than a stroller if you like to do a lot of walking.

MEDICATION

The doctor may prescribe a medicine, for example, liquid acetaminophen or an antibiotic, for your baby if he has a high temperature or infection. Give him the medicine in his mouth using a sterile dropper or medicine spoon. Always give the dosage that is recommended by the doctor or as instructed on the bottle.

TAKING YOUR BABY'S TEMPERATURE

A raised temperature usually indicates that your baby is fighting an infection. Take his temperature with a digital or mercury thermometer by holding it firmly under his bare armpit for three minutes. Bear in mind that the temperature measured in the armpit is about 1°F (0.6°C) less than the actual body temperature. Alternatively, you can use a temperature strip, although these are less accurate. Don't use a thermometer in your child's mouth until he's at least seven years old.

Make sure the bulb is in contact with the skin

CHECKING THE TEMPERATURE
Place the thermometer under your baby's bare armpit and hold his arm across his chest to hold it in place.

CARING FOR YOUR SICK BABY

ALL PARENTS WORRY if their child is sick; it's even more distressing when it's a baby because he's unable to tell you how he's feeling. If you suspect that your baby isn't well, don't hesitate to get medical advice. You're the best judge of when your baby is feeling under the weather because you know and understand his moods and personality.

NURSING YOUR BABY

When babies are sick they are often whiny and fretful, probably waking more frequently at night and needing constant attention and cuddles. However, a very ill baby will become listless and unresponsive. If your baby has a cold, it might make feeding difficult because he won't be able to breathe properly through his nose. Be patient and let him come up for air when feeding, but if this becomes a real problem ask your doctor or pharmacist for nose drops.

RECOGNIZING A FEVER
The best way to recognize a fever is to lay your hand on your baby's brow. If his skin is hot, red, and clammy he has a fever. When his temperature is very high, he may also shiver.

LOWERING TEMPERATURE
If your baby has a very high fever, you should lower it to prevent overheating. Remove all his clothing, lie him on a towel, and sponge him down with tepid (not cold) water. Don't let him get too cold. If he's over three months, you may also give him liquid acetaminophen (see above left).

TEPID SPONGING
To cool down your baby, apply tepid water with a sponge or cloth to his face and body.

Soak a soft cloth or sponge in tepid water, squeeze it out, then dab it over your baby

PREVENTING DEHYDRATION

Dehydration in babies under 12 months can be dangerous, and steps must be taken to replace lost fluids, sugar, and salt. Signs of dehydration in babies are general listlessness and a sunken fontanelle (the soft area of skin on the top of the skull). Your baby may also wet his diaper less frequently. When your baby has a temperature, or when the weather is hot, make sure he doesn't become dehydrated by offering the breast more frequently or giving him cooled boiled water in a bottle or on a sterile spoon.

If your baby suffers from vomiting and diarrhea for more than 24 hours, always consult your doctor. If you are bottle-feeding, stop formula feedings for 24 hours and give rehydration solution (this is available from your doctor or pharmacist) by bottle. If you're breast-feeding, give rehydration fluid in a bottle, if possible, before the feeding. If your baby won't take a bottle, you will need to breast-feed more often to maintain fluid intake.

Mild diarrhea can sometimes occur when you introduce new types of solid food (see p. 94) – if you suspect this is happening, stop giving your baby that particular food and then try again after a couple of weeks.

RECOGNIZING AN ILLNESS

AILMENT	WHEN TO CALL THE DOCTOR
HIGH OR LOW TEMPERATURE	• If your baby's temperature rises above 100°F (38°C) and he's obviously sick, or if it rises above 103°F (39.4°C) although he doesn't seem sick. • When your baby's temperature goes up and down. • If your baby is unusually quiet and limp and his skin is cold, although his hands and feet are pink (see p. 103).
BREATHING DIFFICULTIES	• If your baby's breathing becomes difficult. • The rate of breathing speeds up and you notice his ribs being drawn sharply in with each breath.
LOSS OF APPETITE	• If your baby is under six months and refuses to feed either at the breast or from a bottle. • If your baby has been weaned and refuses food when he is normally a good eater.
VOMITING	• If your baby is burping up whole feedings or the vomiting is violent, prolonged, or excessive, it can cause rapid dehydration and medical help should be sought immediately. However, all babies regurgitate a little milk from time to time after feedings.
DIARRHEA	• If the stools are watery, possibly greenish in color, foul-smelling, and abnormally frequent. • If diarrhea is accompanied by a raised temperature, you should always consult a doctor.
RASHES	• If you notice an unusual rash it can be a sign of infection, especially if it's accompanied by a raised temperature, or it might be an allergic reaction. Your baby's doctor will want to examine the rash. • One type of rash caused by meningitis is very serious and should be treated as an emergency (see above right).

MENINGITIS

This is an inflammation of the membranes that cover the brain, resulting from an infection. Viral meningitis is relatively mild; bacterial meningitis is life-threatening and requires immediate action. The main symptoms can develop over a matter of hours.

SYMPTOMS
In a baby under 12 months the main symptoms are general irritability, a slightly tense and bulging fontanelle (see p. 56), fever, and a rash consisting of flat, pink or purple spots that don't disappear when you press them. There may also be listlessness, vomiting, loss of appetite, and pain in the eyes from light.

WHAT TO DO
Press a glass to your baby's skin to see if the rash remains visible through it. If you think your baby may have meningitis, get him to a hospital immediately.

101

FEBRILE CONVULSIONS

These occur in young children (mainly aged from six months to five years) if there is a rapid increase in temperature due to an infection. The sudden rise causes the brain cells to discharge impulses to muscles, which contract jerkily. It does not indicate an underlying brain defect. The symptoms can be frightening to witness, but febrile convulsions are relatively common and rarely serious. The risk of epilepsy developing is very small.

SYMPTOMS
Loss of consciousness and uncontrollable twitching of the arms and legs. There may also be frothing at the mouth and the eyes may roll back.

WHAT TO DO
Clear a space and sponge your baby down to lower his temperature (see opposite). Call a doctor.

EMERGENCY FIRST AID

FIRST-AID MATERIALS

In preparation for an accident or emergency, keep a box of first-aid materials in your home. Make sure that any caregivers, such as a baby-sitter, know where this is kept. It should include the following:

■ Adhesive bandages.

■ Sterile dressings – do not open these until you need to use them.

■ Bandages.

■ Cotton.

■ Scissors and tweezers.

■ Adhesive tape or safety pins.

YOU NEED TO KNOW what to do if your baby is seriously injured or sick. The following is not a substitute for proper first-aid training, but you should familiarize yourself with the techniques and information detailed here so that you know what action to take in an emergency. Although it may be difficult, always try to stay as calm as possible.

AN UNCONSCIOUS BABY

If your baby does not respond when you gently shake her shoulders or pick her up, she is unconscious. She may have stopped breathing, in which case no oxygen is reaching her brain, and her heartbeat may have slowed down or stopped altogether. You need to act quickly to open your baby's airway and resuscitate her if necessary (see below).

Calling an ambulance If you have a helper, ask him or her to call an ambulance. If not, resuscitating your baby for one minute before you call for help could save her life. When you call an ambulance, take your baby to the telephone with you; give the dispatcher as much information as you can.

102

WHAT TO DO IF YOUR BABY IS UNCONSCIOUS

If you think that your baby is unconscious, act as quickly as possible. Look, listen, and feel for breathing so that you can decide on the best course of action, and then follow the relevant procedure outlined below.

IF SHE IS BREATHING

MAINTAINING AN OPEN AIRWAY
If your baby is unconscious, there is a chance that she could choke on her tongue or vomit. To prevent this happening, cradle your baby with her head lower than her chest, as shown above, so that her airway remains open. While you're waiting for help, keep checking her breathing and pulse (see right); if either or both are absent, follow the procedure for not breathing (see right).

IF SHE IS NOT BREATHING

RESCUE BREATHING
● Place one finger under your baby's chin, and your other hand on her head, and tilt her head back very slightly to open her airway.
● Keeping the airway open, remove any *obvious* obstruction from her mouth.
● Seal your lips tightly around her mouth and nose and breathe into her lungs until her chest rises. Then remove your lips and let her chest fall back.
● Continue to do this for one minute, aiming at one complete breath every three seconds.
● Check the pulse (see right). If it is absent, begin resuscitation by alternating chest compressions (see right) with rescue breathing.

PULSE CHECK
● Place two fingers on your baby's inner arm to find the pulse.
● Watch for other signs of recovery.

CHEST COMPRESSIONS
● If the pulse is absent, position your index finger in the center of the nipple line on the lower breastbone.
● Place the next two fingers on the lower breastbone, just below the nipple line and press down sharply to a depth of ½–1in five times in three seconds.
● Give one rescue breath (see left). Continue cycle for one minute.

A CHOKING BABY

If your baby is choking on something she may turn blue and make strange noises because she is trying to cry. *Do not* turn her upside down or shake her. Take the following action before calling an ambulance:

● Lay your baby face down along your forearm and keeping your hand flat, give her five sharp slaps between the shoulders.

● If the blockage has not cleared, turn her face up along your other arm, place two fingers on the lower half of her breastbone, and press down sharply five times (abdominal thrusts).

● Check her mouth and remove any visible obstruction.

● If the blockage has not cleared, call an ambulance. Continue the cycle of back slaps and abdominal thrusts while you are waiting.

● If consciousness is lost, continue the above cycle and give rescue breaths after each cycle.

BACK SLAPS
If your baby is choking, lie her face down along your forearm and give her five sharp slaps between the shoulders, keeping your hand flat.

HYPOTHERMIA

Hypothermia occurs when the body temperature falls below 95°F (35°C). The temperature-regulating mechanism in babies is immature, so they can lose body heat rapidly in a cold place.

THE SYMPTOMS
A hypothermic baby will look misleadingly healthy because she will have a pink glow to her skin, but it will feel cold. She may refuse to feed, and be limp and quiet.

WHAT TO DO
Call a doctor. Warm your baby gradually: take her into a warm room and wrap her in blankets. Put a hat on her head, and hold her close to your body so that she benefits from your warmth.

103

EMERGENCY FIRST AID FOR ACCIDENTS

INJURY	WHAT HAPPENS	BEFORE YOU GET MEDICAL HELP
SEVERE BLEEDING	If your child has an accident that causes severe bleeding, you must act quickly to stop the bleeding before seeking help.	Press firmly on the wound, keeping the injured part raised. Cover the wound with a sterile dressing and bandage it in place.
HEAD INJURY	If your baby hits her head she may become concussed, which usually leads to a brief loss of consciousness.	Make your baby comfortable and treat any bleeding (see above). Take her to a doctor, even if she appears to be fully recovered.
ELECTRIC SHOCK	Your baby may get an electric shock if she plays with electrical outlets or cords. This can cause her breathing and heart to stop, and cause burns on her body.	Immediately switch off the current at the fuse box. Stand on dry insulating material, such as a telephone directory, and push the source away from the baby with a broom.
DROWNING	An inch of water is enough to drown a baby if she falls forward. Never leave her in a tub alone, even if she can sit unaided.	Carry her with her head lower than her chest. If she is unconscious, begin resuscitation immediately (see opposite).
EYE INJURY	If a foreign body enters your baby's eye, wash it out as soon as possible and try to prevent her from rubbing her injured eye.	Tilt her head and pour water into the inner corner of her eye. If it is stuck under the eyelid, lift the upper eyelid over the lower.
BITES	Bites can range from minor insect stings to animal bites and the treatment will differ accordingly.	Wash an insect bite thoroughly and cover it with a bandage. For an animal bite, follow the procedure for bleeding (see above).
BURNS AND SCALDS	If your baby is burned or scalded, you need to act quickly to cool the burn and remove any clothing from the affected area before it begins to swell.	Cool the burn with cold water for ten minutes. Remove restrictive clothing from the area and cover it with clean material. Don't apply anything to the burn.

YOUR SPECIAL BABY

FORTUNATELY, FEW PARENTS ever have to hear the words they may dread: "I'm sorry, but your baby has a problem." But that doesn't make it any easier for the minority of parents who have to face the fact that their baby has a condition that is going to affect, and perhaps dominate, his life and theirs too.

SIGNS TO LOOK FOR

Although the rate of normal development is enormously varied (see p. 127), it may become apparent that your baby's development is delayed. Don't jump to conclusions, but as parents you are likely to be the first to recognize some of the signs that your baby needs help.

HAND AWARENESS
A baby becomes aware of his hands at about eight weeks (see p. 136). He'll watch fascinated as he wiggles his fingers and grabs his toes. At 12–16 weeks this interest wanes, but may last up to 20 weeks in a baby whose development is delayed.

GRASP REFLEX
From birth to about six weeks, your baby wraps his fingers tightly around anything placed in his palm, then the reflex fades as he begins to gain control of hand movements. In a developmentally delayed baby the grasp reflex is retained for longer.

EXPLORATION WITH THE MOUTH
At around four months a baby puts everything in his mouth, stopping at about a year old. Mouthing goes on longer in a developmentally slow child.

"CASTING"
From 8 to 16 months, all babies go through the stage of "casting" – dropping things to see where they fall – but this lasts longer in a baby whose development is delayed.

DRIBBLING
Most babies achieve mouth control at 12 months; slow babies dribble for much longer.

CHEWING
Most babies develop the ability to chew (even if they haven't grown teeth) by about seven months. A developmentally delayed baby will take longer.

DIAGNOSIS

Your baby will be examined by the midwife at birth and by a pediatrician before you leave the hospital (see p. 57); they may find something that requires further investigation at this point. If not, you may be the first to spot something isn't quite right (see left). Talk to your family doctor, who should refer your baby for an expert assessment: insist that this happens if you're concerned. Among the first things to exclude are impaired hearing or vision; these should be tested at your baby's developmental checks (see p. 133).

COMING TO TERMS WITH THE NEWS

Whenever you find out about your baby's disability, you'll need time to adjust to the shock and pain. Every new parent has expectations and hopes for their child, and it's as though all of these are dashed in the space of a few minutes. In many ways, it is like a bereavement; you need to mourn for the baby you thought you were expecting, the perfect, able-bodied child you longed for, and come to terms with the special baby you have. In time, of course, this child will be your perfect child, and you'll feel ashamed that you ever thought him second-best: but in the early days, it is almost impossible not to feel a sense of loss.

TALK TO OTHERS

Many of the congenital conditions that affect children and babies are extremely rare, but it will help you enormously if you can find other parents to talk to who have a child with exactly the same problem as your own. Your family doctor, health center, or local community services department can help put you in touch with specialist organizations. These may have self-help groups that include other parents in the same or a similar position to you (see p. 163) and may be able to provide you with counseling and information on where to go for further help and advice.

PHYSICAL PROBLEMS THAT CAN BE CORRECTED

With advances in neonatal pediatric surgery, many physical problems with which babies are born can be corrected – even in the first months. This is a worrying time because it is distressing to see your baby having to undergo a series of operations. It can also be a strain emotionally (and financially), particularly if the hospital treating your baby is a long way from your home, but it helps to know that there is every chance that your baby will be able to grow up to be a normal, healthy child.

RECOGNIZING DEVELOPMENTAL PROBLEMS

A baby with a developmental problem is going to reach his milestones (see p. 126) at a slower than average rate, and in some cases may not reach them at all. You may notice quite early on that your baby is behind from signs such as unusual quietness, lack of alertness, no interest in his surroundings, floppiness (lack of muscle tone), docility, and sleeping for long periods. Sometimes a baby who's been termed "good" turns out to be a baby with a problem, because this kind of baby cries rarely, makes little noise, and does not interact well with his environment. He'll be late in losing his primitive reflexes like the grasp reflex (see p. 134) that should have disappeared by six weeks, he'll be late in smiling and responding to his name, and he'll be slow in learning to chew. Feeding may be a problem from the start, because muscles may not be developed enough for sucking.

LATER SIGNS

As your baby grows older, at around seven or eight months you may notice that his attention span is very short and he'll spend time moving quickly from one toy to another instead of examining one slowly and carefully as most babies do. Later still, he may be overactive and have difficulty concentrating on a single activity. He may also be reserved and unresponsive to people, even when he knows them very well.

AVOID COMPARISONS

Comparing one baby with another is never a good idea, but if you have a baby with delayed development it's doubly important to see your baby for himself, rather than measuring him against the standard of other people's children. With perseverance, the support of specialists, and encouragement from you, your baby will reach some of his milestones (see p. 126) eventually, and the reward of seeing him do so will be a huge satisfaction.

OTHER PEOPLE'S ATTITUDES

Most people don't have direct experience of a disability, and have little idea of how to react to a disabled person or child. Indeed, this may have been your own position until recently. It is inevitable that your family, friends, and neighbors will become aware of your baby's disability, and many of them will not know how to react appropriately. Almost inevitably there will be those who will say the wrong thing, make a crass comment or remark without thinking; you'll just have to remind yourself that their insensitivity comes from ignorance and embarrassment and they probably don't mean to be offensive. Try not to let this get you down; be open about your baby's disability so that it does not become a taboo subject when you're with others.

GIVING A LEAD

What you'll find is that many of your family and friends will take their lead from you in learning how to relate to your child. Make it clear that although his disability may be permanent, he is in no way inferior to anyone else and has the same right to love, understanding, and support as any child. You'll need courage, but you'll discover, like many other parents of disabled children, that you've got an inner strength that you never thought you would have. If you can be positive and hopeful about your child, and show by example how much you value his individuality and personality, other people will learn to do the same.

HOW YOU CAN HELP

If and when your baby is diagnosed with developmental delay or any other disability or learning difficulty, you will be given specialist advice on how to stimulate him both physically and intellectually. Here are some ideas that will help any baby, and are easy to fit into your daily routine:

■ Stimulate your child from birth. Do this visually by making sure he can see your face close up as much as possible and having a picture of a face hanging down the side of the crib. Stimulate him aurally by playing music or a heartbeat on tape, by talking and singing, and by using touch with different textures, such as lambskin, cotton, rubber, or plastic.

■ Talk and sing to your baby in pronounced rhythms and rhymes, such as "Jack and Jill."

■ Read and talk to him as much as you can.

■ Make him aware of his body with gentle clapping games and baby massage (see p. 92).

■ Find toys that are educational and enjoyable to a young baby and join in so you can show him how to play with them (see p. 126).

■ Introduce him to as many people as possible.

■ Give him all the love you have and make him feel secure.

■ Praise him often.

■ Give lots of cuddles, nuzzles, and kisses; make sure others do, too.

■ Never scold or punish his slowness.

■ Encourage him to be independent – help him try to do things, even if it's hard.

■ Be patient when he's frustrated. Remember, life will be a bit more difficult for him, especially when he's older and he begins to realize that he is not able to do things other children of his age can.

105

ADAPTING TO PARENTHOOD

In addition to mastering the practical care of your newborn baby, you need to think about your lifestyle and your relationship so that you're able to get the most out of being parents and a family. Your baby will undoubtedly be your main priority and it's easy to let her soak up all your emotional and physical energy. But to maximize the many joys of parenthood, it's worth making sure that you have time for each other and time for yourself. You are, after all, still individuals and still in a loving relationship and it would be wrong to think that your baby could fulfill all your needs. How easily you adjust will depend on your individual circumstances: having a good and equal relationship with each other already and an adequate support network (especially if you're a single parent) can make the transition to parenthood that much easier. If you have difficulty in adjusting at first, don't worry. Parenthood is full of ups and downs, but if you work together to get the balance right, hopefully it will turn out to be all that you wanted it to be.

HELPING EACH OTHER

MOTHER

If you've been at home with your baby for a few months while your partner is at work, you may begin to feel that you know your baby better than he does; at the same time you may feel resentful that you don't get enough help from him. Think about how your attitudes may affect your partner.

SUPPORTING YOUR PARTNER

■ Resist the tendency to think that your partner isn't as "good" as you are at caring for your baby. His role is vital and by encouraging him to get involved with the baby care and share the workload, you'll all benefit.

■ If your partner is tired after work, be patient. Let him wind down, then encourage him to spend time with your baby as a way of relaxing, not as a chore. Bathing the baby is often a good way for him to look after the baby and wind down at the same time (see p. 81).

■ Try to keep communicating. Tell him about your day with the baby. If it's been difficult, don't bottle it up resentfully, but, equally, don't convey it accusingly as if it's his fault.

BUILDING YOUR SELF-ESTEEM

■ Be proud of your achievements. As the main caregiver, you should justifiably take pride in the upbringing of your baby.

■ Stay in contact with colleagues at work so that you can keep in touch with career developments and gossip! That way it's less of a shock when you return.

■ Make sure you have some time away from the baby, on your own and with your partner (see p. 114).

YOU BOTH WELCOME YOUR BABY. His presence is a shared joy that cements your relationship. However, new parenthood is a testing role, when both of you are faced with a new set of priorities and when expectations come up against hard realities. So spare a thought for each other's needs, as well as those of your baby.

THE INITIAL IMPACT OF THE BABY

As first-time parents, you may seriously underestimate the amount of work and disruption that is entailed in caring for a baby and the extent to which this affects your relationship. Many couples are shocked to find that, rather than bringing them closer together, their baby can bring to light differences that drive them apart. This is normal and very much part of your growth into parenthood, when you begin to lay the foundations of your new parental relationship with your baby and with each other.

DIFFERENT PATTERNS OF BONDING

While two-thirds of mothers bond with their babies almost immediately or within a few days, many fathers admit that intense paternal feelings take much longer to develop. Many mothers are overwhelmed by the depth of their feelings for their baby. Unfortunately, some fathers view this as an obsession, to which they are not sympathetic, and they resent being excluded from their partner's affection and attention. If his partner breast-feeds, the father often feels excused from nurturing as a consequence, driving a wedge between himself and his baby. Fathers who are involved in their baby's daily care will strengthen their paternal bond in the early weeks and close the gap between how fathers and mothers feel differently about their baby.

SHARING THE CARE
Your baby needs the protection and love of both his parents. Sharing his daily care will help you and your partner to really understand each other's needs and feelings.

108

DEFUSING AREAS OF CONFLICT

WHAT TO DO	HOW IT HELPS
DISCUSS WHO DOES WHAT	You probably both have views about what roles men and women should play; this can be a powerful hidden agenda. Discuss how you feel and be prepared to have your views challenged.
TALK ABOUT YOUR EXPECTATIONS	Disappointed expectations may result in disillusionment, so it's best to give and take in those areas where your views diverge, even though you won't escape hard choices.
LISTEN TO EACH OTHER	Try to talk openly about your feelings and think about how to express them. Do this in a way that avoids accusation, sarcasm, or belittling your partner. Give "I" rather than "you" messages.
RESOLVE CONFLICT IMMEDIATELY	Resolve conflict by determining the cause and coming to a mutually agreed solution. A common area of conflict is when you have differing views on division of labor (see below).
PUT YOUR FAMILY FIRST	Self-denial isn't a very popular concept these days, but if you're to turn your trio into a family you'll each need to forego some individual pleasures in the interest of building your family.
LEARN TO COPE WITH STRESS	Reactions to stress differ from person to person. Try to evolve together a pattern of "stress management" for difficult periods, to minimize any possible damage to your relationship.

DIVISION OF LABOR

By far the biggest bone of contention between new parents is how they should share caring for the baby and the workload that goes with it. Only about one in twelve fathers takes on a full 50 percent of the load (even allowing for work commitments). Even when some mothers return to full-time work, they frequently have to shoulder more than half – and in some cases virtually all – the baby care and running of the home outside their working hours. Some fathers help with the fun and rewarding tasks, such as bathtime and bedtime stories, but may be less enthusiastic about changing diapers, washing clothes, and getting up in the middle of the night. They may also be more reluctant to make lifestyle changes and sacrifices, such as giving up a hobby or spending time with friends. This attitude is inappropriate: parenting is a partnership and a father must make sure he doesn't miss out on invaluable time with his baby.

AN EQUAL RESPONSIBILITY
Find ways of sharing the drudgery and the delights of caring for your baby. Look positively at your baby's development and how you can stimulate and enjoy it together (see p. 126). You and your partner should consider parenthood one of the most demanding jobs you can have, and reinforce each other's equal responsibility to succeed in this new role.

FATHER

If you're at work and your partner is at home looking after the baby, try to see things from her point of view. Although you'll miss your new family when you're at work, you'll have the usual challenges and friendships of working life to stimulate you during the day. Your partner may well be missing these if she's stopped work to look after your baby and she may be finding the change in lifestyle difficult.

SUPPORTING YOUR PARTNER
■ Telephone her at different times of the day – several times a week. If you're near enough, go home for lunch on occasion.

■ Let her know what time you're going to be home and stick to it. She'll need a break in the evenings and this is valuable time for you to spend with your baby.

■ Share the ups and the downs. If you've had a rotten day at work, talk to her about it, but listen to her and be sympathetic if she's also had a bad day.

■ Make sure she has time out to relax away from the baby and to see her friends (see p. 114).

BECOMING MORE INVOLVED
■ If your partner is at home with the baby most of the time, don't think that she's the only one who can care for him. Your role in caring for your baby is vital and will be very rewarding for you.

■ Talk through what happened at home during the day and find out what milestones your baby may have reached – then spend time with your baby so that you can experience them for yourself.

■ Try to use your weekends and days off to have extended time with your baby. Continue caring for him just as you did when he was first born.

109

LEARNING TO COPE

MINIMIZING STRESS

Most family arguments occur at stressful times. Early in the morning, when you're only half awake and you have to do too many things too quickly, you can become clumsy and irritable. If you have a full-time job, it's easy and natural to bring the stress home with you, making it more difficult to cope with the demands being made on you at home. It's at times like these that you and your partner need to work together to help each other; if you take out your stresses on each other or on the baby it will probably only make matters worse.

■ Try to find ways of relaxing with each other and by yourselves (see p. 114).

■ Try to be honest about how you're feeling to help prevent any misunderstandings.

■ Don't try to do too many things at once: you'll only get frustrated and overtired.

■ Try not to bring work home with you – physically or mentally.

NEGATIVE FEELINGS

You may experience a cocktail of emotions that conflict with your ideas of what it's proper to feel. Having negative thoughts toward your baby because she's kept you up all night or because she's crying is normal. There's no point in refusing to accept how you feel; it doesn't make you a bad mother. It's abnormal, however, to use violence as a way of expressing yourself; if your temper is really being pushed to the limit, talk to someone or take time away before you harm your child.

CARING FOR A BABY tests all parents. If you get upset, angry, argue with your partner, or if you can't comfort your baby, you may feel that you have in some way failed, but you haven't. Getting through these times is part of being a parent; you'll learn from every occasion and be a better parent and partner for having come through it.

DEALING WITH ANGER

It's paradoxical that some of our strongest negative feelings are directed toward those we love most. On closer examination, of course, this is easily explained: the extent to which we are hurt, angered, disappointed, or disillusioned by others is an index of how strongly we feel about the people concerned. You're probably never going to feel more strongly about anybody than about your children. Your love for them will not be diminished by the fact that you're sometimes angered or disappointed by them, but at such times you'll be besieged by conflicting emotions, especially when you're dealing with a baby.

WHY ANGER IS NORMAL
If your baby cries for long periods or sleeps only for brief intervals, you're bound to feel concerned and worried. If this worry is then compounded by a feeling of impotence, it often expresses itself as anger. You may sometimes be seized by acute feelings of helplessness, guilt, and inadequacy when nothing you do seems to pacify your baby. At such times it's difficult not to feel victimized and the worry can often quickly escalate to resentment and then anger. You may also feel angry that nothing you do seems to work, and resentful that you're left with little time or energy for your own needs. You both have to accept that these feelings are very natural.

BREAKING THE CIRCLE OF NEGATIVITY
The knowledge that your tension and frustration can be communicated to your baby will only increase your anxiety, which will in turn make the baby feel more insecure. It's very easy to become locked into a vicious circle of negativity. Your baby will express this in the only way she knows, by crying, and her crying will further unnerve you. This circle must be broken.

Talk to someone Telephone someone in whom you can confide; just getting your feelings out in the open will help you put everything into perspective. Talking to other parents in the same situation is often useful – you'll realize your feelings are very normal. You should also talk to your partner, but remember he or she may also be feeling exasperated; try to talk to each other when you're able to go out without the baby or when the baby is asleep. If none of the above is possible, speak to your visiting nurse or doctor.

A change of scene If you're alone with your baby during the day, get out of the house. The change of scene will help you relax, and being driven in a car, wheeled in a carriage, or walked in a sling can often soothe a baby. In the short term, if you feel yourself being engulfed by anger, leave the room or put the baby in another room until you feel calmer. When your baby is older, make sure you have adequate time away from each other (see p. 114).

IF YOUR BABY IS DIFFICULT TO LOVE

Just like both of you, your baby has her own personality. She may be happy and smiling all the time, or she may be reserved and seemingly unsociable. She may be independent and not very affectionate, or clingy and easily upset. Remember, your baby doesn't choose to behave in a certain way to spite you – it's just how she's made. As with all relationships, you need to keep the communication channels open with your baby. You have to get to know what makes her tick, and accept that you're not going to have an easy relationship with her all the time.

MAINTAINING AFFECTION

Some babies don't like to be handled or cuddled very much; others go through phases of being unsociable. If a baby does not want attention, she will tend to stiffen her body and cry when you hold her. Most babies will become more sociable with time, but if you're particularly worried, seek advice from your visiting nurse. Try to do the following:

● Accept that babies are sometimes just difficult and don't blame yourself.
● Don't thrust unwelcome attention on her – it may make matters worse.
● If your baby is more affectionate with your partner, be grateful! Don't take this personally; babies often go through periods when they prefer or cling to one partner and this will pass with time.
● Remember, your baby will respond to you so make sure you're smiling and being affectionate toward her.

WHEN YOUR BABY MISSES YOU

If you have invested time in your baby and bonded closely, you'll have created a feeling of rightness when you're together that is shattering when you're apart. An upheaval such as returning to work, the preferred parent being away for a period of time, or the introduction of a baby-sitter may make your baby unsettled. This is most likely to reveal itself in her being fretful, fussy, needing more cuddles than usual, and a change in her eating and sleeping patterns. If your baby appears to be genuinely unhappy, reassess the situation; for example, it could be that she's unhappy with her baby-sitter. To help your baby when you're away from home:

● Telephone frequently.
● Ask your partner or baby-sitter to talk about you to your baby.
● Leave an item of your clothing for your baby to hold.
● Tape yourself singing and talking to your baby.
● Leave photos of yourself.

KEEP IN TOUCH

A baby will love to hold the telephone, hear Mommy's voice, and "talk" to her when she's away.

A FRETFUL BABY

Most parents experience one or more periods during which their baby is consistently fretful and demanding for no apparent reason. This inability to communicate what is wrong can be very frustrating for both of you and your baby.

WHY SHE MAY BE FRETFUL

■ Your baby may not be receiving as much stimulation as she needs. Babies who can sit up and who would like to explore their environment but who can't yet crawl can become particularly frustrated.

■ If your baby is teething, she may be experiencing discomfort or even pain (see p. 132).

■ If you're particularly stressed, your baby may be picking up your heightened tension.

GETTING THROUGH IT

■ Remember, you haven't produced a monster – your baby's behavior is normal. Much of your frustration stems from her inability to communicate. This is part of the human condition and not a failing in her or you.

■ The fact that your baby is going through a bad period doesn't mean that you're inadequate: difficult periods are experienced by the majority of parents.

■ If you accept your feelings rather than getting angry with yourself, you'll find it easier to retain an overall positive attitude. This will help you resolve your difficulties.

■ If you can share your negative feelings with each other, or with a friend, without shame or blame, it will help you to keep things in perspective.

■ There are particular ways that a crying baby can be comforted: try some of the suggestions outlined on pages 88 to 91.

111

HELPING EACH OTHER

In the days following the birth, when "baby blues" may be rife, you'll both need to pull together to be able to support each other. This can range from working as a team as you share the day-to-day care of your baby, to just listening and being there for each other.

WHAT FATHERS CAN DO
■ Encourage your partner to talk about the things that are getting her down. Give her lots of "I care" messages and as much attention and affection as possible.

■ Tell her you love her often to boost her self-esteem – she may dislike her body and feel she's unattractive; tell her that she's beautiful to you.

■ Take her shopping specifically for clothes and flatter her until she regains her prepregnant figure. Be patient and tell her she looks good. Don't push her to lose weight.

■ Encourage her to join a mother and baby support group and make it easy for her to go.

■ Encourage people to visit if that's what she wants, but, if not, help maintain her privacy.

WHAT MOTHERS CAN DO
■ If you've got the blues, try your best not to take out your tensions on your partner. Try to express how you're feeling rather than blaming or arguing. If you need a cuddle, tell your partner – remember, he's not a mind reader.

■ Remember that your partner also has some big adjustments to make. He may be finding it difficult, too.

■ Make sure your partner has time with the baby; it will create problems if he feels left out.

■ Try to limit the number of people that visit. It may make your partner feel like an outsider if your house is crowded with your friends and relatives cooing over your baby.

FEELING LOW

IT'S CERTAINLY TRUE that nothing can prepare you for caring for a new baby. The physical and emotional upheaval is bound to have an impact; quite often when most mothers think they're going to be happiest, they often feel very low – the "baby blues." In most instances this only lasts a few days but, sadly, in others these feelings can continue for months due to a condition known as postpartum depression. It's important for a father to be aware of the symptoms and recognize the difference between the normal "blues" and real depression so that he knows how to help and when to seek medical advice.

BABY BLUES

The "baby blues" are mood swings caused by hormonal changes. In all likelihood this period of feeling low one minute and euphoric the next won't last beyond the first week, but you'll still need a lot of support to get through it. Maybe the "baby blues" are a natural sign to those around you that you need time and space to come to terms with being a mother. That's certainly how a concerned partner, relative, or friend should deal with it. You may also find that, because your hormones are all over the place, you'll cry when someone's nice to you as well!

WHY YOU GET THE BLUES
Your hormones, progesterone and estrogen, will have been high during pregnancy. After you have had your baby, these hormone levels drop and your body may find it difficult to adjust. This can have a marked effect on your emotions. With this, and the fact that you're probably completely exhausted from labor and lack of sleep, it's not at all surprising that you may not be feeling on top of the world.

WHAT YOU CAN DO
● Give yourself time: accept that you'll feel like this for a short time and that what you're going through is incredibly common.
● Accept offers of help and don't try to do everything yourself.
● Try to talk about your feelings and have a good cry if it helps.
● Tell your partner you need a lot of love and affection, but remember this is a time of upheaval and change for him, too.

WHEN FATHERS GET THE BLUES

Most fathers feel an anticlimax after the birth. There are the extra responsibilities and sudden changes in lifestyle. If your partner is feeling low, you'll be called on to be a tower of strength, which can be a huge strain. Try to think of the first few months as a period of rapid change that is testing for both of you; when you come through it, you'll both emerge closer than you were before. If you get really unhappy, talk things over with your visiting nurse, doctor, or a close friend.

POSTPARTUM DEPRESSION (PPD)

If symptoms that started out as the common "baby blues" don't go away and, in fact, start to become worse, you could be suffering from postpartum depression. This is a temporary and treatable condition that varies from woman to woman. It can develop slowly and not become obvious until several weeks after the baby's birth, but if it's diagnosed and addressed early enough, there's a good chance of a fast cure. Visiting nurses are trained to recognize the symptoms and treatment ranges from something as simple as talking to a friend, nurse, or doctor about how you feel, to taking medication, such as antidepressants, for more severe cases.

WHY POSTPARTUM DEPRESSION HAPPENS

There are many reasons why postpartum depression occurs. It depends on you as a person, your personal circumstances, and the way your baby behaves. Research shows that the following risk factors may make you more susceptible to postpartum depression:
- If you enjoyed a senior position at work or a high-flying career before the birth, it can be difficult to adjust to the status change.
- If you already have difficulties in your relationship, the baby may make them worse; this in itself may lead to disillusionment and low self-esteem.
- If you had an unexpected difficult birth experience (see p. 48), you could easily feel demoralized and feel that you've, in some way, failed.
- If you've had depression in the past.
- A very demanding, sleepless baby can trigger postpartum depression from sheer exhaustion.
- If you have particularly difficult living conditions and no support network, this can exacerbate postpartum depression.
- If you've bottled up your emotions and not sought help early on.

SEEKING HELP

Many women are too embarrassed to admit how they feel, fearing that it will appear that they have somehow failed. Talking about how you feel is the most important thing you can do; once you accept that you're not "mad" and that there are things you can do to help yourself, you are one step on the road to recovery. Once you seek help you'll be guided to:
- Understand how you feel and learn to express this.
- Learn to prioritize and go with the flow.
- Devote more time to yourself and find ways to relax.
- Visit your doctor or nurse more regularly and seek support.
- Begin taking medication if your postpartum depression is very extreme.

WHAT FATHERS CAN DO

You may feel helpless because you don't understand postpartum depression. Remember, it's temporary and treatable, so try to be patient. You can be a huge help if you make an effort to understand and do the following:
- Talk and listen to your partner. Never tell her to pull herself together – she can't. Don't assume she'll snap out of it – she won't.
- Take care of her and encourage her to rest and eat and drink properly.
- Encourage her to be with the baby as much as she wants so that she can take things slowly and gradually work out how the baby will fit in.
- Make sure she's not alone too much because she'll fear isolation.
- See the doctor alone for advice since your partner may refuse to accept that she's ill. The doctor may arrange to visit her informally at home.

PPD SIGNS TO LOOK OUT FOR

The signs and symptoms of postpartum depression vary from woman to woman, but include:

- Anxiety: in particular, a mother may worry about her baby and refuse to be parted from him.

- Irrational fears, for example, about being left alone.

- Loss of appetite.

- Insomnia.

- Fatigue.

- Lack of concern with appearance.

- Making mountains out of molehills.

- Withdrawal from social contact.

- Feeling negative and inadequate.

- Growing feelings of despondency and helplessness.

POSTPARTUM PSYCHOSIS

Postpartum – or puerperal – psychosis is the rarest and most serious form of postpartum depression. It affects about one in 1,000 women and usually occurs in the first three months after the birth. This illness should not be underestimated, but it is curable. Urgent medical help should be sought and hospitalization will be necessary. Where possible, the mother and baby should be kept together. The symptoms the mother may have include:

- Sleeping all day.

- Long periods of crying.

- Tension and anxiety.

- Manical happiness and odd behavior.

- Paranoia and hallucinations.

- Thoughts of harming herself and the baby.

113

MOTHER

It's vitally important, for the sake of all your relationships, that your partner also has time out. He needs his own time with the baby, time alone with you, and a chance to relax away from the workplace and home.

HOW TO HELP YOUR PARTNER

■ Encourage him to have an occasional night out with friends or to continue a hobby, even if he's been out of the house all day. It's good for anyone who works to reduce the pressure this way as long as it doesn't take over his life to the exclusion of you and your baby.

■ Make the most of your time at home with your partner. He may feel left out, so make the effort to make him feel special, particularly when the baby is asleep.

HOW THE BABY GAINS

Spending short periods of time away from your baby can make you a better parent, so don't feel guilty about leaving her every now and then. You should see your occasional separation as something positive for the following reasons:

■ You'll appreciate your baby more when you see her again.

■ A break will help you feel relaxed and rested, which will mean you'll be better able to cope and the baby will benefit.

■ It's good for her to get used to you going out (she'll soon learn that you always come back), and being with others will stop her from becoming too dependent on you.

■ Your baby will learn the seeds of confidence and develop her social skills by having to relate to others.

TIME OUT

BEING A NEW PARENT is unarguably a tiring and time-consuming experience. Finding five minutes of peace and quiet may seem impossible to begin with, but it's essential that your routine includes time out for you and your partner – both individually and together. It will be good for your relationship and good for your baby.

TIME TO YOURSELF

Making time for yourself is not a luxury, it's a necessity. You both need time when you're not being parents or partners, but are just being yourselves. To ensure that you have time away from your baby you'll need to be well organized and divide your life into areas: baby, partner, work, and yourself. That doesn't mean you should put yourself last. Having time to yourself should be high on your list of priorities, especially if you're feeling tired or stressed. Otherwise, you may become unhappy, which will be upsetting for everyone, including your baby, and not what you expected at all.

MAKE TIME FOR YOURSELF

● If you're the primary caregiver, incorporated into your daily timetable should be at least half an hour devoted entirely to yourself, when you can have a soak in the tub, read a magazine, or just visit with a friend.
● When your baby is asleep, take the opportunity to rest; if you're feeling tired, having a catnap is more important than cleaning the house. Don't be hard on yourself – it's okay to sleep in the middle of the day, especially if you're having to get up during the night.
● Time away doesn't only mean half an hour away from your baby when she's asleep; it means time away from the home environment. If you arrange to see a friend, suggest that you visit her or meet her somewhere – if you're at home you are more likely to become involved with your baby.
● Arrange a "baby swap" with other parents: they look after your baby along with their own on a particular day or evening, and then you do the same for them. Ask friends and relatives to help out, if they live nearby.
● Find out if the local community center or gym has a nursery – and use it!

BE FLEXIBLE WITH YOUR DAILY ROUTINE

You can roughly plan your day, but don't be too regimented and inflexible. The needs of a young baby change all the time, and if your baby wakes up unexpectedly you may not be able to have the half-hour you wanted. Try to be relaxed about it and take a break later in the day.

ACCEPT HELP FROM OTHERS

It will be much easier to make space for yourself if you learn to accept offers of help. Don't be stoic and don't feel you're somehow a failure because you let someone else look after your baby. Just say yes gratefully, then do your own thing – you deserve it. It's very normal to feel strange about leaving your baby to begin with, but this will pass with time once you have learned to trust your helpers. Your baby will also benefit in many ways by not only being with you all the time (see left).

SPENDING TIME TOGETHER AS A COUPLE

An important part of keeping the communication channels open with your partner is to find time when you can be alone together. Doing this is possible, but may require planning. It will seem odd to book a time to see your partner, but if you try to be spontaneous about it, you'll always find an excuse or decide that your baby is more important. Sometimes it may only be possible to spend time together in the house, but try to find times when someone else can look after your baby so that you both have the opportunity to go out and have uninterrupted time.

AT HOME
● Try to continue any rituals you had before your baby was born, such as having a drink together in the evening, sharing a bath, or just doing the crossword puzzle. Try not to talk about your baby all the time.
● Cuddle up together for half an hour on the sofa; this precious time together will help you to keep some semblance of normality and act as a reminder that you're still a couple, as well as being parents.

GOING OUT
● Don't turn down invitations and, if possible, try not to take your baby with you all the time (although it may be easier to do so in the first 6–8 weeks). Find a reliable baby-sitter and, if you're breast-feeding, express milk (see p. 72) so that you don't have to cut your evening short.
● When your baby is a bit older, find people you can rely on – such as grandparents – to look after her for a longer period of time so that you can take the opportunity to have a weekend away together.
● Continue hobbies you enjoyed together before the baby was born, such as playing sports (see p. 62). If you can't find a baby-sitter, go swimming, which you can all enjoy together (see p. 119).

GRANDPARENTS

Your baby's grandparents can loom large in your life both positively and negatively. If they respect your privacy and your right to bring up your children your way, grandparents are unquestionably the best friends, helpers, and supporters you and your baby will have.

MAKING THE MOST OF THEIR HELP
Grandparents are the people most likely to encourage you to have time off, not least because they'll want to spend some time with their grandchild. Make the most of this. Let them be a part of your baby's life and have their own relationship with her – the bond between grandparents and grandchild can be priceless for your child and for them. It is, however, important to get the balance right, not least because you don't want to fall out with the people who are your best helpers:
● Don't let bossy parents or parents-in-law take over, pop around every five minutes, or turn up uninvited. If they live nearby, try to get into a routine that suits everyone – for example, choose a particular day of the week for them to look after your baby.
● Be clear from the outset about how you want to bring up your baby to prevent any misunderstandings later on. Make sure that when grandparents look after your baby they do things the way you like them done, and not the way they think best.

FATHER

If you're not used to domestic work, looking after a baby will come as a bit of a shock. It should, however, give you a better understanding of how your partner feels and how important it is for her to have some time off.

HOW TO HELP YOUR PARTNER
■ Take your baby out shopping with you or just for a walk in the carriage on weekends to give your partner some space.

■ Be fair to your partner: if she has stayed in looking after the baby while you've been out with your friends, make sure you offer to do the same for her.

■ Share the cooking, even if you have been at work. Make a habit of treating yourselves to takeout occasionally so that neither of you has to cook.

115

BABY-SITTERS

Use a baby-sitter who has experience with babies and young children, and preferably one who is recommended by friends. Don't ask a person under 16 years old to look after your baby in case a problem arises that he or she may be too inexperienced to handle. When you go out the baby-sitter will need:

■ Telephone numbers for you and a relative or neighbor.

■ The location of the first-aid kit (see p. 102) and an explanation of how to use the baby monitor.

■ An idea of your baby's routine and what to do if she wakes up.

■ Feeding equipment and details of what your baby should be fed.

■ Diaper-changing equipment and a change of clothes.

SEX AND PARENTHOOD

YOUR SEXUAL RELATIONSHIP with your partner will, for a short time, be one of the many aspects of your partnership that has to adapt. The last thing either of you will want, while you're caring for your new baby, is for this to become an issue. So try to talk openly to each other about your sexual needs and expectations.

YOUR FEELINGS ABOUT SEX

Don't just have sex because you think it's what your partner wants and don't expect to have sex after a certain point. It's normal to feel sexually different now that you're in the dual and contradictory roles of being a parent and a lover. You may even feel guilty about wanting or thinking about sex because you feel you should be looking after and thinking about your baby. Don't take sexual rejection personally. Talk to each other and try to understand the reasons for wanting or not wanting to resume intercourse. Sex can only become a problem if you let it, and it should be easily resolved if you keep talking to each other about how you feel.

How sex can help Taking care of a baby can cause tensions and problems: having intercourse at the right time, when you're both ready for it, may be just what you need to bring you closer again, reaffirming your desire and affection for each other.

PHYSICAL CONSIDERATIONS

Today, the general advice is that you can resume sex whenever you both feel ready (unless you have been advised to wait for any particular reason), but there could well be physical problems that will deter you from resuming sex in the first few weeks after the birth.

Vaginal discomfort It's normal to feel too sore and tender to resume penetrative sex. The vagina will be bruised, making sex painful even if the childbirth was free of intervention. If you had an episiotomy (see p. 45), you may not be able to tolerate anything rubbing against the site for many months. In addition, the glands that normally lubricate the vagina will not function effectively because of hormonal changes, so it's advisable to use a lubricating cream, available from your pharmacist.

The lochia (see p. 60) Don't resume penetrative sex until this discharge has stopped, which will not be for at least three weeks.

Breast-feeding Your breasts may leak milk during intercourse, especially when you reach orgasm, which can be a shock if you're not prepared for it.

Tiredness Given the choice between having sex or sleeping, most new parents would choose the latter. Until you have more of a routine, and have found ways to have time to yourselves, it's difficult to resume a normal sex life. Try to be understanding if either one of you is too tired for sex.

Libido It appears that the sex drive in both new parents is much lower than normal and it returns slowly over a matter of months.

Cesarean Although you won't have any vaginal discomfort, a cesarean is major abdominal surgery. You're likely to feel very tender for about six weeks and should not resume sex until you're fully recovered.

MOTHER

Your life has gone through a big change and it will take time to adapt. Given your new responsibilities and possible physical discomforts (see below right), having intercourse is unlikely to be a high priority.

YOUR BODY IMAGE
You may feel unattractive if you have stretch marks and feel bloated, but your partner is likely to be less bothered about these things than you think. However, you do have to start liking yourself again before you can give and receive pleasure from sex. Consider exercising (see p. 62); if nothing else, it will make you feel better about yourself. If you're breast-feeding, you may be uncomfortable with your partner touching your breasts. Tell him – he may share your feelings.

YOUR BABY
You're likely to be completely preoccupied with your baby and having sex may be the last thing you want to think about. This is normal, but once you decide to resume sex, try to put the baby in the back of your mind. It's pointless to assume you're going to be interrupted every time.

YOUR PARTNER
Don't put up with discomfort, even pain, because you mistakenly feel dutiful. Your main duty is to your baby and, although your partner needs to feel loved, you don't have to show that by having uncomfortable sex. Remember, however, that although you are preoccupied and fulfilled by your baby, your partner may not be to the same extent. Explain to him how you feel and how it affects your attitude toward sex.

116

CONTRACEPTION

The last thing you're likely to want when you're looking after a newborn baby is to find that you're immediately going to be parents all over again! So do start thinking about contraception as soon as you can after the baby is born. The midwife or family planning adviser will ask you about contraception before you're discharged from the hospital and you will also be asked about this at your six-week check (see p. 60). You can become pregnant even if your periods have not started and you can be fertile as early as three weeks after the birth of your baby.

Breast-feeding Although breast-feeding does reduce fertility, you have to be breast-feeding very regularly (at least every four hours and, for some women, more frequently) to prevent ovulation from occurring. Breast-feeding is not a contraceptive; don't rely on it.

METHODS OF CONTRACEPTION

TYPE	ADVICE
PILL	Those containing estrogen are not prescribed for women who are breast-feeding because they reduce milk production.
MINI-PILL	These contain only progestogen, which does not inhibit milk production, but they may worsen any postpartum depression (see p. 113) by inhibiting the natural production of progesterone. The mini-pill must be taken at the same time each day.
CONDOM (MALE AND FEMALE)	These should be used with a contraceptive gel for comfort and security. A female condom may cause discomfort if you're bruised and sore after childbirth.
IUD (INTER-UTERINE DEVICE) AND DIAPHRAGM	Your cervix may have enlarged and won't return to its normal size for 2–3 months. If you used an IUD or diaphragm before you were pregnant, you'll need a new one. Some doctors will fit this at the six-week check (see p. 60), although others prefer to wait a bit longer.

HAVING SEX

Without it being an automatic prelude to sex, you should both feel that you can engage in physical contact whenever you feel like it. It's important that you continue to enjoy sex and find what is right for both of you – talk about your preferences and be open to trying new things.

Foreplay It's good to build up your sex drive through foreplay: touch and caress, massage each other with aromatic oils, or take a bath together.

Nonpenetrative sex For the first few times, maybe quite soon after the birth, try bringing each other to orgasm through gentle manual and oral sex. Consider being experimental: for example, try sex toys such as a vibrator.

Comfortable positions Once you feel confident enough to try penetrative sex, experiment with different positions to find the ones that put least pressure on the sore areas. Stop at any time if the mother feels discomfort.

FATHER

It's quite natural to have a low sex drive (see below) for a short time after the baby is born. It's often a good thing, because it allows you to concentrate all your energies on your baby. However, many men are ready to resume sexual activity sooner than their partners feel prepared to do so.

REASONS FOR A LOW SEX DRIVE
■ Being too tired and preoccupied with the baby.

■ Having witnessed the birth.

■ The baby sharing a bedroom with you and your partner.

■ Feeling that your partner's body (especially her breasts) belongs to the baby and finding it difficult to think of her sexually.

■ Being frightened of physically hurting your partner.

UNDERSTANDING YOUR PARTNER
■ Start being closer and more affectionate gradually and you'll soon begin to see your partner as your lover and not just as the mother of your baby.

■ Don't expect too much from your partner too soon. Sex will be much less enjoyable for you if she's not ready or comfortable enough to participate fully.

■ Remember, from the moment of birth your partner's ear is attuned to the baby's cry (and yours may be, too). This means that she may find it difficult to relax when she's having sex. Be understanding and try to find a time when you can be alone without your baby (see p. 114).

■ If your partner cuddles you or you are just being affectionate with each other, don't read it as an open invitation to have sex. If you do, it will only upset her, disappoint you, and probably cause an argument.

117

YOUR NEW WORLD

PLAYGROUPS AND NURSERIES

Playgroups and nurseries range from informal arrangements between several parents to professionally organized sessions, where a trained superviser, with the help of the member parents, offers a wide variety of play-based activities:

■ The playgroup acts as an information exchange center, giving you a chance to meet other parents, and your baby an opportunity to make friends with other children and adults.

■ A child of two and a half can be left at a playgroup for a couple of hours, but many also have a mother and baby group attached to them where parents can go along with their babies. You must, however, stay with your baby because the playgroup won't have the resources to look after her.

■ Many community centers, supermarkets, and shopping centers have nurseries where babies and children can be left for a couple of hours. You must stay in the vicinity in case you're needed.

BEING A PARENT will become the core not only of how you see yourself, but of how others view you. Your obligations to your baby will take precedence over any other and, whatever your other responsibilities, being a parent is the first role you assume every morning and it can't be shaken off at the end of the day. This shift in priorities can take some getting used to, especially if you have, until this point, lived a very independent and career-driven life. To avoid isolation you need to join forces with other parents and use the facilities designed to help make caring for a baby easier and more fun.

OTHER PARENTS AND CHILDREN

Being a parent will extend your range of friends to include those who have children. In addition to counteracting the demoralizing effect of mid-morning and early-afternoon isolation that can be the curse of solitary child care, making friends with other parents benefits you in many ways:

● It gives you the opportunity to mix with other people who are equally focused on being a parent.

● It's a good way to introduce your baby to relationships outside the family, which helps to develop her social skills.

● Parenting is a learning process: you'll be breaking new ground every day and be able to exchange tips with the friends you've made.

● You'll have people who understand the difficulties you're going through because they're going through them too.

Your babies will enjoy interacting with each other

HOW TO MEET PEOPLE

A good way to make friends who have children is to stay in touch with some of the parents you met while pregnant, particularly if you live in a rural area where there may be fewer activities. Swap telephone numbers at prenatal classes or in the maternity ward, and don't think twice about getting in touch. If you have a spring or summer baby, you'll probably meet people in the park or playground. However, if your baby is born in the winter, find out about activities from your nurse or local library.

MEETING PEOPLE
Forming friendships with other parents and their babies can be beneficial to both you and your baby.

WHEN PARENTHOOD IS NOT ENOUGH

It used to be thought that motherhood and domesticity were satisfying ways for a woman to spend her most creative and active years; the same would rarely be thought of a man. But nowadays many women would be far from fulfilled by simply being a parent. Some who have tried to do it, because they believe that it is the best start they could give their child, have found the experience quite limiting, especially when they don't have the support network of the extended family.

LEARNING TO ADAPT

In a society where the worth and freedom of the individual, the opportunity for self-development, and an obligation to be oneself are constantly cited as legitimate goals, it's not surprising that most people are ill-prepared for the narrowing of horizons that comes with caring for a baby. You and your partner simply won't have as much of yourselves left over as before and this doesn't sit easily with the kind of ambitions bred by modern society.

Finding fulfillment Women who want to take an active part in the wider world, and have been educated and trained to do so, can hardly be expected to substitute an intimate relationship with the washing machine for the stimulation and satisfaction they derived from their work. The thousand joys of nurturing babies and children don't, for some women, entirely compensate for the loss of a fulfilling life outside the home because the joys are not the same. You can't make up for a lack of vitamin A by taking large doses of vitamin B. It goes without saying that full-time parenthood is a worthwhile career for a person who is happy in it, but anyone who desires more out of life than pure domesticity need never feel ashamed. Just because you have interests beyond day-to-day child care does not mean you don't love your baby and it will not harm her.

Avoiding isolation Many people decide to become parents with the view that it will be a temporary – never total – denial of their needs and ambitions. This is why it is important – and, ultimately, in the baby's best interests – that you do not feel trapped by your parenting role. What most of us understand as isolation is the absence of other people and for those who spend their days caring for children, this means other adults. However wonderful the communication between you and your baby, it's important to have the stimulation of adult interaction, which is why it's essential that you get out and meet people.

WORKING FROM HOME

To make the transition to being a parent easier and less of a shock to the system, some women try to keep some of their old self by working from home. The information technology revolution has made this possible for more women than ever before, but it's not as easy as it sounds, especially if it's attempted too early on:

- You must have a routine with your baby in order to do justice to your work and to make sure you don't end up working in the evenings.
- It's important to make sure you're not just dividing your time between work and your baby; you must still have time for yourself to rest, relax, and spend time with your partner.
- It's likely that you'll still need to organize some form of proper child care (see p. 150) and this could mean that you miss precious time with your baby in her early months.

ACTIVITIES AT HOME

It's unrealistic to be out of the house all the time, especially in the winter months. Team up with other parents and take turns hosting social activities at home. This is also a good way for your baby to get used to strangers coming into the home. Some suggestions are:

- Coffee morning: this is a good and cheap activity, giving you the chance to chat as your babies play.

- Lunch party: provide simple snack food since it's not realistic for everyone to sit down to a meal and baby watch at the same time. Ask friends to bring a contribution (especially for their babies) or just take turns to host lunch.

- Home-selling party: this is a good way to be sociable and earn some money. It involves presenting and taking orders for products, such as household goods or books, and earning a commission on what is sold. Before embarking on this, always check that the company you're working for is reputable.

119

COMMUNITY CENTERS

A good way of getting out is to go to a community center. Find one that has a nursery (see opposite) so that you can take your baby with you – some have a "soft room" where your baby can play safely. Most swimming pools offer parent-and-baby sessions and your baby, equipped with suitable buoyancy aids, will enjoy dabbling with you in a heated pool as soon as she can hold her head up confidently (at about four months). She should also have had her first vaccinations (see p. 162). Remember, you should avoid high-intensity exercise for the first nine months and while breast-feeding.

ACCEPTING HELP

Most couples struggle to bring up a baby without help, so as a single parent don't think you have to do it all yourself, and don't let pride come before your baby's welfare. You need to know that you'll have some guaranteed respite at regularly scheduled times each week, and it's good for your baby to interact with other people:

■ Try to build up a small network of people on whom you can rely.

■ If you have several helpers, spread their time with your baby throughout the week.

■ If possible, ask a relative or friend who is not working to stay once a week so that you're guaranteed a good night's sleep, especially if you're working.

■ Seek the help of volunteer organizations (see p. 163) if you don't have a network of people on whom you can rely.

■ Make sure you're getting all your financial benefits and any child-support payments from the absent parent, if applicable.

■ If you know other single mothers, "baby swap" with them so that you both get a chance for some time to yourselves.

■ Don't be embarrassed or too proud to accept gifts – people would probably have given them to you even if you weren't single.

NEGATIVE REACTIONS
There will be people who judge you, and your ability to bring up your baby – especially if you have chosen to have a baby outside of a committed relationship. Dealing with this can have a positive effect: many single parents become determined to prove that they are just as capable of raising a happy and contented child. However, criticism can also put pressures on single parents, making them feel that to ask for help is equal to admitting failure. It isn't, so do try to resist this.

SINGLE PARENTS

IF YOU ARE A SINGLE PARENT, you won't have the luxury of a partner to share the day-to-day care of your baby or the joys of watching him develop. Without a good support network, it can be physically and emotionally exhausting, but the knowledge that you've done it alone can also be hugely rewarding for you and beneficial to your baby.

SINGLE PARENT BY CHOICE?

If you've chosen to be a single mother, you may be more prepared emotionally, practically, and financially for looking after a young baby and look forward to the prospect. If you've split with your partner during the pregnancy or soon after the birth, you may have more difficulties. Coping with the emotional problems of separating from someone while looking after a young baby is bound to have an impact on your ability to cope. In this situation, it's more important for you to ask for and accept help.

LONE PARENTING CAN BE POSITIVE

Being a single parent is by no means all doom and gloom. You and your baby can benefit in many ways from the special relationship you'll form:
● Single parents tend to develop a much closer bond with their babies; they do not have to share their love between a partner and a child.
● Extended family – grandparents, aunts, and uncles – often get more involved when there's only one parent. The baby can greatly benefit from this network of support and love.
● Looking after a baby alone is a great achievement. You'll strengthen as a person as you watch your baby develop.
● If you're single because your relationship has broken down, you have made the right decision; it's better for the baby to live with one fairly contented person than two people who are at war with each other.

BALANCING YOUR RELATIONSHIP WITH YOUR BABY

I'm a firm believer in showing boundless affection to babies, but as a single parent you do need to balance your relationship with your baby: some lone parents may invest all their emotions and energies into their baby and use him as an emotional crutch. Don't think that you have to be a mother and father; being a responsive parent is good enough. Your baby has no notion of lacking a second parent; he's happy enough with you, so there is no need for you to overcompensate.

ENCOURAGING INDEPENDENCE
You and your baby will have a very close and important one-to-one relationship and no one can take that away from you, but babies need and thrive on exposure to others and should be encouraged to interact with a wide range of people. It's essential that you introduce him to other adults and children, so he gets used to being without you now and then. This will make it much easier for you and him whenever you need a babysitter.

POTENTIAL DIFFICULTIES

DIFFICULTY	HOW TO DEAL WITH IT
FINANCIAL	With only one income, you're more likely to struggle financially and be unable to provide your baby with as many toys and clothes as you would like. Make sure you are getting all the benefits to which you are entitled, especially from your ex-partner. Remember that material possessions are not the most important things you can give to your baby.
FATIGUE	If you are looking after your baby alone, the physical and emotional strains will be more of a problem. Catnap whenever your baby does. Try to take breaks and ask for and accept offers of help.
CONCERNS ABOUT THE BABY	If your baby gets sick, you're unlikely to have someone there to reassure you and keep things in perspective. Look at pages 100–103 and consult your doctor as early as possible to minimize your worries.
CHILD CARE	Affording child care (see p. 150) can be a struggle for single parents. You may find that local day-care centers make special provision for babies of single parents. Look into sharing a nanny with another parent. If there is a nursery at work, or if one could be set up, this would minimize having to transport the baby around.

FEELING ISOLATED

All single parents are bound to experience feelings of loneliness and yearn for adult company. When the baby is very young, he won't be the best company because he only sleeps, cries, and feeds; as he gets older and begins to develop skills, you'll want the company of others so that you can share the pleasure and joy of this with someone else.

HAVING A SOCIAL LIFE

It's important that you have adult company outside of work as well as time away from your baby and, of course, if you want to build future relationships you have to get out and meet people:
- If it's difficult for you to go out for financial or child care reasons, invite people to your house for a meal – ask your guests to bring a dish.
- Get to know other mothers – they'll probably also be glad of the company.
- Ask people if they will baby-sit – you don't know unless you ask.
- Find hobbies, classes, and events that have nursery facilities.
- Find out about local activities so that you can meet other parents.

SHARING YOUR BABY'S DEVELOPMENT

As your baby develops new skills (see p. 126), don't be afraid to share your joy with your relatives and friends – if they're close to your baby, they'll love to hear about it. Keep your own record of when each milestone occurs; when there is only one of you it will be more difficult to remember them.

THE SINGLE FATHER

There are very few men who are the sole caregivers of a young baby, but for those that are, the pleasures and most of the problems will be the same as those of a single mother. Single men are at no more of a disadvantage in the practical care of their baby because they are male; the only thing they can't do that a woman can is breast-feed.

THE BENEFITS

Although it's not an ideal situation to be caring for a baby alone, a single father may benefit in ways that would not have happened had he been sharing the care with his partner. Research has shown that single fathers are more satisfied parents, feel closer to their child, and are more confident and effective than the average father.

THE PROBLEMS

The main problem that may occur for a single father is that of isolation. As for a father who chooses to stay at home while his partner works (see p. 154), a single father will find that he has to battle for recognition in female-dominated environments and, sadly, there will be those who question his ability to bring up his baby properly.

121

THE ABSENT PARENT

Whatever happens, try to keep the communication channels open with the absent parent:

■ Try to reach an agreement on access arrangements and on how you want to raise your child.

■ Make sure that he or she is clear about financial support required. Seek legal advice if necessary.

■ Try to spend time together as a family occasionally, and, if appropriate, encourage the other grandparents to see your baby.

THE INSTANT FAMILY

Adopting a baby is a big decision. You are bound to have doubts and fears about this new responsibility.

WHAT IF I CAN'T COPE?
All new parents have days when they can't cope (see p. 110). As an adoptive parent, you may have the added pressure of feeling that you are responsible for someone else's child and have had less time to prepare yourselves. Don't be afraid to admit that you're having difficulties; use the adoption services because they're there to help you make the transition to parenthood as easy as possible.

WHAT KIND OF CHILD WILL I RAISE?
No one can predict the kind of person a child will turn out to be, not even couples who are the biological and social parents of that child. Genetic makeup makes each individual unique, so even biological parents have no guarantee that their offspring will resemble them either physically or in terms of personality.

WILL I BE A GOOD-ENOUGH PARENT?
Your motives for wanting to adopt and your suitability as parents will be analyzed before you're accepted as adoptive parents and you're bound to question whether or not you'll be good parents. It's natural to have doubts, but in my opinion, the most important aspects of being a parent have nothing to do with being the birth parents. These are:

■ Your feelings and actions toward your child.

■ Your sensitivity to your child's individual needs.

■ Your capacity to be consistently loving and accepting.

■ Your ability to be fair and to set firm limits for your child.

MORE PEOPLE ARE FINDING THEMSELVES part of an unorthodox family structure. An "instant family" may be created through adopting a baby or by joining an already-existing family and taking on responsibility for stepchildren. A new baby brought into either situation can raise emotional and practical issues that aren't present for most new parents.

ADOPTING A YOUNG BABY

If you're fortunate enough to adopt your baby when she's very young, then everything said about bonding in earlier chapters applies to you as well. Babies come equipped with a strong urge to bond with their parents, or to anyone who gives them loving care, so you'll be off to the same promising start as everyone else. You'll be just as capable as a biological parent of caring for your baby: changing a diaper and comforting a crying baby are not innate skills – they are learned, and caring for your baby will become easier the more you do it and the better you know her. What may be difficult is that you won't have had the nine-month build-up to the birth and the internal bonding in the same way as a pregnant mother. On the other hand, you may have a stronger yearning for a baby than a natural parent (there's rarely such a thing as an unwanted adopted baby); this makes you ideally placed to be a generous and loving parent, so be confident.

ADOPTING AN OLDER BABY

If you adopt a baby when she is a few months old, it's really important that you find out as much as possible about the circumstances of her life up to the time when she came to you. This will help you compensate for any experiences on which she has missed out and for any delay in the developmental stages you would normally expect her to have passed through. Read the chapter on development carefully (see p. 125) to get a rough idea of where your baby stands in relation to the majority of babies of her age. If you find any deficits, decide how you can adapt your nurturing to make up for them. Do not, however, worry about her development too much; your baby may not have been affected at all by not being with her natural parents. Even if it has affected her, in the right loving environment your baby will soon be able to catch up.

BONDING WITH AN OLDER BABY
Trust is the basis of all good relationships between babies and their parents; if you have adopted an older baby, you may have to work harder to establish this trust than parents who have had their babies with them from birth. An older baby is likely to have been placed with foster parents for the first few months of her life and will have formed a strong attachment to them. Bear in mind that your baby may not immediately react as you had hoped; she has to learn how to respond to and accept your love and affection, and this takes time. Rest assured, however, that if you are relentless in offering your baby love, comfort, and affection, she will eventually learn to trust you and to accept and reciprocate your feelings and actions.

A NEW BABY IN THE STEPFAMILY

If partners with a stepfamily decide to have a baby together, the dynamics of the family will change. While the baby may act as a uniting force within the family, her advent may equally provoke some of the anxieties and tensions that were present at the formation of the family.

HOW STEPCHILDREN ARE AFFECTED

Your stepchildren's reaction to your baby will depend on how old they are, their relationship with you, and their past experiences. If their parents have split up recently, it may be more difficult; they're again being asked to adjust because of the actions of their parents.

Insecurities The news of the baby may remind the children of a previous breakup, and feelings such as rejection and fear of losing a parent may resurface. They may worry about the baby being seen as more precious and more desirable because she is a product of the present (your preferred) relationship, rather than of the past (your rejected) union.

Realization Many children from broken marriages live in hope that their parents will reunite. A new baby is a clear sign of commitment between their parent and step-parent, which often brings the truth home.

Relationship with step-parent If you and your stepchild have already established a good relationship, the arrival of your baby will cause fewer problems. If there are underlying tensions, the new baby may be the catalyst for resentment and anger.

Second time around A man who has a child later in life may change his priorities and be a more devoted father. Older children may resent not having received this attention when they were growing up. It's also common for children to find it distasteful for a parent to start a new family, especially teenage boys who are often embarrassed by their mother's pregnancy.

HOW YOU CAN HELP

Once the baby is born, your stepchild may become more accepting. To minimize problems, however, talk to him as early as possible. Ask him to tell you his concerns and reassure him that you still love him and that there's space and time for everyone to enjoy the baby. Encourage him to develop his own relationship with your baby. He may enjoy being given responsibility for the baby, but don't abuse this: older stepchildren may resent constantly being used as convenient helpers and babysitters.

INVOLVING STEPCHILDREN

Help your stepchild develop his own relationship with your baby. Let him help out and be involved.

DECIDING TO HAVE A BABY

Couples make the decision to bring a new baby into the stepfamily for a variety of reasons. One partner may be childless and want a baby of his own to feel fulfilled. The other partner, who is already a parent, may feel less of a need for a new baby. Even if both partners have children, they may feel that a baby will unite them as a couple and the stepfamily as a whole.

PLANNING AHEAD

■ There may be financial obligations to ex-partners and children from a previous relationship, which can make the expense of a baby more difficult than for most couples. Also, be aware that stepchildren living with you will resent having to sacrifice new clothes or going out because of the baby.

■ Do you have room in the house for the baby? Will it mean that stepchildren have to move out of, or share, a bedroom? If so, discuss this as a family rather than just telling the children it's going to happen. If you have to move, will it make it more difficult for visiting stepchildren to stay?

TELLING AN EX-PARTNER

It's always better for your ex-partner to hear the news that you are having a baby from you; whatever your relationship, it's difficult to hear it from someone else. He or she definitely should not be told by the children. Some people are shocked at the strength of their feelings when they find out that their ex-partner is having a baby and worry that their own children will in some way lose out. However, if you have a good relationship with your ex-partner and he or she reacts positively to you having a baby, this could also have an effect on how your children handle the news.

123

Your baby is developing from day one and one of the most fulfilling aspects of parenthood is to watch him grow and learn. You'll become fascinated by his skills and amused by how he tries to copy your actions. In just twelve months, he'll change from a tiny helpless newborn into a sturdy and sociable toddler who has a mind of his own. Your role as his parents is crucial in your baby's development: you are his first teacher and friend and by being aware of the stages of development you can encourage certain skills at certain times. It's important, however, for you to remember that your baby's physical and mental development is individual to him, so you should never push him beyond his capabilities. Your baby learns primarily through play: he'll love it if you're his playmate and, although you should show him how things work, it's essential to his sense of self and independence that he finds out how to do things for himself. He also learns by watching other children, so encourage your baby's social skills — getting to know other people is crucial to his development.

YOUR BABY'S DEVELOPMENT

HOW BABIES DEVELOP

NEW SKILLS

Your baby will give you clear signs that a "milestone" (the acquisition of a skill) is on the brink of emerging. Be on the lookout for signs of progress. Then, and only then, match your efforts to your baby's development and give her games to help her acquire that skill – it's almost pointless to try before. With correct timing she will acquire skills at 100 percent of her potential. If you force her too early or leave it too late, she'll acquire the skill, but not at her full capability. The main milestones are:

■ Smiling at a distance (6 weeks).

■ Discovering her hands and feet (3–4 months).

■ Blowing bubbles – this is your baby's first sign of proper speech (5 months).

■ The ability to transfer an object from one hand to the other (6 months).

■ Knowing her name (6 months).

■ Sitting unsupported (7 months).

■ "Getting" a simple joke like peek-a-boo (8 months).

■ Wanting to feed herself (9 months).

■ Crawling (9 months).

■ Pointing to an object with her forefinger (10 months).

■ Picking up objects with her finger and thumb (10 months).

■ Swiveling around while sitting to reach a toy (10 months).

■ Putting things into containers and taking them out again (11 months).

■ Saying her first word with meaning (11–12 months).

■ Walking unsupported (12–13 months).

ONE OF THE MOST FULFILLING aspects of parenthood is to watch and share in your baby's physical and mental development. To help your baby develop happily and to her maximum potential, you need to stimulate her to encourage her to learn new skills, while also allowing her to develop at her own pace.

NEWBORN BABIES

Your baby begins to develop from the very second she's born and she'll be longing to learn. You'll see evidence of this if you watch an infant just after birth: every baby enters the world in a state of "quiet alertness" and this state of intense focus on her surroundings can last up to an hour. She's a sponge ready to soak up information about her new environment:

● She recognizes your voice – and your partner's – immediately. She's heard these voices for seven months and switches on to them instantly.

● When your baby is born, her sight is fixed at a focus of 8–10in (20–25cm); if you hold her at this distance from your face at birth, she can see you clearly and she will smile at you.

● She has an acute sense of smell and will be able to inhale and register the natural scent (pheromones) from your body.

● She'll "mouth" in response to you if she can see your face and your lips moving (at a distance of 8–10in/20–25cm); she's attempting conversation.

STIMULATING YOUR BABY

Both of you are your baby's first teachers and playmates. You must feed her with all kinds of stimulation, through play and through the way in which you interact with her, if you want to help her develop to her full potential. Your job is to teach her to be imaginative, adventurous, curious, helpful, and generous. There is no limit to the amount of praise and encouragement you should give her as she learns new skills and begins to discover her world.

BEING A PLAYMATE
Show your baby how toys work. This will help her learn more quickly and she'll enjoy you joining in.

Your baby will learn by copying your actions

HELPING YOUR BABY TO DEVELOP HAPPILY

WHAT YOU CAN DO	HOW IT HELPS YOUR BABY
SET REALISTIC GOALS	Set appropriate goals for your baby: for example, don't expect her to be able to play properly with toys designed for older babies. If you do this, it will outstrip her skills and she will become unhappy, frustrated, and demoralized. Always concentrate on accomplishments, not deficiencies, and praise your baby with exaggerated gestures.
BE A PLAYMATE	You are your baby's first playmate as well as her teacher. Make time to play with her whenever you can – even if it means the dishwashing has to wait another hour! Babies have to be shown how to do things, so get down there and join in – your baby will love it. But don't interrupt when she is engrossed in something; it's hard enough for her to concentrate and see a job through to completion, without being distracted.
ENCOURAGE SPEECH	Encourage your baby to talk – even when she's only gurgling. Keep her eyes 8–10in (20–25cm) from yours when she makes noises, especially when feeding and talking to her. That's her first experience of feeling valued, and a valued baby will grow up to be a child who talks to you about everything – good and bad.
REPEAT EVERYTHING	Repeat words and actions until you're sick of it. You must tell your baby the same thing over and over again – using the same even tone of voice – and show her how to do things. It will all be worthwhile once she understands and begins to copy.

RULES OF DEVELOPMENT

Although it's wonderful to watch your baby develop, it's important not to push her beyond her limitations. She has her own timetable and it's pointless trying to set a different one. Remember the following:

● No two children develop at the same rate so don't compare your baby to other babies – even if they did walk or talk before her.

● Development is continuous, although certain skills will be acquired in a spurt while other skills slow down. For example, while a child is mastering walking, she may turn into a sloppy feeder.

● A baby won't learn to say words with meaning before she is about ten months old and won't speak until much later. She will make her own brave attempts at "talking" with babble, cries, and giggles and she'll "mouth" from birth, but she'll be unable to say proper words.

● Development of the whole body is dependent on how mature the brain is and whether or not brain, nerve, and muscle connections have grown. This is individual to your baby so she can't learn a skill like walking or talking until all the connections are in place. Bladder control is not possible until 18 months (see p. 157). If you have expectations of potty use any earlier, this is very likely to lead to failure and could slow down your baby's progress when she tries to acquire this skill later.

● Development proceeds from head to toe (see p. 130) so a baby can't sit until she can control her head and she can't stand until she can sit.

● Skills gradually become finer: for example, at about five months she "grasps" with her open hand; at eight months she can pick things up with her fingers and, when all the nerves and muscles have connected, she can pick up an object with her index finger and thumb.

● Be aware that overstimulation is as bad as understimulation; if there is a constant barrage of noise and movement, your baby may become very confused and gain very little in terms of development.

POSITIVE DISCIPLINE

Teaching your baby right from wrong starts at the very beginning, but it is the way in which you teach her that will affect her physical and emotional well-being. You can discipline your child positively in the following ways:

■ Praising and rewarding her good behavior and ignoring bad behavior, especially during mealtimes.

■ Disciplining your baby through love, praise, and encouragement. Never use anger and spanking – this can have a damaging effect on young children.

■ Setting useful tasks to help her understand the discipline of a daily routine – for example, encourage her to feed herself and brush her hair.

■ Holding your finger up and firmly saying "no" if your baby is likely to harm herself, others, or cause damage. She'll understand this from around four months.

127

128

NEWBORN BABIES

From day one there are distinct differences between the behavior and development of baby boys and girls; these differences continue as your baby grows and develops (see p. 158). When babies are newborn, the gender differences are revealed mainly by how they use their senses to perceive things and by the kind of things in which they show an interest.

HEARING
Hearing in boys is less acute than in girls, which causes them to have more difficulty in locating the source of sounds. Girls are more easily calmed down by soothing words because of their acute hearing. Whisper close to your baby boy's ear as you speak to him to stimulate his hearing and to help calm him down.

SPEECH
A baby girl uses her own voice to get her mother's attention earlier and more often than a boy. If a newborn boy hears another baby cry, he'll join in but stop crying quite quickly, whereas a girl will cry for longer.

SIGHT
A newborn girl responds enthusiastically to visual stimuli from birth. A boy, however, quickly loses interest in a design or picture that is placed in his crib, and requires much more visual stimulation up to the age of about seven months.

SOCIAL SKILLS
Boys are as interested in things as they are in people, whereas girls show a clear preference for the human face above anything else. Later in life this female trait reveals itself as an ability to intuitively read facial expression. To encourage your son to get used to people and to help develop his social skills, hold him 8–10in (20–25cm) away from your face from birth onward so that he's able to see you clearly.

BOYS AND GIRLS

THERE ARE FACTORS IN PLACE at birth that create the differences in behavior and development between boys and girls – that's a biological fact and no amount of campaigning for political correctness will ever change it. Male and female brains work differently and we do our children a disservice if we try to force them to go against their biological grain. You can encourage your baby's individual ability if you are aware of his or her innate strengths, and by not enforcing stereotypes. Instead, help your baby develop skills that don't come as naturally, such as language for a boy and spatial skills for a girl.

DIFFERENCES IN BRAIN DEVELOPMENT

Gender differences stem from the way the brain develops in male and female embryos. For a baby to learn and develop, certain connections have to have taken place between the right and left halves of the brain. Girls grow these connections earlier than boys (many are already in place when girls are born), which enables them to adapt faster to their new environment after birth. Connections form in a boy's brain more slowly and because of this later development, a baby boy will need slightly more help from you to reach his milestones (see p. 126).

AVOIDING STEREOTYPES

Stereotypes influence children and, worse, they tend to make people label certain qualities as inferior or superior – the latter usually being attributed to males. When children are taught to think, feel, and act in line with a stereotyped model, it can stunt their personal growth. Individuality should be encouraged, regardless of gender.

DISCOURAGING STEREOTYPES IN A GIRL
● Encourage physical activities usually associated with boys; these will help your baby's muscle development.
● Make her feel important through eye contact and by using her name; this helps her develop a sense of self.
● Don't always whisper baby talk to her.
● Don't provide her only with soft toys.
● Don't give her only dresses and pink clothes to wear.

SPATIAL SKILLS
Help your daughter develop spatial skills by encouraging her to play with practical toys.

Encourage her to do things for herself

DISCOURAGING STEREOTYPES IN A BOY
● Stress gentleness from when he's very young.
● Let him have a doll and soft toy to cuddle.
● Don't stereotype him into the traditional male role with over-boisterous games, loud talk, loud toys, and by dressing him only in blue clothes.
● Don't burden him with all that "big boys don't cry" "stiff upper lip" stuff; big boys do cry, and he's only a child!
● Little boys are naturally very loving – make him proud of that and don't sneer.
● Play down aggression by being gentle, but firm.

BEING A ROLE MODEL
You can positively influence your son by actively joining in with pastimes traditionally associated with females.

Encourage your son in a wide range of activities

FATHER

Fathers tend to be slightly guiltier than mothers of stereotyping their children. As a father you have a big influence on how your children develop and how they come to view themselves. Think about your attitude to your son or daughter and the type of activities you're encouraging.

INFLUENCING YOUR DAUGHTER
As a father, you may consciously or unconsciously reinforce your daughter's femininity. You are stereotyping her if you encourage her in activities like ballet and drama, rather than giving her a free hand or suggesting some traditionally masculine pastimes, such as soccer. Fathers often involve boys in "rough and tumble" games, whereas they'll be gentler with girls. Expose your daughter to all kinds of activities and let her choose. Don't fall into the trap of believing some behavior is acceptable in boys and not in girls – you diminish your daughter if you do this. You should also be aware that your daughter is very likely to feel devalued if she sees you devaluing her mother.

INFLUENCING YOUR SON
Research has shown that your son looks to you to set his own standards of behavior and that's a serious responsibility for you. You can encourage your son to develop the more attractive male qualities (such as gentleness and a sense of responsibility) rather than the less desirable ones (such as being aggressive, dominant, and confrontational) simply by the way in which you behave – your son will be influenced by watching your actions. He will imitate you in every respect and the quality of fathering that he receives from you is the most critical factor in how he views himself as a male.

129

GENDER DIFFERENCES UP TO AGE SIX

WHAT DEVELOPS	GIRLS	BOYS
NATURAL ABILITY	Girls are better at language skills like talking, reading, and writing and they tend to keep this ability.	Boys are slower to develop language skills, but from a very early age they show superior spatial skills.
SOCIAL SKILLS	Girls are more sociable than boys: they are more interested in people and feelings and display this regard for others even in the first 12 months.	Boys are generally more interested in objects than people and feelings. Unlike girls, they tend to look after themselves rather than groups.
BEHAVIOR AND PERSONALITY	Girls cope better with stress and are more conciliatory. They tend to have fewer behavioral problems than boys.	Boys tend to be more aggressive, competitive, and rebellious than girls. They are more likely to develop behavioral problems.
PHYSICAL GROWTH	Girls walk earlier than boys. They grow faster and more steadily – they do not tend to have growth spurts. They gain bladder and bowel control earlier.	Boys shoot ahead physically after five years. They develop faster during growth spurts, when many skills tend to emerge over a short time.

CONCERNS ABOUT WEIGHT GAIN

A baby's growth is an important indicator of health and well-being, but don't become obsessed with weight gain – it isn't the only issue. Any real discrepancies between length and weight should be picked up at your baby's developmental checks (see p. 133) but, if you're concerned, speak to your doctor beforehand.

WHAT IF MY BABY IS NOT GAINING WEIGHT?

Some babies remain the same weight for a while and then have a growth spurt. So don't worry if your baby does not gain weight over one week or appears to have lost weight. This could be due to something as simple as her being weighed at a different time of day or because she's eaten less. If your baby is sick for any period of time, she may lose weight rapidly but will regain it quickly once she's well. If she appears lively it's a good sign that she's getting enough to eat. Don't be tempted to switch to bottle-feeding in the hope of improving "slow" weight gain. In fact, if you breast-feed your baby she's likely to grow faster, especially in the first few weeks.

WHAT IF MY BABY IS OVERWEIGHT?

Some babies are naturally fatter than others, which may lead to some physical development happening slightly later. If you're concerned that your baby weighs too much for her age, seek medical advice, but do not reduce her intake of food, which could affect her growth and development. The aim should be to maintain her weight at the current level until her length catches up. Research does, however, show that the pattern of heart disease and obesity in adulthood can be set very early in life by being overweight from overfeeding, so never press your baby to finish off the last drops of a feeding or bottle.

HOW YOUR BABY GROWS

YOUR BABY'S PHYSICAL DEVELOPMENT will be monitored closely at the developmental checkups (see p. 133): growth (centile) charts, which show the rate of growth expected for your baby's weight and gestational age at birth, will be used to map her progress. Your baby will grow faster in the first year than at any other time in her life. Physical development starts at the top, which is why her head looks large, and from the inner parts to the extremities, which is why her hands and feet look tiny. Remember, your baby's development is individual to her; don't worry if she appears to be growing faster or slower than other babies.

WEIGHT

When a baby is born, the question "How heavy was she?" comes only second in the West to "Is it a boy or a girl?". Although people will place importance on your baby's weight, it is not the only sign of growth and it is important not to use this as the only way to judge her well-being (see left). Your baby's weight will be monitored at the developmental checkups (see p. 133); you can also have her weighed at your local baby clinic or doctor's office. Babies are normally weighed naked and before a feeding. One feature all babies have in common is chubby arms and legs; this is due to uneven fat distribution and your baby will not lose this until she begins to use her limbs and becomes active.

THE NORMAL PATTERN OF WEIGHT GAIN
- In the first few days your baby may lose 10 percent of her birth weight.
- By the tenth day she'll have regained her birth weight.
- In the following six months, she'll gain weight rapidly, at a rate of about 2lb (1kg) each month.
- In the second six months, weight gain slows down and she'll put on around 1lb (500g) each month.

Most newborns look quite scrawny – they fill out at about 4–5 weeks

A newborn's head is disproportionately large compared to his body

LENGTH (HEIGHT)

Your baby's size is partly due to inheritance – if you're both tall, the chances are you'll have a long baby. The biggest increase in length occurs in the first six months, after which growth slows down. If your child appears well and healthy, there's no reason for you to worry about her growth rate; any pronounced disproportion between length and weight will be investigated at the developmental checkups (see p. 133).

AN APPROXIMATE GUIDE TO A BABY'S GROWTH RATE
- A newborn full-term baby is on average 20in (50cm) long.
- Her length will increase by 10–12in (25–30cm) in the first year.
- On average, boys tend to be taller than girls for the first two years.

HEAD SIZE

A newborn baby is top-heavy, with a disproportionately large head – this gradually changes over the first four years. Head circumference is monitored at developmental checkups; if the proportions do not even out, it could alert doctors to certain rare medical conditions.

HOW THE PROPORTIONS CHANGE
- A newborn baby's head circumference is about 14in (35cm), which is disproportionately larger than the rest of her body. By the time she is 12 months old, the size of her chest and head should have evened out.
- When a baby is born, her head makes up one quarter of the length of her body, compared to an adult's head, which makes up around one eighth.

12 MONTHS OLD

She "feels" the shape and texture of objects with her lips and tongue

A baby has to learn to sit before she can stand

SEVEN MONTHS OLD

HOW THE SENSES DEVELOP

In the first year, your baby will begin to discover her world through her senses.

VISION
Your newborn has limited, but excellent, vision; at a distance of 8–10in (20–25cm) she sees clearly, so keep your face at this distance from hers when talking or smiling and she'll respond. At six weeks her eyes focus at any distance and both eyes work together. By three months she has full perception of colors; at six months she sees more detail; and by one year her vision is well developed.

HEARING
She recognizes your voice and your partner's from birth, and will turn her head when you speak, so talk to her from the very first day.

TOUCH
Babies begin by "feeling" the shape and texture of objects with their lips and tongue and then explore with their hands.

TASTE AND SMELL
Newborns have a complete set of tastebuds and can recognize their parents' smell. They only like sweet tastes and smells, which is why they love breast milk, but they gradually accept different tastes and make their likes and dislikes known.

131

YOUR BABY'S FIRST YEAR
A newborn baby is floppy and has no head control. As bones and muscles develop she learns to control her head, which is the first step toward walking. Once this skill is acquired, she will learn to sit and then, by the time she is 12 months old, she should be able to stand unsupported.

Brain, nerve, and muscle connections have to be in place before a baby can learn to stand

NERVE AND MUSCLE DEVELOPMENT

WHAT DEVELOPS	HOW IT DEVELOPS	WHAT IT MEANS FOR YOUR BABY
NERVE CONNECTIONS TO LIMB MUSCLES	Nerves grow slowly from the brain and spine to reach the different muscle groups in the limbs. In a newborn, connections between these nerves have not been formed so movements are uncontrolled and crude. As the nerves grow and forge connections, movements become finer and more precise.	Your baby progresses from picking something up with his fist at four months to picking up objects with his finger and thumb by ten months. As nerves grow outward and down from the brain and spine, your baby will achieve head control and then sit, crawl, and stand, before finally walking.
NERVE CONNECTIONS TO BLADDER MUSCLES	It takes at least 18 months for nerves to grow as far as the bladder. Prior to that your baby cannot have any control over how his bladder works – so don't expect it.	Once nerve connections to the bladder are in place, your baby has to "train" the bladder muscles to hold urine and then let go. This takes several months and can't be hurried.

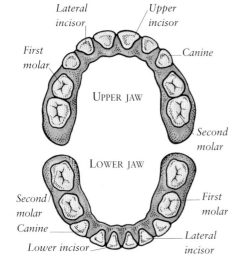

Lateral incisor   *Upper incisor*

First molar   *Canine*

UPPER JAW

Second molar

LOWER JAW

Second molar

Canine

Lower incisor

First molar

Lateral incisor

THE ORDER TEETH APPEAR
The age when teeth are cut varies, but they always come through in the same order: incisors, first molars, then canines.

HOW YOUR BABY'S TEETH DEVELOP

A first tooth is an exciting milestone – an indication that your baby is ready for foods other than milk, in other words, for weaning (see p. 94). Teeth usually start to come through from six months, but the age varies from baby to baby (a few babies are born with a tooth already through, while others are still toothless on their first birthday). During teething, your baby may be more irritable and more wakeful than usual (see p. 91).

HOW TEETH COME THROUGH
● The first tooth to appear is usually a lower incisor, followed almost immediately by its neighbor.
● Next come the upper incisors, followed first by the upper lateral incisors, then by the lower lateral incisors. There may be a delay before the first molar appears.
● After the two first molars come the canines, and finally the second molars appear.

PREVENTING PROBLEMS

You can help prevent your baby developing any teething problems:

■ Buy your baby a small, soft toothbrush and get him into the routine of brushing his teeth in the morning and at bedtime.

■ Don't give him drinks and snacks that contain added sugar. Give him plain water to drink sometimes instead of juice.

■ Never add sugar to fruit juice, and always give him undiluted juice in a cup, not a bottle.

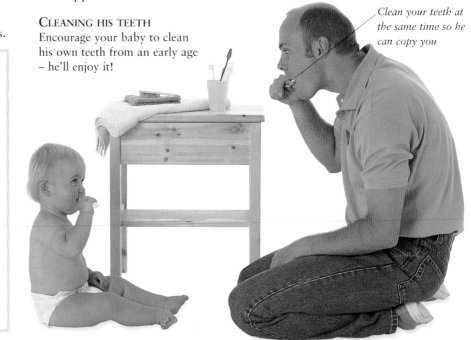

CLEANING HIS TEETH
Encourage your baby to clean his own teeth from an early age – he'll enjoy it!

Clean your teeth at the same time so he can copy you

132

DEVELOPMENTAL CHECKUPS

You will be asked to take your baby for a developmental checkup twice in the first year: at 6–8 weeks and at 8–9 months. As well as discussing any issues with you, the nurse will weigh your baby, and measure his length and head circumference, and then a doctor will check the baby's general health and carry out specific medical checks (see charts below).

WHAT IS THE PURPOSE OF THE CHECKUPS?

Many health professionals feel that "testing" babies at certain stages to see whether they are "up to the mark" is crude; now they are much more interested in the wellbeing of the whole child. When you're at the doctor's office, or perhaps have a nurse in your home, you'll be asked a series of questions to establish how you're all getting on together, how you are managing, and whether you've noticed any specific problems with your baby. You should view it as an opportunity to discuss any aspects of your baby's life (not just his development) or of your life with him that seem relevant: baby checkups aren't, or at least they're not supposed to be, just a rote procedure.

PREPARING YOURSELF BEFORE YOU GO

Make a list of questions and concerns you'd like to discuss. For example, you may have problems feeding or difficulty coping with sleepless nights. Don't be afraid to highlight problems – being a new parent is not easy for anyone and you should take the opportunity to get expert advice.

WHAT IF MY BABY HAS A PROBLEM?

It's worrying to have doubts cast over your baby's development (see p. 104). If you have any concerns or a problem is found:

■ Ask for time to sit down and talk through exactly what is wrong with your baby. Ask as many questions as necessary, especially if it is not clear what the doctor is saying. Don't let yourself be dismissed by being told that the doctor doesn't have time at the moment or that you are worrying for no reason.

■ Don't accept that you should "wait and see" – if there's any question of a problem, your baby should be referred for tests or to see a specialist immediately.

■ Get a second opinion if you are not satisfied or are still concerned.

133

6–8-WEEK CHECK

WHAT IS CHECKED	WHY IT IS CHECKED
HEART AND LUNGS	The breathing rate and heart rate are checked, particularly to rule out a heart murmur.
PALATE	The palate is checked at birth, and now, for completeness and to test the sucking reflex.
VISION	Your baby will be tested to see if he can follow movement and look toward light.
HEARING	A simple check will be made to see if your baby is startled by a sudden loud noise.
MOBILITY	Your baby's hips are checked for displacement and any correction needed. Head control is checked.
TESTES	If you have a baby boy, the doctor will check to ensure that his testes have descended.

8–9-MONTH CHECK

WHAT IS CHECKED	WHY IT IS CHECKED
SPEECH	Your baby should be making a range of sounds by now and his ability to do this will be noted.
VISION	Any problem should have become apparent, but the doctor may check for a squint.
HEARING	You will hold your baby while the doctor makes noises behind you to check his response.
COORDINATION	The doctor will give your baby a toy to hold so that he can check the baby's skills.
MOBILITY	The doctor will check that your baby can sit up and is able to stand supported.
TESTES	The testes will be checked again. If they have not descended, an operation may be needed later.

BABY DEVELOPMENT
0–1 MONTH

GRASP REFLEX Your baby will grasp anything put into her fingers and her grasp is so strong, she can take her weight.

WHAT TO LOOK OUT FOR

WHAT DEVELOPS	HOW SHE PROGRESSES	HOW YOU CAN HELP
HER MIND	• At birth, she can see clearly at a distance of 8–10in (20–25cm). • She will respond to your voice by moving her eyes and turning her head. • She will gaze at you and recognize you. • She will become quiet when you speak soothingly and distressed when you are loud.	• When talking to her, hold your face 8–10in (20–25cm) away from hers. • When you speak, let her see your mouth moving, make interesting faces, and smile. Make eye contact at 8–10in (20–25cm). • Use your voice: speak in a sing-song voice, sing lullabies, and laugh a lot.
HER MOBILITY	• She will turn her head: this control is the first step toward learning to walk. • By the end of the first month, the most she may be able to do is lift her head about an inch off the surface when lying on her tummy.	• Do gentle exercises to make her aware of her body (see p. 57). • Her neck and back muscles are too weak to lift her head so give her something to look at when she is lying on her back.
HER COORDINATION	• Your baby is born with "the grasp reflex," which means she will keep her fists tightly closed and grasp anything put into her fingers. • If she's startled, she'll spreads her arms, fingers and legs to protect herself.	• Your baby can't purposely hold onto anything until she loses the grasp reflex. • Gently open her fingers one at a time. • If she grasps your fingers, she'll take her weight if you pull her up a little way.
HER SOCIAL SKILLS	• Your baby is born ready to love other people and asks for love. She longs for company and takes immediate delight in you. • She'll respond instantly to your voice and your smell. She is upset by a harsh-sounding voice.	• Let her have contact with other people from when she's very young. • Be physical: make skin-to-skin contact with your baby; use your body to express love; rock, sway, and dance with her.
HER SPEECH	• She "mouths" if you speak to her from a distance of 8–10in (20–25cm) because she is trying to imitate your gestures and expressions. • She's born longing to communicate and will start to make little burbling noises as a mark of pleasure and contentment.	• Talk to your baby all the time so she gets used to your voice. • Make facial expressions to match what you're saying.

STIMULATING PLAY

● Stimulate her senses with songs and by talking to her.
● Move your fingers or a brightly colored toy through her line of vision so that her eyes and head follow your movements.
● Put a mobile over her crib.
● Do gentle knee bends and straighten her legs when you're changing her diaper; this will encourage your baby to straighten out her body.
● Place a small mirror or a clear, cartoon-style drawing of a face in her crib where she can see it when she is lying down.

Make eye contact

Talk to her

Hold her where she can see you when talking to her, ideally at 8–10in (20–25cm)

BABY DEVELOPMENT
1–2 MONTHS

SMILING
Your baby's eyes have learned to focus at any distance so, however far away you are, he'll now begin smiling at you.

WHAT TO LOOK OUT FOR		
WHAT DEVELOPS	**HOW HE PROGRESSES**	**HOW YOU CAN HELP**
HIS MIND	• Your baby begins to smile at you from a distance and bobs his head when you talk to him. • He starts to be interested in his surroundings, looking in the direction of sounds and staring at objects as though "grasping" with his eyes.	• Prop him up slightly with cushions or put him in a baby chair. Place lots of brightly colored toys within his view. • Put a mobile over the crib – it's good if it makes a sound or has a musical box.
HIS MOBILITY	• He can raise his head to 45 degrees when he's lying on his tummy. • By the end of this month he can support the weight of his head if you hold him upright with your hands around his chest.	• Hold a colored toy close to his head so that he has to lift his head to see it. • To teach your baby about balance, hold him upright on your knee so his legs take his own weight for a second.
HIS COORDINATION	• Your baby will no longer have a grasp reflex. • His fingers are open most of the time and he's starting to become aware of them.	• Touch, tickle, and massage his hands. • Give him toys and encourage him to bend his fingers over them.
HIS SOCIAL SKILLS	• He's starting to notice people, but knows you from all others. • He smiles from a distance at six weeks and moves his whole body with excitement when he sees you.	• Make sure you give your baby frequent skin-to-skin contact and maintain eye contact when you're talking to him and, more importantly, when feeding.
HIS SPEECH	• He will begin by answering you with small throaty sounds and by the end of two months he will make grunts and cries, and move his whole body in his desire to communicate with you. • He knows your voice – and your partner's – and turns his head and neck when he hears you.	• The more your baby is stimulated to talk by being talked to and encouraged to respond, the earlier he'll learn to talk and the better his quality of speech. • Talk nonstop, be expressive with your conversations, and ask questions.

135

STIMULATING PLAY

● Sing nursery rhymes and rock and sway while you hold him. Sit in a rocking chair with him or put him in a cradle.
● Show him his hands and demonstrate how to wiggle his fingers. Play "This little piggy."
● Gently rub a soft brush over his hands and fingers, especially at the tips.
● Sit him up supported at an angle of 45 degrees – this helps increase his concentration span. Use cushions or a bouncing baby chair on the floor. Let him touch toys or objects of different textures, shapes, and materials.
● Dangle, kick, or bat small soft toys quite close to him, within striking distance of his hands.
● Have a special walk, talk, and sing time with your baby every day. Carry him in a sling (see p. 69).

Make eye contact as you talk or sing to him

He'll wriggle with excitement when he sees you

BABY DEVELOPMENT
2–3 MONTHS

HEAD CONTROL
She can hold her head up for a short time when lying on her front.

WHAT TO LOOK OUT FOR

WHAT DEVELOPS	HOW SHE PROGRESSES	HOW YOU CAN HELP
HER MIND	• She's becoming familiar with her own body, staring at her fingers and then moving them. This is her first lesson in cause and effect. • She has a repertoire of responses to you: she smiles, mouths when you speak to her, nods, squeaks, yelps, and blows raspberries.	• Show your baby her fingers so that she can study them. • Answer her with responses that are exaggerated and larger than life. • Reward her attempts to relate to you with hugs, kisses, and squeals of delight.
HER MOBILITY	• She can keep her head up steadily now when in a standing or sitting position or while lying on her front, but not for long. • When she is lying on her tummy, she can hold her head in line with her body.	• Encourage her to reach out for soft toys, especially when she's on her tummy. • Teach your baby about balance: hold her in a standing position with your hands around her chest, for a few seconds at a time.
HER COORDINATION	• She begins to discover her hands – she keeps them open and looks at them. • She'll hold a rattle for a few seconds if you place it in her hand.	• Encourage her to look at her fingers and to hold a rattle. • Put toys over her crib or give her a baby gym to encourage her to reach out.
HER SOCIAL SKILLS	• She turns her head to your voice and smiles because she is happy to see you. • She expresses her joy in you by waving her arms and kicking her legs.	• Keep eye contact with her when feeding – it's heaven for her to have food and your attention at the same time! • Respond positively to her overtures.
HER SPEECH	• She will begin to make simple vowel sounds, such as "oh," "ah," and "uh." • She has a repertoire of easily recognized cries to express how she is feeling: hungry, tired, lonely, bad-tempered, frustrated, angry, impatient, or just wanting to be left alone.	• Imitate all the sounds she makes back to her. • When your baby cries, it is her way of communicating with you – always respond to it (see p. 88).

STIMULATING PLAY

● Act out nursery rhymes and play pat-a-cake.
● Play lots of simple physical games, such as gentle jerks, knee bends, arm pulls, and tickling feet.
● Introduce her to toys with different textures and say out loud to your baby how they feel.
● Lie on the floor opposite her while she lies on her tummy and looks at you – this will encourage head control.
● Encourage her to reach out for soft objects.
● Take her into the bath with you for a skin-to-skin soak and lots of water games. Encourage her to kick and splash. Make her aware of her hands by splashing them in the water, and splash your own.

Introduce her to different types of toys

Encourage her to reach out for objects

BABY DEVELOPMENT
3–4 MONTHS

FEET
In this month, your baby will discover his feet.

WHAT TO LOOK OUT FOR

WHAT DEVELOPS	HOW HE PROGRESSES	HOW YOU CAN HELP
HIS MIND	• He's curious and wants to join in. • He can recognize places and faces as familiar. • He loves the breast or his bottle and shows it. • He'll laugh by the age of four months.	• Offer a wide range of toys. • Explain everything you see and do. • Pin photographs of yourselves in his crib with a safety pin.
HIS MOBILITY	• He loves sitting up now with a little support from you or cushions. • If you gently pull him into a sitting position, he will bring his head up in line with his body. • If he is lying on his tummy, he can look straight at you now.	• Sit him up with cushions for support. • Pull him gently up into a sitting position to strengthen his back and neck muscles. • Play games that make your baby swivel from the waist and offer toys that he is able to reach easily.
HIS COORDINATION	• He's starting to control his hands and feet and will start reaching for his toes. • He moves his hands and feet together. • He crosses his feet and puts a foot on the opposite leg.	• Put toys in his hands when he reaches for them or he will overshoot. Make him reach for things in every position. • Give him rattles so that he can make noises with his hands.
HIS SOCIAL SKILLS	• He looks at and smiles at people who talk to him – he hasn't learned shyness yet. • He knows you and your partner and people he sees regularly, such as grandparents. • He loves company and cries if left alone for long. He knows warmth and love – and the opposite.	• Encourage his sense of humor. Laugh with him, share the joke, and imitate everything he does. Don't be afraid to over-act in all your responses. • Encourage emotional development: laugh when he laughs and cry when he cries.
HIS SPEECH	• He squeals with pleasure. • He's learning all the basic tones of voices. • He says "m," "p," and "b" when unhappy and "j" and "k" when happy.	• Repeat sounds back at him – "M, m, m you're not happy are you." Speak in a tone of voice that is appropriate.

137

STIMULATING PLAY

● Play "peek-a-boo" and hiding your face games. When playing "peek-a-boo" stay slightly to one side so that your baby has to swing his trunk to find you.

● Put objects on a string over his crib and carriage so that he can examine them – one day he'll reach out and knock one.

● Amplify his experiences by talking to him about what you see and do. Add as much detail about each object and activity that you can.

● Place a rattle in your baby's hand and shake it a few times. He will be intrigued by its texture and by the sound that it makes.

● Play tickling games to encourage his laughter.

Gently pull him up when he is lying on his back

BABY DEVELOPMENT
4–5 MONTHS

EXPLORING WITH HER MOUTH
Your baby will put everything into her mouth, especially her hands. She is exploring with her lips and tongue.

WHAT TO LOOK OUT FOR

WHAT DEVELOPS	HOW SHE PROGRESSES	HOW YOU CAN HELP
HER MIND	• Your baby loves games – she learns skills from them by copying what you do. • Her concentration is expanding. She spends a long time examining things. • She smiles at herself in the mirror. • She moves her arms and legs to attract you. • She pats her bottle when feeding.	• When she attracts your attention respond to it; this will encourage good behavior. • Turn your body toward her. Let her know you're attending to her by focusing on her: make it obvious by moving toward her, bending down, and making eye contact. • Call her by her name all the time.
HER MOBILITY	• She has now mastered full control of her head. Although it's quite steady, it may wobble if she moves suddenly.	• Give her plenty of rocking motion. This will promote head stability and aid her when she begins walking.
HER COORDINATION	• She puts things into her mouth, such as toys, her fist, and feet, since it's the most sensitive area. • She grasps large toys with both hands and begins to use the little finger side of her hand to grip things. She sometimes can't let go.	• Don't try to stop her putting her hand in her mouth – it's natural. • Play with her toes and guide them to her mouth. • Play give-and-take games with toys.
HER SOCIAL SKILLS	• Your baby is beginning to be shy with strangers (this is the first sign of her emerging "self"), but she still smiles at people she knows.	• Introduce her to all visitors so that she gets used to strangers and the concept of friends.
HER SPEECH	• Her language is very colorful: she tries to "talk" by blowing, babbling, squealing, laughing, and she says "ka" in an attempt to sound like you. • She uses facial expressions to communicate.	• Imitate all her sounds with changes of pitch and volume. If she listens, stimulate her with new sounds and name them.

STIMULATING PLAY

● Play lots of games with her, especially those that involve clapping.
● She loves crumpling paper – give her sheets of old brown wrapping paper or lots of tissue paper that crackles.
● Hide her face under a towel for a second then whisk it away and say "peek-a-boo" – she'll squeal with delight.
● Look out for your baby holding her hands up and her arms wide – this means that she wants to play.
● Let her look at herself in a mirror while you hold her – talk to her and help her recognize herself and you.
● Play rocking games while she is sitting on your lap, dance with her, and gently swing her.
● Encourage her to open her fingers by playing giving and taking away games. Always give her the object when she reaches out.
● She will reach for her bottle to feed herself. Let her hold it and then try to get her to give it back to you.

Gently rock her on your lap to help develop balance and mobility

She now has head control

BABY DEVELOPMENT
5–6 MONTHS

SITTING SUPPORTED Encourage him to sit by propping him up with cushions.

	WHAT TO LOOK OUT FOR	
WHAT DEVELOPS	**HOW HE PROGRESSES**	**HOW YOU CAN HELP**
HIS MIND	• He gets excited if he hears someone coming. • He expresses his discomfort or insecurity. • He makes lots of attention-seeking sounds and raises his arms to be picked up. • He loves mealtimes, showing preferences for different foods and making his particular likes and dislikes very clear.	• Respond to his call as soon as you hear it. Shout out that you're coming, then go toward him and say his name. Hold out your arms as you approach him. • Keep using his name every time you speak to him. • Encourage him to try different foods.
HIS MOBILITY	• He's now strong enough to take the weight of his upper half on his arms. • He can sit for a few minutes supported on the floor with lots of cushions.	• Play bouncing games with your baby. Get a baby bouncer if he likes it. • Lie next to him on the floor and crawl around. It will encourage him to copy.
HIS COORDINATION	• He now has the ability to transfer objects from one hand to another. • He'll drop a toy he's been holding to grasp another toy. • He'll hold his bottle.	• Show him how to let go and drop things and how to pass a toy from hand to hand. • Play give-and-take games – this will also encourage him to share. • Give him finger foods, such as biscuits.
HIS SOCIAL SKILLS	• He starts to make assertive advances: pats your cheek, scratches, and slaps. • He explores your face with his hands – it means "hello," so say "hello" back and smile. • He's possessive of you and may be very wary of people he doesn't know.	• Show your baby new gestures; stretch out your arms to him, and he'll lift his too. • Make expansive gestures and pitch your voice to match. He will copy you. • Avoid leaving him in a room with strangers.
HIS SPEECH	• He blows bubbles (this is his first real speech). • He now says "ka," "da," and "ma" all the time and a new sound emerges: "ergh." • He seems to understand a bit of what you say.	• If he appears to understand you, ask if he does, repeat what you said, and praise him.

139

STIMULATING PLAY

● Demonstrate cause and effect. Push a ball to him while he's sitting up and say "the ball is rolling."

● Play weight-bearing games: these encourage him to take more and more weight on his legs, which helps to strengthen them. Hold him on your lap or on the floor, gently bounce him up and down and you'll feel him push off.

● Blow "raspberries" at him when you're changing his diaper or getting him dressed after a bath – encourage him to copy the different noises you make.

● Reward him for holding out his arms by playing lifting games – squeal with delight as you lift him and swing him around.

Weight-bearing games will strengthen her legs

BABY DEVELOPMENT
6–7 MONTHS

MOBILITY
Your baby can now bear her weight on one hand when she's lying down on her tummy.

	WHAT TO LOOK OUT FOR	
WHAT DEVELOPS	**HOW SHE PROGRESSES**	**HOW YOU CAN HELP**
HER MIND	• She starts off conversations and you'll understand many of her own sounds. • She knows her name and who she is. • She may want to feed herself. • She anticipates repetition and imitates you.	• Encourage her sense of self by showing your baby her reflection in the mirror and repeating her name over and over "That's Katie, that's you." • Have conversations with her.
HER MOBILITY	• She can now bear weight on one hand when she is lying on her tummy. • She can lift her head when lying on her back. • When you hold her up she can take all her own weight on straight legs and hips.	• To encourage her to take her weight, play lots of standing games. • Place a toy above her while she's on her back and encourage her to lift her head to reach out for it.
HER COORDINATION	• She reaches out for objects using only her fingers now. • She holds onto a toy if she reaches for another. • She bangs the table. • She's becoming much more accurate when she feeds herself with finger foods.	• Let her try to feed herself from a dish with her own baby spoon. Continue with finger foods (make cheese cubes smaller and smaller) to encourage fine finger movements. • Give her plenty of toys that are easy for her to hold.
HER SOCIAL SKILLS	• Your baby loves other babies and stretches out to them in friendship. • She may cry if she's left with anyone other than you or your partner, especially if it's someone who she doesn't know.	• Give her physical affection; she can't be loving to anyone (including herself) if she doesn't have a bank of love to draw on. • Keep introducing her to strangers and give her time to adjust.
HER SPEECH	• She now has very clear syllables with actions, "ba," "da," and "ka." • Cries have high and low pitches and a nasal sound has appeared.	• Make every sound back to her to make her feel important.

STIMULATING PLAY

● Encourage her sense of self by playing games with her things and using her name: for example, say "That's Katie's dress" and "Whose teddy is this? It's Katie's."
● If she's wary of strangers now, introduce them gradually.
● Develop her sense of humor with simple jokes like tickling; play "Pop goes the weasel."
● To encourage her to pull her tummy off the floor, play at airplanes. Lie side by side on your front and lift your arms and body – and your baby's – off the floor.
● Play touching games: use every opportunity to touch your baby and let her touch you; for example, she'll love it if you let her explore your face.

Hold a mirror up so that she can see herself, and say her name

140

BABY DEVELOPMENT
7–8 MONTHS

FINGER-THUMB GRASP
Your baby will try to pick up objects using his thumb and fingers in a "pincer" movement.

WHAT TO LOOK OUT FOR

WHAT DEVELOPS	HOW HE PROGRESSES	HOW YOU CAN HELP
HIS MIND	• He's showing signs of determination; he'll keep going after toys he can't quite reach. • He concentrates hard on discovering what he can do with his toys – he's learning all the time about the properties of various objects.	• Encourage him to retrieve a toy for which he has to stretch. • Play water games in the bath. • Give him plastic containers to pour, empty, and fill over and over.
HIS MOBILITY	• He'll sit rocking his body backward and forward to reach a toy. • He loves standing when supported. If you stand him on your lap, he'll bounce around. • Lying on his front, he'll try to wriggle forward.	• While he's sitting, sit a little way from him and hold your arms out. He'll try to shuffle along on his bottom to reach you. • Hold him upright as much as possible. • Get him to reach a toy while on his front.
HIS COORDINATION	• He loves making any noise by banging. • He'll try to copy you if you clap. • He can hold any toy firmly in his fingers, and will shake a rattle. • He will point to objects – this is the first stage of him learning the finger-thumb grasp.	• Give him spoons, pan lids, or a toy drum so that he can use his hands to bang and make a noise. • When he's sitting on the floor or in his crib, make sure that he has lots of toys to reach for, pick up, and explore.
HIS SOCIAL SKILLS	• He will respond fully to sociable games such as "Pat-a-cake" or "This little piggy." • He doesn't like it when you're angry and will respond accordingly. • He understands "no" and responds to it.	• Make him feel valued by using his name in every situation. This will help him to develop a sense of himself. • When you need to say "no," say it firmly and use a different tone of voice.
HIS SPEECH	• He plays games with his mouth and tongue, blowing "raspberries" and smacking his lips. • He may combine two syllables such as "ba-ba" and "da-da," although not with meaning.	• Play sound games to convey meaning – "quiet" (whisper) or "loud" (shout).

STIMULATING PLAY

● Play and sing word games to encourage him to vocalize. Say rhymes over and over again, always with the same emphasis, and move your body; he'll start to copy you and use his.
● Use all kinds of safe household items as toys, for example, plastic or wooden spoons, pans, and brushes. Show your baby how to use each one. Banging games will be lots of fun.
● Always answer his needs and cries; this breeds self-confidence and self-esteem.
● Sit with your baby on the floor and encircle your legs around him. Fill the circle with his favorite toys.
● Lie on the floor and encourage him to climb over you.
● Play clapping games – encourage him to copy you.

He'll try to copy clapping games

141

BABY DEVELOPMENT
8–9 MONTHS

LEANING FORWARD
Your baby will have mastered the skill of leaning forward to reach objects.

WHAT TO LOOK OUT FOR

WHAT DEVELOPS	HOW SHE PROGRESSES	HOW YOU CAN HELP
HER MIND	• Your baby loves familiar games and rhymes and laughs at the right times. • She can anticipate movements. • She will turn her head to her name and hold out her hands to be reached.	• Help her understand life on a day-to-day basis by explaining all routines. Use meals and bathtimes as cues for special activities – "Now it's time for lunch," "Now it's time to have your bath."
HER MOBILITY	• She can take her weight on her legs, if supported. • She can sit for 10 minutes, lean forward and sideways, and stay balanced. • She can roll from side to side, but can't get up from a sitting position to stand.	• Help her to stand from a sitting position, bend her hips, and knees for her. • Help her to move around the furniture by having pieces close together. Encourage her to hold on to a low piece of furniture.
HER COORDINATION	• Her movements are becoming more refined. • Her fingers are used for exploring – she puts things in her mouth much less. • She has the ability to lean forward and pick up small things easily.	• Show her how to stack bricks on top of one another or side by side – she's learning about volume as well as fine movements. • Give her a soft cooked pea to pick up between her finger and thumb.
HER SOCIAL SKILLS	• She's shy with new people and may be reluctant to be picked up by those she doesn't know. • She remembers people she knows well, even if she hasn't seen them for a few days.	• Talk to her on the telephone when you have to be away from home. • Get her a toy telephone to play with. • Help her get to know the baby-sitter.
HER SPEECH	• She's understanding more and more of what you say so repeat "Yes, that's what daddy means: it's cold outside, brrrr." • She'll start to add "t," "d," and "w" sounds. • She might make one animal sound if you do.	• Repeat words that start with t, d, and w. • Repeat all her sounds back to her. Name everything. • Read animal stories and make the noises.

STIMULATING PLAY

● Read a book or magazine – babies especially love color supplements with commentary from you.
● Get lots of noisy toys (wooden spoons, metal pots and pans, or a toy drum). These help her understand how to exert some control over things and herself and develops her understanding of cause and effect.
● Name parts of your body and ask her to repeat after you.
● Crawl beside your baby and imitate her movements to encourage her to do the same.
● Show her how to put one brick on top of another.
It takes great skill and she won't achieve it by herself for at least another month or so, but she'll enjoy knocking the bricks over and scattering them around the floor!

Playing with bricks will help her to develop her hand control

She can pick up small objects easily

142

BABY DEVELOPMENT
9–10 MONTHS

CRAWLING
He will begin by leaning forward onto his hands and knees.

	WHAT TO LOOK OUT FOR	
WHAT DEVELOPS	**HOW HE PROGRESSES**	**HOW YOU CAN HELP**
HIS MIND	• Your baby is getting used to rituals; they order his life and make him feel secure. • He'll wave bye-bye. • He'll put his foot out for a sock – he's longing to be helpful! • He knows teddy and dolly. • He'll look around corners for a toy.	• Try to keep to some sort of routine so that your baby can get used to it. • Show him how to dress and undress, so that he begins to understand the concept of a daily routine. • He should have toys such as teddies or dolls that are "like baby."
HIS MOBILITY	• He's discovered mobility. • He moves forward on his hands and knees and loves changing positions. • He can twist his trunk around quite confidently.	• Hold out your arms, call his name, and encourage him to crawl to you. • Offer your fingers for him to pull himself up on, then lift his foot on and off the floor.
HIS COORDINATION	• He reaches for objects with his index finger and will master picking up something small, such as a raisin, with his thumb and index finger. • He'll let go of objects deliberately. • He can build a tower of two bricks.	• Point to objects for him. • Put toys on the tray of his high chair and encourage him to throw them over; you can tie them on. • Ask him to roll a ball to you.
HIS SOCIAL SKILLS	• He shows affection by pressing his face and head against yours and hangs on to you tightly. • He'll give you a toy if you ask him for it, but become angry if you take it away.	• Teach about hugs – hug each other – he's learning reciprocity. • Teach sharing: ask him for a bit of food and show him how nice he is for sharing it.
HIS SPEECH	• Your baby begins to make lots of consonant sounds. • He chatters away in the rhythm of speech, without meaning.	• Name absolutely everything. • Face your baby when you speak to him so that he is able to read your lip movements.

143

STIMULATING PLAY

● Rock him on your knee and pretend to drop him – he'll enjoy "falling" as long as he's safe.
● Set aside a time each day for reading: read real storybooks and point out pictures. He'll learn to look at pictures the right way up and begin to recognize pictures of objects.
● Play hide and seek by hiding yourself or a toy.
● Give him lots of bath toys – plastic jugs, beakers, and sieves as well as floating toys like boats and ducks.
● Give him his own doll and teddy and show him how to dress and undress them.
● Give him squeaky toys, horns, and bells.
● Stack blocks or cubes of the same size on top on one another and side by side for him to see.

Encourage him to pull his sock off; he wants to help

BABY DEVELOPMENT
10–11 MONTHS

CONTAINERS He'll love to put items into containers and take them out again.

144

WHAT TO LOOK OUT FOR

WHAT DEVELOPS	HOW SHE PROGRESSES	HOW YOU CAN HELP
HER MIND	• Your baby will point things out to you. • She loves dropping toys off her high chair, then looking for them. • She asks to be picked up. • She learns through opposites: keep showing her examples, such as in and out, here and there, and over and under.	• Read different kinds of books and magazines to her. • Increase her concentration span by telling her a simple storyline. • Pick her up if she reaches out to you. • Keep demonstrating cause and effect, by pushing over bricks or splashing water.
HER MOBILITY	• She's crawling or shuffling at great speed. • If you support her standing, she'll lift one leg. • She's completely balanced while sitting.	• Place a toy right behind her to make her twist around – it's okay, she's got the skill. • Position her so that she can crawl or shuffle.
HER COORDINATION	• Your baby loves taking things out of containers and putting them back. • She will hold something out to you if you ask for it.	• Play giving things to each other and then taking them away, but don't *force* her to relinquish something. • Take her hand and point to objects.
HER SOCIAL SKILLS	• She knows her name and knows who Mommy and Daddy are when you use the words. • She's got a wonderful sense of humor: play little jokes all the time and laugh at her attempts to make you laugh.	• Use laughter to show your approval and silence to mean the opposite: this is gentle baby discipline and she'll soon catch on. • Demonstrate social rituals, such as kissing and waving goodbye.
HER SPEECH	• Your baby is now beginning to imitate real speech sounds. • She may start to attempt one word with meaning – "Dada" when Daddy appears is often the first.	• Keep saying "Mama." • Repeat "Dada." Use association, for example: "Dada has gone to work."

STIMULATING PLAY

● Play games using the hands, such as "Itsy-bitsy spider" and "Jack and Jill" – buy a book that shows you the movements.
● When reading, name several items on each page and go over them in the same order each time you read. Let her turn the pages.
● Babies love babies, so introduce the concept of parenthood through pictures of other babies, puppies, and kittens.
● Encourage her to practice putting in and taking out by giving her a wooden spoon and bowl or bricks and a basket.
● Play games with bricks: she will attempt to make a tower of bricks and you can demonstrate cause and effect by knocking them down and saying "all fall down."
● Encourage her to pull herself up to standing by holding a favorite toy just out of reach.

Help her to learn by showing her how toys work

BABY DEVELOPMENT
11–12 MONTHS

FEEDING
By this age your baby will be much more adept at feeding himself.

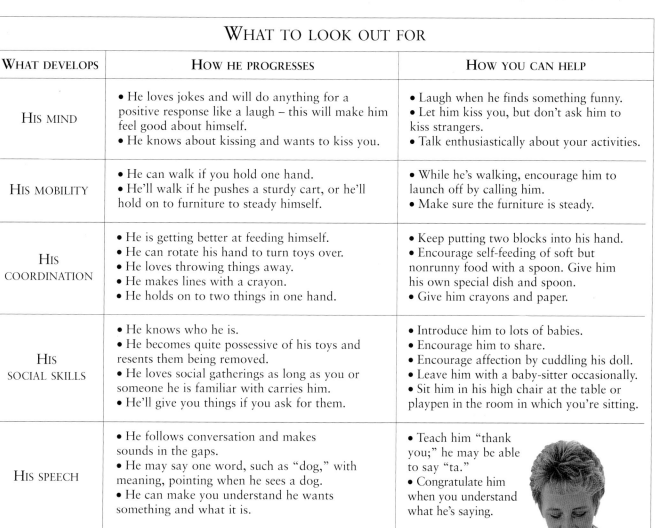

WHAT TO LOOK OUT FOR

WHAT DEVELOPS	HOW HE PROGRESSES	HOW YOU CAN HELP
HIS MIND	• He loves jokes and will do anything for a positive response like a laugh – this will make him feel good about himself. • He knows about kissing and wants to kiss you.	• Laugh when he finds something funny. • Let him kiss you, but don't ask him to kiss strangers. • Talk enthusiastically about your activities.
HIS MOBILITY	• He can walk if you hold one hand. • He'll walk if he pushes a sturdy cart, or he'll hold on to furniture to steady himself.	• While he's walking, encourage him to launch off by calling him. • Make sure the furniture is steady.
HIS COORDINATION	• He is getting better at feeding himself. • He can rotate his hand to turn toys over. • He loves throwing things away. • He makes lines with a crayon. • He holds on to two things in one hand.	• Keep putting two blocks into his hand. • Encourage self-feeding of soft but nonrunny food with a spoon. Give him his own special dish and spoon. • Give him crayons and paper.
HIS SOCIAL SKILLS	• He knows who he is. • He becomes quite possessive of his toys and resents them being removed. • He loves social gatherings as long as you or someone he is familiar with carries him. • He'll give you things if you ask for them.	• Introduce him to lots of babies. • Encourage him to share. • Encourage affection by cuddling his doll. • Leave him with a baby-sitter occasionally. • Sit him in his high chair at the table or playpen in the room in which you're sitting.
HIS SPEECH	• He follows conversation and makes sounds in the gaps. • He may say one word, such as "dog," with meaning, pointing when he sees a dog. • He can make you understand he wants something and what it is.	• Teach him "thank you;" he may be able to say "ta." • Congratulate him when you understand what he's saying.

STIMULATING PLAY

• Read simple stories about animals and their young to encourage his interest in other "babies." All babies love this and you can use this opportunity to make references to you and your baby and how much you love him and will protect him.

• Give him nontoxic colored crayons and large sheets of plain paper on the floor, to encourage him to draw.

• Encourage him to stand unaided by holding him steady, then letting go for a second or two.

• Concentrate on the names of objects and name parts of the body. Point to parts of your body and he'll copy.

• If he uses the furniture as support to get around the room, place it slightly farther apart to encourage him to bridge the gap. Be ready to help in case he loses his balance.

As you are reading, point to objects and name them

145

GOING BACK TO WORK

Just as you've settled into being a mother and found a routine that's right for all of you, you may find yourself thinking about returning to work. For many women, this is a financial necessity and for some it's a relief after months of diapers and baby talk! Going back to work requires some reorganization and a change of priorities, and it's sensible to consider all the options quite soon after your baby is born. Try to decide as a family what arrangements suit you best. You may, for example, have the option to return part-time or work from home some days, or your partner may decide to give up his job to care for your baby, especially if you earn more money. If you both work full-time, you'll have to arrange child care and accept that on weekdays you're going to see your baby for only a couple of hours in the morning and evening. This is never ideal or easy, but as long as you maintain your baby's routine, and she has your undivided attention while you're with her, she won't suffer from having working parents.

WORK AND PARENTING

WHEN IS THE RIGHT TIME?

Aside from legal requirements (see p. 160), your baby's needs and your feelings will, to an extent, dictate when you're able to return to work:

■ If you want to continue breast-feeding, practice expressing enough milk for your baby's needs (see p. 72). If you intend to stop breast-feeding, you need to introduce the bottle in good time.

■ Think carefully about whether you feel ready – physically and emotionally – to return to work.

WORK OPTIONS

Look at all your options to work out which would suit you best.

PART-TIME/JOB-SHARING
Part-time can be the best of both worlds, since you have time with your baby and the stimulation of work, but also have the pressure of both. If you can be part of a job-share, you may be better able to continue to build your career.

WORKING FROM HOME
You have to be self-disciplined and that necessitates arranging some child care (see p. 150). If the baby is in the house, you're more likely to be easily distracted.

CAREER BREAK
You may decide to take a career break for a couple of years. Make sure that putting your career on hold is what you really want and that you've thought clearly about all the implications.

FATHER AT HOME
If you want to return full-time, your partner may be primary caregiver (see p. 154).

IF YOU PREPARE for returning to work well in advance, the transition period should be easier for all of you. As a couple, you need to make sure that you've made adequate child care provisions, decide how you'll adjust your routine, and accept that the change in lifestyle may be unsettling at first, especially for the baby.

MAKING THE DECISION

You may decide while you're pregnant that you want to return to work at the end of your maternity leave (see p. 160). Once the baby is born, however, it's normal to feel unsure about leaving him, especially since this is likely to coincide with the time that you're just settling into being a mother. On the opposite end of the scale, you may be surprised to find that you actually miss work and are ready, after a few months, to take a break from the domestic routine and return to an adult environment. Of course, there may simply be no decision for you to make – financially, you may have to work.

WHAT TO CONSIDER
Whatever you decided while pregnant, it's important to look at your financial and domestic situation once the baby is born and for you and your partner to weigh up the advantages and disadvantages of your returning to work:
● What type of child care can you afford? Have you checked what is available in your area?
● After covering the cost of child care, does your salary leave enough extra to make it worthwhile? (Don't forget to take travel costs into account.)
● Is it feasible to return to your old job as it was and also devote enough time to your baby? For example, does your job involve lots of overtime or travel away from home?

CONCERNS
For the past few months you'll have been focused on preparing for the birth and then looking after your new baby. Once you have to think about returning to work, you're likely to have concerns and mixed feelings.

Feeling guilty You may feel guilty (especially if you can't wait to get back to work), but don't. Just because you're a working mother doesn't mean you're a bad mother. There is no point in staying at home with your baby if it doesn't fulfill you – it will be more beneficial to him if you're happy and contented when he does see you. Also, don't forget that your baby will benefit from the additional income.

Losing your confidence If the last few months of your life have consisted mainly of diaper changing and entertaining a baby, you may doubt your ability to readjust to a working environment. You may worry that you have lost your touch and that everyone got on fine without you. A couple of months after the birth, try to ease yourself back into the work mode by catching up on what has been going on in your industry and by talking to colleagues. Nearer the time, go into the office (without the baby, if possible), even if it's just to meet someone for lunch, so that it isn't such a shock when you return. You'll soon realize that not much has changed in the time you've been away.

WHEN YOU'RE BACK AT WORK

It may take a few weeks to settle back into work. You'll just about have worked out a routine with your baby at home and then suddenly have to adapt to a different timetable and concentrate your mind on a different set of priorities. You'll also, for the first time, be doing your job while having to handle added pressures and responsibilities at home.

MAKING THE TRANSITION

AREA OF CHANGE	HOW TO MAKE IT EASIER
PREPARING YOUR BABY	Introduce your baby to the babysitter, starting with a couple of mornings each week and gradually building it up, or take him to the nursery for a trial run. You should also start to adapt his feeding routine in good time.
ADAPTING TO A CHANGE OF ROUTINE	Trying to juggle work and looking after your baby can be difficult. Establish a routine in the mornings and evenings so that you are sharing the baby care and chores equally. You'll soon find a routine that works.
COPING WITH FATIGUE	No one who is consistently deprived of sleep can be expected to cope adequately with a job, so you must take turns caring for your baby during the night. Even if one of you is in part-time work, you should still organize a prorated arrangement.
FOCUSING ON WORK	It's an acquired skill not to think about your baby while you're at work. If you've made the best arrangements you can for his welfare, any energy you now dispense on worrying is wasted and cheats both you and your employer.
SETTLING YOUR BABY	The fact is your baby will *have* to settle and he will. What you can do is prepare yourselves for his reaction and, during the time he's with you, be reassuring and comforting to him. Make sure he has whatever comfort object he loves.

CAREER CONSIDERATIONS

People often assume that a woman's first priority will be her child and, in some situations, they're right: when push comes to shove, it's quite often the mother's employment that takes the strain and not the father's. If your partnership is different, you're probably going to have to demonstrate this several times before it's recognized. How your career is affected may also depend on your employer's attitude: set the ground rules early on by talking to your manager and telling him or her that you're committed to your job, but that your responsibilities at home will necessitate a certain amount of flexibility. Explain that you need to leave on time (although, ideally, picking up your baby should be equally divided with your partner), but that with sufficient notice you're prepared to work extra hours, if necessary.

FATHER

If you've agreed as a couple that your partner should go back to work, then you must be accommodating. The routine at home will change if you're both working full-time and you must prepare yourself for this.

HOW YOU CAN HELP
■ Be supportive to your partner. She's very likely to find the transition to going back to work a strain and she may be distressed by having to leave the baby. Try to plan in advance as much as possible and give her time to adjust.

■ Share the responsibility. Don't just assume that your partner will sort out child care problems. The caregiver or nursery should have telephone numbers for both of you (including any mobiles), so that you can easily share the responsibility if a problem arises.

■ Share the chores. Your partner may have been doing most of the caregiving while she was at home full-time, but now that she's back at work this should become more equal. Alternate doing the domestic chores, getting up during the night and collecting your baby from the babysitter.

EMERGENCIES

You both have to agree on a strategy for emergencies, such as your baby or the babysitter being ill. In the absence of a replacement caregiver, such as a grandparent, there's no alternative to one of you taking time off work. If either of you feels that your job merits priority, then this is something that must be stated and agreed in advance of the problem arising.

HIDDEN COSTS

When you're weighing up the cost of child care, don't just look at the daily or hourly rate. It's worth considering the following:

■ Are there transportation costs?
■ Are your baby's meals provided?
■ What are the additional costs associated with a live-in caregiver?
■ Would it be cheaper to employ a nanny if you have twins?
■ Are there hidden emotional costs, such as feeling indebted, if you're using a friend or relative?

CHILD CARE

WHEN CHOOSING CHILD CARE, most parents are restricted by what they can afford. Ideally, as part of your decision to have a baby, you will have discussed your options or, if not, have some idea of what would suit you once the baby is born. Finding and choosing a caregiver is mainly dictated by practical and financial considerations, but there are also emotional issues involved: leaving your baby for several hours each day with someone new is difficult so, for your own peace of mind, it's essential that you're as happy and confident as possible about the type of care and caregiver you've chosen.

CHILD CARE OPTIONS

TYPE OF CARE	DESCRIPTION	ADVANTAGES	DISADVANTAGES
RELATIVE	You may decide to leave your baby with a member of your family, such as a grandparent. Encourage him or her to involve your baby in outside activities, such as a playgroup.	• Usually a cheaper option. • Your baby is with someone who loves her. • You are less likely to have strict time restraints, but don't abuse this.	• It can be difficult if there are disagreements. • You may worry more about your baby forming a close relationship with that person.
HOME DAY CARE	A home day care provider looks after several children in her own home. She is often very experienced, especially if she has her own children.	• You can often pay by the hour to suit your budget. • Your baby will mix with lots of children, which will help develop social skills.	• No training is required. • She may have limited resources. • You can't take your baby if she's sick.
NANNY	A nanny cares for your baby at home and may live with you. Interview a prospective nanny together – you both have to get on with her and observe her with your baby.	• A nanny is professionally trained and qualified. • Care takes place at home, which will help your baby to settle and is more convenient for you.	• A nanny is expensive (you're responsible for her taxes and Social Security); consider a nanny share. • Domestic tensions may arise if she lives with you.
DAY NURSERY	There are very few local nurseries, so you'll probably have to pay for private care. If you're lucky, an all-day nursery may be available at your workplace.	• Your baby is with other babies and care is based around developing skills. • Nurseries must be registered and often employ qualified caregivers.	• Can be expensive and there will be limited places. • You'll have to collect your baby at an agreed time. • You can't take your baby if she's sick.
AU PAIR OR MOTHER'S HELPER	This is a student, possibly from another country, who lives with you as part of the family. She may want to attend classes and is suitable only if you work part-time or from home.	• Care is provided in the home, which is convenient. • Cheaper than a nanny. • When your baby is older, the au pair may be able to teach her a second language.	• Not professionally qualified, and not suitable for the full-time care of a baby. • Works limited hours. • There will be additional live-in costs.

WHAT TO LOOK FOR IN A CAREGIVER

Once you've decided on the type of child care you'd prefer, you need to look around for the best caregiver. If you plan your child care well in advance, you'll have more choice. If you leave it too late before you finish maternity leave, you may be restricted by what is available. Ask the person or institution that you're considering lots of questions to find out the type of care that will be provided, and thoroughly check the facilities. If you're unhappy or unsure, follow your instincts and look elsewhere.

Qualifications and references A nanny or nursery nurse should have accredited training with a proper qualification. If you're using home day care or a nursery, check that the person or institution is registered with a local authority. Remember, au pairs are not professionally trained. Ask a potential au pair for the name of another employer you could speak to and at least two written references. Always try to talk to the referees on the telephone to gauge a better idea of the person's suitability.

Level of care Check how many babies are looked after at one time and the caregiver-to-child ratio. Even if your baby will not be receiving individual care (with a nursery or home day care), she should still be given enough care to be stimulated and to encourage her development. Check the space and resources available, such as the cleanliness of the kitchen, the play area, and the types of toys offered. With all types of care, ask what kind of activities your baby will be involved in on a day-to-day basis.

Interaction with your baby Always invite a potential caregiver to spend time with your baby so you can see how they interact. Watch to see what she says while holding your baby and how your baby reacts. Ask her questions, such as her thoughts on discipline to check that they match your own.

Commitment It can be confusing and distressing for a baby to have a change of caregiver. Check that the person or institution will be able to provide relatively long-term care. An au pair may be available for only a short time and is likely to have other commitments while she is staying with you.

YOUR RELATIONSHIP WITH YOUR CAREGIVER

However sure you are about employing your caregiver, it's advisable to discuss and agree on all aspects of caring for your baby from the outset:
● A trial period before you agree to a full contract is a good idea.
● Write down your requirements so that you can agree on some ground rules; especially with regard to telephone use and visitors for live-in caregivers.
● Find out the caregiver's thoughts or the institution's policy on discipline.

THE CAREGIVER'S RELATIONSHIP WITH YOUR BABY
Leaving your baby with a caregiver is likely to come at a time when you've just settled into being a parent and feel particularly close to your son or daughter. Your caregiver will also form a close relationship with your baby, but this doesn't mean you're any less important and you're by no means replaced. Your baby is capable of being close to – and accepting the attention of – more than one person: in fact it's beneficial if this happens because the more love, attention, and stimulation she receives, the better she'll develop. Babies often go through periods of time when they favor certain people (see p. 111); if your baby seems closer to her caregiver it's probably only a phase. Your baby may also seem unsettled now and then, but don't read too much into this. However, if it continues for more than a week or two, spend time with the caregiver and your baby together to try to pinpoint any problems.

TRIAL PERIOD

Investing money in nursery fees or your caregiver's wages before you return to work, so that you can settle in your baby gradually, will pay huge dividends:

■ Your baby will have time to become familiar with new surroundings and new caregivers.

■ You'll be able to gauge the impact of the new regime on your baby and find ways of soothing her if she becomes unsettled.

■ You'll be able to sort out logistics problems without the pressure of neither of you being available.

■ If you introduce your baby to her new caregiver gradually, the emotional impact of handing her over should be less once you actually return to work.

151

IF THINGS GO WRONG

If the child care situation doesn't work out, it can be disappointing and problematic, especially if your caregiver lives with you. You should, however, try to treat the problem professionally as you would with a working relationship:

■ It's best if issues are dealt with quickly; ignoring problems will only make matters worse and lead to resentments building up.

■ Talk to the caregiver and try to reach a compromise. Agree to see how things go and, depending on the problem, set a time limit. If, after this period, you have not resolved the matter, it may be in everyone's best interest to terminate the employment.

■ Decide on a set notice period at the beginning; this is also advantageous to you because, if your caregiver is the one who decides to leave, you won't suddenly be left in the lurch.

MOTHER

Remember, play does not have to involve sitting down and playing with toys; often just being with you is fun for your baby.

WHAT YOU CAN DO
■ When you get home from work, make a habit of picking up your baby right away and keep him on your hip as you walk around the house doing things.

■ Exaggerate your pleasure at seeing him, talk to him the whole time, make eye contact, laugh a lot, play little jokes, and enjoy each other.

■ Try to spend ten to fifteen uninterrupted minutes playing with your baby each evening.

■ Later in the evening, read the paper or a book together so that you both relax. Read out items and show your baby pictures to involve him.

■ If you're really tired, have a bath together. A skin-to-skin soak is good for both of you.

152

AN HOUR EACH DAY

An hour of time spent playing with your baby each day becomes rewarding and fulfilling for all of you. What's more, a baby who gets the undivided attention of his parents for an hour a day acquires self-esteem and self-confidence and becomes a generous, loving, and well-adjusted child. This does not have to be a solid hour – in fact, your baby will not concentrate for this length of time; it could be two half-hour periods or four quarter-hour periods as long as he has your undivided attention at these times. Your baby loves routine and will get excited as her playtimes approach.

SPECIAL TIME WITH YOUR BABY

IF YOU'RE WORKING PARENTS, the time spent at home as a family becomes not just important, but precious – and that applies as much to fathers as to mothers. Play is essential to your baby's mental and physical development, and nothing will make him happier than to play and have the attention of his parents at the same time.

THE IMPORTANCE OF PLAY

In addition to being a parent, you are your baby's playmate; this is especially true in his first year when he may not have had much opportunity to interact with other children. Every game you play with him is magical and every lesson becomes worth learning, so time spent in games, no matter how simple, ensures that your baby is avidly learning and acquiring skills. Do not underestimate how important play is to your baby: it's his full-time job; a job that requires great concentration and expenditure of energy. It's harder than most adult work because everything is new and fresh lessons are learned all the time. These lessons, however, are made easier and are more fun if he can enjoy them with his favorite playmates – his parents.

WHY PLAY IS ESSENTIAL
● Your baby investigates his world through play.
● It stimulates and excites him and is the best use of his time.
● For the first few years of his life it is the only way he learns.
● It is an integral part of his physical and mental development.

GETTING THE MOST OUT OF PLAY
To maximize the rewards that play can bring, it's important to make the time to join in activities with your baby and encourage him in play that will stimulate his development.

Investing time Formal play isn't necessary, but some planning does reap dividends so try to make play a part of your morning, evening, and weekend routine so that your baby is getting at least an hour of playtime in total from each of you every day (see left). A baby has a very short attention span, so don't expect him to sit playing happily while you cook the dinner. Fifteen minutes invested in playing with your baby before you begin a chore will pay off; if you give him only five minutes of your time he's more likely to want your attention when you're busy doing something else.

Stimulating development Babies start acquiring skills from the very moment of birth. These mental and physical milestones (see p. 126) emerge at particular stages as your baby's brain and body develops. It follows that these are optimum moments for you to introduce games that encourage particular skills to flourish, so make sure you vary the activities that you play with your baby: for example, physical games encourage mobility; singing helps develop speech; playing with toys such as building blocks helps your baby become more dextrous.

MAXIMIZING YOUR TIME

If you work full-time, try to take advantage of any spare moments you have to spend time with your baby. It helps if you're organized and can prioritize: if you're both in high-pressured jobs it's easy to let your career take over and work an extra hour at the beginning or end of the day, but this hour is invaluable time you could be spending with your baby.

WEEKENDS

If you're at work all week, your weekends will be very precious. Don't bring work home with you; if it's not there you can't do it, so you can spend time with your baby without feeling guilty. Try to get out as a family at least one of the days of the weekend; if you're in the house, you're more likely to get distracted with other things. Keep to your baby's weekly routine as much as possible – at around nine months he'll begin to understand that certain things happen at certain times.

MORNINGS

It can be one mad rush in the mornings if you're trying to get yourselves and your baby ready, but most babies do wake up early so use this opportunity to spend time together. If you don't have time to play, sing and talk to your baby as you change and dress him. Try to sit down to breakfast with him – he'll enjoy you being sociable.

EVENINGS

Working full-time will make you tired in the evenings. Try to establish some sort of routine for when you get home because, in addition to having time with your baby, it's important that you both have time to yourselves and time together as a couple (see p. 114).

Leave work on time Try to get into the habit of leaving work on time. It's unfair to your partner and the baby if either one of you is always home late, leaving one parent to do everything. Don't take advantage of the baby-sitter – an extra hour in the evening is a lot when she's been looking after the baby all day.

Divide the chores One of you should cook and the other wash up so that you both have time to spend with the baby.

Choose relaxing activities It will be difficult to get your baby to bed if he's very excited. Read or sing to him to calm him down before you put him to bed. Remember, he's had a busy day playing and he's probably tired too!

RELAXING TOGETHER

Play doesn't always have to be energetic. Settle into a comfortable chair in the evening and read a story to your baby. This is a relaxing and enjoyable activity for both of you.

FATHER

Your baby will look forward to you coming home in the evenings. Reward him by showering him with attention and showing him how special he is to you.

WHAT YOU CAN DO

■ Develop a special routine that becomes a welcome ritual when you get home from work. It could be holding out your arms for your baby to walk or crawl to you, or picking him up immediately, walking around with him, and telling him about your day.

■ Try to find time each evening to spend ten or fifteen minutes playing a game.

■ If you like to read the paper in the evening, let your baby sit with you, read to him, and let him have his own piece of paper to crumple.

■ Have a bath with your baby (see p. 81) before getting him ready for bed; this can be relaxing for both of you.

■ If you don't have much time with your baby on weekday mornings, try to make a special effort to dress him and give him breakfast on weekends.

153

TIME-SAVING TIPS

To maximize time with your baby in the evenings:

■ Try to prepare some weekday meals over the weekend.

■ Record any early-evening programs and watch them once your baby has gone to bed.

■ Save any long telephone calls until your baby is asleep.

■ Eat a late lunch sometimes so that it's possible for you to wait later for your evening meal.

FATHERS AT HOME

154

MOTHER

Being the breadwinner while your partner stays at home can lead to conflicting emotions, even when it's a decision you're sure about.

HOW TO HELP YOURSELF
Society as a whole still pressures women to be the main caregiver and it's difficult not to be affected by this. You may feel guilty, and envy other women who have more time to spend with their babies. Be confident in your decision or accepting of your predicament, and spend as much of your spare time as possible with your baby. It can be stressful if your family relies on you for its income; find ways to relax and try not to let this pressure turn into resentment.

HOW TO HELP YOUR PARTNER
Make sure your partner has time out to relax, see his friends, and spend time with you (see p. 114). Don't leave all the chores to him just because he's the main caregiver.

HOW FRIENDS REACT

Most of the flak that fathers at home have to dodge comes in the form of ridicule from male friends. Many traditionally minded men find it threatening that the "house husband" is independent and strong enough to flout the social conventions that are sacrosanct to his more macho brothers. They like to hang onto these conventions because it gives them security. But if you're a man who is strong enough to have made the decision to be a full-time parent, you'll no doubt be strong enough to take the flak!

SOME COUPLES ARE SUFFICIENTLY LIBERATED – and brave enough – to avoid the traditional pattern of family life. They're opting for a reversal of roles in which the mother becomes the breadwinner, while the father acts as a "house husband," caring for the baby and running the home. Just as women only needed the opportunity to demonstrate their competence in the workplace, men who become the main family caregiver are finding that they only needed to be given the chance to demonstrate that they are just as capable as women of loving and bringing up their children at home.

MAKING THE DECISION

For many couples, the decision to reverse roles is made because they feel that their baby will benefit from having a full-time parent at home and, because the mother is earning more, it makes sense for the father to be that person – especially if his work is something he can do from home. When a parent stays home full-time, a couple will be financially worse off than if both work, but this is often compensated by an improvement in their quality of life and is seen as a worthwhile investment in their child. A man may be forced to stay at home because of a job loss; even if this is only short-term, it can often be an invaluable opportunity for him to spend time with his child and take on the role of primary caregiver.

A LEARNING PROCESS

Those people who make a stand on the traditional roles of father and mother as being "natural" are missing the point completely – to divide parental labor along the lines of gender is completely redundant. Looking after a baby is a learning process for all new parents, whether they're male or female, so don't let anyone tell you otherwise. Remember the following:
● Women are not born with an innate ability to change diapers and dress babies: they possibly appear more confident at it because they're made to feel that they should know what to do.
● Looking after and nurturing a baby is a learned skill and to begin with it's as difficult for a mother as it is for a father.
● Men are not at a disadvantage when it comes to caring for a baby: if you're a father who has decided to stay at home to be the main caregiver, you have as much chance at being good at it and raising a happy, confident, and intelligent child as your partner.

PARENTING
If you're a couple who has chosen the father-at-home option, you are presumably committed to parenting in general rather than "fathering" or "mothering" (see p. 11). It's only sensible to base your family set-up on your mutual strengths rather than be captive to stereotypes that may well conflict with your personalities.

THE ADVANTAGES

As a father who chooses to stay at home, you'll form a close bond with your baby and have a chance to watch and enjoy her development at an age that most men miss out on. This role will enable you to express your affection and feelings in ways that are difficult when you're in the more traditional male role. Giving up a full-time job to be a caregiver will enable you to change your priorities and release you from the pressures of being the main provider for your family. This leaves you with more of yourself to offer your baby and partner, which can be hugely beneficial to the family as a whole.

HOW YOUR CHILD IS AFFECTED

To a baby her mother and father are interchangeable. The baby only knows parental love and care – it doesn't matter who is doing the giving. The advantage of a man being the main caregiver is that he can offer a positive role model to his children free from the most common kind of stereotyping. A son will grow up feeling comfortable with the emotional side of his personality and he'll follow his father's lead in having an independent spirit unpressured by prevailing social mores. A daughter, of course, will seek out the same well-balanced kind of men as her father – and that's no bad thing.

BEING THE LONE MAN

The main problem for most full-time parents is isolation and since a large proportion of people are working during the day, adult company can be found largely with others looking after children. Since these are usually women, this can cause a problem for the full-time father. It's pointless to pretend that people interact with the opposite sex in the same way as with their own, but it's likely that a man with enough flexibility and confidence to become the main caregiver in the first place will move fairly easily into this predominantly female world. While some mothers may be surprised to find their ranks as full-time child caregivers joined by a man, few will be hostile. The "house-husband" is usually a bit of a nine-day-wonder whose presence is very shortly taken for granted. Most men are welcomed, although some are the victims of maternalism of the "let-me-help-you-love" variety, which can be as irritating as the "leave-that-to-me-darling" paternalism practiced by some men.

AN EQUAL SHARE

Some couples decide that they'll both work part-time or one or two days at home, so that they both have a mix of parenting and work. This is possible if the job can be done at home or part-time, but with the technological revolution it is becoming an option for more and more people. The downside is that it may mean both of you putting your careers on hold, but many couples feel that it's the right choice; at least it prevents either person having to give up a career altogether. The advantages include:

■ Both of you have real quality time with your baby a couple of days each week, which will enable you to form an equally close bond with her.

■ You'll both have a strong appreciation of the frustrations involved in being in sole charge of your baby and the problems of juggling work and home.

■ The baby benefits from building close relationships with both of her parents.

■ You become a real team by dividing things equally; this prevents the resentments that often build up in the classic mom-at-home set-up.

155

BEING ACCEPTED
Over time, a full-time father will stop being the token male and become just another parent, who shares the same pleasures and problems of parenthood as his female friends.

LOOKING TO THE FUTURE

YOUR CONSTANT ROLE

Your role as nurturer entails respecting your child and offering support without foregoing your own principles. It takes many forms.

COMFORTER
You can only help your child to cope with emotional or physical pain by acknowledging it, and by offering comfort when it's needed.

PLAYMATE
Play is a serious business for your child, and the best play is inter-active. No amount of passive amusement in front of a television set can compensate for active play with other people, the most important of whom are his parents.

LIMIT-SETTER
The first limits you set for your baby will be to prevent him from hurting himself; later, these limits will prevent him from hurting others as well. Never be apologetic about consistently setting reasonable limits, but try not to do so in a punitive or accusatory manner. Rather than saying "no" all the time, help him to understand your reasons for restraint.

TEACHER OR ROLE MODEL?
The role of teacher is crucial for any parent; but it isn't formal teaching: you do it by example. Your child will learn behavior from you, so you can't shrug off responsibility for an errant schoolchild or truculent teenager – he learned about life from you.

AUTHORITY FIGURE
Don't confuse authority and power: power results from the use or threat of force; authority comes from a person who has influence over, and receives consent from, others without force. Your child will accept your authority if he also sees that you are competent, fair, loving, and reasonable.

YOUR BABY HAS NOW COMPLETED his first year of life; he's beginning to communicate with language, he's mobile (perhaps even taking his first steps), he's feeding himself, and he's asserting his personality as a full member of the family. He's growing up, so your role as parents will be changing too, and it'll continue to change as he progresses on to school and ultimately to adolescence and adulthood. As the months and years pass, under your care he'll become more and more independent, but he'll always need you both as his permanent bedrock of security, sympathy, friendship, and love.

YOUR BABY GROWS UP

The main change you will see, and must be prepared to accept, is that your baby is becoming a person in his own right, with personality, preferences, and a will of his own. He will gradually acquire a sense of place in the family, a sense of independence, and, most importantly, a sense of self-worth. Not all these changes are straightforward for you. On the one hand, they are all signs of growing maturity and so should be welcomed. On the other hand, some aspects of his growing up may lead to clashes with you and could result in a battle of wills that requires careful handling. Then again, his frustration at wanting to out-perform his ability may express itself as tantrums that leave you bewildered, perplexed, and sometimes helpless (see p. 158). Tantrums, nonetheless, are a crucial milestone; he cannot become a reasonable, self-controlled child without experiencing them.

A HIERARCHY OF NEEDS

Keep in mind the basic needs that will help your child grow and develop normally. Health, of course, is a prerequisite, but you also have to try to provide the right sort of environment for him to reach his full potential – physically, emotionally, socially, and intellectually. All children have a hierarchy of needs, starting from the very basic need for survival. You could think of your child's needs in terms of a pyramid: the solid base is provision of the food, drink, and shelter needed for *survival*; then comes *safety*: protection from harm; a sense of *belonging*: your child feels wanted and secure, leading to *self-esteem*: no one can feel good about himself if he feels unloved. Near the top of the pyramid comes *actualization*: understanding his place in the world – with a fully developed sense of *self* as the pinnacle that can't be achieved without the rest in place.

BUILDING CONFIDENCE These fundamental building blocks help your child reach his full potential.

SELF
ACTUALIZATION
SELF-ESTEEM
BELONGING
SAFETY
SURVIVAL

BECOMING INDEPENDENT

Your child's burgeoning spirit of self-reliance is more important than you may think because so many good things can flow from it. Without a secure feeling of independence, a child can't relate to others, share, be reasonable, outgoing, and friendly, have a sense of responsibility, and eventually respect others and their privacy. Many other qualities stem from his belief in himself – curiosity, adventurousness, being helpful, thoughtful, and generous. If he has such qualities people will relate well to him and he'll automatically get more out of life. What you pour in as love, expresses itself as self-worth and belief in himself. Love, of course, is not the only spur; you can encourage him practically as well.

Helpfulness Ask him to carry things for you, such as the shopping bag or a wastebasket, so that he feels useful.

Decision-making Give him small decisions to make, like which toy to play with or which cup to use, so he can use his judgment and rely on it.

Sense of identity Ask questions about his preferences and solicit his opinion to give him a sense of identity and importance.

Physical independence Give him slightly more and more difficult tasks – like jumping up and down, throwing or kicking a ball, so he can feel pleased with the strength and coordination of his body.

Emotional independence Show him that he can trust you: you always come back after leaving him, you always comfort him when he's hurt, you always help him when he's in difficulties.

Cooperation "We can do it together" is a motto that you should keep repeating – it breeds faith in your baby's own efforts. When he overcomes an obstacle or succeeds in a task on his own, he'll experience the thrill of achievement – especially if you heap praise on him.

ACHIEVING CONTROL OF HIS BODY

Many parents believe that they can set a clock for their baby to achieve bowel and bladder control. Those parents are doomed to frustration. Your baby's timetable has nothing to do with your expectations – only with his speed of development. Bowel and bladder control are undoubtedly important milestones between dependent baby and independent child, but they can't be reached until other areas of development have been achieved. This is why I dislike the term "toilet training"; no child can do something until he's ready for it and, once ready, no child needs training.

WHEN HE'LL BE DRY

At around 18 months and no earlier, your child might start to tell you that he can feel himself passing urine. He can't hold it, he can't wait, he has no control over it. He'll give you a sign; he'll point to the diaper and vocalize to draw your attention to it. Then, and only then, do you start a gentle program of encouragement. Your daughter will probably have achieved bladder and bowel control by the age of two, and be dry at night by three; it may take your son longer. Being dry all night can take some children a long time – it's quite normal for a boy not to achieve full control until he is four or five. Never scold your child for wetting the bed, or having an accident during the day, especially if he's been "dry" for a while. It could be a sign of illness or emotional distress, so think about the underlying causes. Being angry with your child for something over which he hasn't much control will just upset him and make the problem worse.

BEING REASONABLE

This heading disguises a few personal comments on discipline in young children. I have to disguise it because what I believe to be good discipline has little to do with the usual punitive interpretation of the word.

REDEFINING DISCIPLINE
Good discipline has nothing to do with a parent forcing a mode of behavior *on* a child; it's about encouraging reasonable behavior *from* a child. Your aim should be to create a desire to behave well most of the time, rather than to conform to an arbitrary adult code out of fear, weakness, or resignation.

ENCOURAGING GOOD RESULTS
Hitting a child to make him obedient is no more efficient than belaboring a worker on the production line for being too slow. The basic tool of good personnel management is praising for good results, not penalizing poor results, and so it should be for children.

START FROM THE BEGINNING
It's easier if you start how you mean to finish; discipline doesn't just happen at, say, three years old. It's been building from birth and is based on reasonable behavior expressed by you.

PARENTAL RESPONSIBILITY
Children are born with an overwhelming desire to please; if they lose that desire, my view is that we parents must take responsibility. If you think you're doing everything right, but still have a difficult child, you may be being too easy on yourself. Look at what you think of as "right," and ask yourself if it is right for your child.

BEING CONSISTENT
Work out your joint attitude to discipline, and be consistent in your response. A child who gets different reactions from each parent will be confused about what his limits really are, and his behavior will reflect this.

157

158

TEMPER TANTRUMS

By the time she's about two, your child's will is well developed, but her ambitions far outreach her capabilities. The resulting combination of stubbornness and frustration can be explosive, resulting in the classic temper tantrum. There are ways to cope:

■ Accept temper tantrums as normal. Better still, see them as a cry for help. Having your child throw a fit of screaming, kicking, and crying is upsetting at the best of times, and sometimes publicly humiliating. If you're firm, gentle and have a steady nerve, you'll nurse her out of them; to do that you have to realize that she's not being willfully naughty – she simply can't control herself.

■ Don't shout, spank, or get angry. She needs you to help her regain control. A temper tantrum means she's saying, "Help me. Protect me from myself." Your very quietness should calm her down.

■ A really upset child can frighten herself by the sheer strength of her uncontrolled emotions, so cuddle her close; be firm – she will struggle.

■ Be businesslike; she's trying to elicit a dramatic response but she'll calm down if you're cool.

■ If this doesn't work, say you're going to leave the room or walk where she can't see you, but you can see her. Do as you promised and the screaming will stop; it usually does without an audience. (If members of the public form a scandalized audience you may have to carry her outside.)

■ Try to stay where you can see her as much as possible, and be ready to prevent her from hurting herself or others.

CAUTION
Some children develop breath-holding attacks that may be frightening, but most are brought to an abrupt end by a firm tap between the shoulder blades.

GENDER DIFFERENCES IN DEVELOPMENT

It's clear from the previous page that bladder and bowel control is one obvious area of development where there may be a marked difference between boys and girls (although there will always be exceptions to the rule). However, many gender differences are imposed on boys and girls by adults' own prejudices about what boys or girls are expected to be like (see p. 128), and so it's not always clear whether the recognized differences are solely due to nature or nurture. However, differences in the rate of development of certain skills between boys and girls throughout childhood and into adolescence have been measured by researchers (see chart below). Being aware of these may help you understand your children better, which can then enable them to move forward at an appropriate rate and also help overcome any difficulties before they become problems. It can also help to avoid the sort of gender stereotyping that doesn't allow girls to be adventurous or boys to show affection.

SOME DEVELOPMENTAL DIFFERENCES

GIRLS	BOYS
As toddlers, girls are better at hopping, rhythmic movement, and balance.	At school age, boys are usually better than girls at running, jumping, and throwing.
Girls are slightly faster than boys at some aspects of early language ability. They learn to read and write, and understand grammar and spelling, earlier than boys.	Most boys talk later than girls, and take longer to make complicated sentences. They have more reading problems by adolescence, and are less adept at verbal reasoning.
Girls are more emotionally independent than boys and are also more sociable and form close friendships from an earlier age.	Boys are more emotionally dependent than girls, and tend to have more behavioral problems before and during adolescence.
There's little difference in strength and speed between girls and boys until puberty, but from that time fat to muscle ratio is greater in girls.	At adolescence, boys become stronger and faster than girls and have more muscle and bone, less fat, and larger hearts and lungs.
Physical growth is faster and more regular; girls mature at adolescence earlier than boys.	Physical growth tends to go in uneven spurts; boys reach puberty later than girls.
Girls may be slightly better at arithmetic than boys before they reach adolescence, after which the trend reverses.	At every age boys are better at spatial visualization and, from adolescence, may be better than girls at mathematical reasoning.
In early childhood, girls generally appear to be more willing to obey adults' requests.	From toddlerhood, boys are more aggressive socially, and more competitive than girls.

WIDENING HORIZONS

As your child grows and develops, she'll become increasingly sociable and need contact with other people in order to develop natural curiosity and intellectual growth. She'll get these from the everyday interaction she has with you, your friends and their children, with grandparents, and other relatives. But it's also a good idea to let her meet other children of her own age with you at a parent and toddler group, and later to think about playschool or nursery as a way of preparing her for formal schooling in the future. Although your child may not start to form strong attachments – real friendships – until she's approaching three years old, she'll enjoy playing alongside other children. This will enable her to start finding out about giving and sharing, and to begin exploring the enormous potential for creativity in joint imaginative play.

EXTENDING YOUR FAMILY

Once you're settled as a family with one child, it's natural to think about whether or not you're going to extend your family and, if so, how long to wait. As with all family matters, there's no hard and fast rule about this. It suits some couples to wait until their first child is old enough to attend a nursery, or even until she's at school full-time. For others, a smaller gap seems better, but bear in mind that children have been found to benefit from a minimum gap of two and a half years. You also need to take into account work commitments and financial considerations, as well as your own health; a mother who had a strenuous labor and birth, or perhaps a cesarean section, would probably want to feel that her body is completely back to normal and has had time to become "hers" again before embarking on another pregnancy. Age is also significant, although today this doesn't have much bearing on the ability to bear and look after children. However, biology is against you: the older you are, the longer it's going to take you on average to conceive again (see p. 18), so you may not want to wait too long before trying for another baby.

THE IMPACT ON YOUR CHILD

Whatever the length of time between the two (or subsequent) births, it's important that you think carefully about the impact on the older child, and that you introduce the idea to her sensitively and in good time. Even a teenager can feel displaced by the arrival of a new baby, something that may well happen if you've entered a new relationship and one of you already has children (see p. 123). Your decision to extend your family must always be inclusive: your first child is a fully paid-up member of your family unit and deserves to be treated as such, whatever her age.

A FINAL WORD

Long after your child can cook herself a meal, iron her own clothes, and has left home, she'll still need both her parents to nurture her. True nurture caters not only to her material wants but also offers continuing and unconditional love, and it's a lifelong commitment. If this unconditional love is combined with reasonable limits and guidelines, you'll help her to mature into an individual who is sensitive to the needs of others, but remains independent of mind, confident, and open to all the possibilities that life can offer.

SIBLING RIVALRY

Jealousy is a normal emotion for a small child if her security appears threatened by the arrival of a new baby. Although you can't guarantee to avoid some jealousy, the best way to help her cope is to prepare her for the new arrival and to keep on showing her that her place in your affections is quite safe.

BEFORE THE BIRTH
Talk to her about the new baby as soon as your tummy looks really swollen. Let her touch your tummy whenever she wants to, but especially to feel the baby kick. Refer to the baby as *her* baby, and ask if she'd like a brother or a sister to get her involved. If you know the sex in advance, tell her so she can start to identify with the new baby. Get her to show love and affection openly by reading parent and baby animal books together, by encouraging her to be gentle with other babies, and by exchanging lots of cuddles.

AFTER THE BIRTH
When she visits you in the hospital for the first time, make sure you aren't holding the baby – have your arms free for her and wait for her to ask to see the baby. Give her a present from the baby. Share bath and feeding times so that she can show you how helpful she is and be praised and rewarded by you. Put aside at least half an hour a day when you give her your full attention one-on-one, without the baby. Keep telling her how much you love and treasure her.

THE FATHER'S ROLE
Some feelings of displacement are inevitable, but a father really comes into his own when the new baby arrives. You'll be able to reassure your elder child that you still love her. You're ideally placed to arrange special treats and activities. With your attention and love, you'll enable your first-born to negotiate the choppy waters of sibling rivalry and you'll have cemented a lifelong friendship.

159

USEFUL INFORMATION

MINIMUM RIGHTS

Regardless of how many hours you work or how long you've been employed, you're entitled to:

■ Working conditions that are safe for your unborn child: any risk must be removed, or you must be removed from it, if necessary by moving you to a suitable alternative job or suspending you on full pay.

■ Time off work without loss of salary to attend prenatal appointments and classes.

■ The right to keep your job; you cannot be dismissed as a result of your pregnancy.

■ Minimum maternity leave and pay (see right and opposite).

ADDITIONAL BENEFITS

If you work, you may be eligible for other benefits to help you support yourself and your baby:

■ **Disability** Benefits are available to many women, although they vary from state to state. Consult your state disability office or your employer's personnel department regarding local coverage and obtain the application form.

■ **Health insurance** If you receive insurance through your company, check the coverage before you become pregnant. If not, the insurance may not cover any bills resulting from your pregnancy.

■ **Government assistance** State and local health departments have information on any government programs that help mothers and young children, such as well-baby clinics and immunization programs.

THE FOLLOWING SECTION provides information to help you maximize the resources and benefits available to you during your pregnancy and after the birth. It also includes a summary of the health care procedures and recommended immunization schedule for your baby, and details of specialist organizations that offer help and support.

FINDING OUT YOUR MATERNITY RIGHTS

Becoming a parent entails changing your status from a legal and economic point of view, as well as a personal one. Sometimes the changes that are made in your working and economic life seem very complicated, but help is available. The important thing is to start making inquiries and getting help from the relevant agencies early on in your pregnancy – don't leave it until you're 35 weeks pregnant, or you may find yourself losing out. Women are legally entitled to certain benefits under the Pregnancy Discrimination Act of 1978. Many employers also provide additional maternity rights. It's a good idea to read your contract and staff handbook, especially if you work in a large company, so that you can check the company's benefits. If you are confused about anything, make an appointment with your personnel manager to find out exactly what is offered by your company and to discuss any alternatives. To qualify for maternity leave you need to obtain the appropriate forms from your personnel office and apply by the deadlines (see chart, opposite).

MATERNITY LEAVE

Eligible employees have the right to at least 12 weeks of unpaid, job-protected leave for certain family and medical reasons under the Family and Medical Leave Act of 1993. In order to be eligible, you must have worked for your current employer for at least one year, and for 1,250 hours over the past twelve months. However, companies with fewer than 50 employees within 75 miles may be exempt from this requirement. When you return to work you're entitled to return to the same position, or to a similar one that provides equivalent benefits, salary, and other terms of employment. Although you cannot lose benefits that you have already earned, salary and seniority benefits cannot be accrued during your maternity leave. Most states have their own family leave laws, which may be either more or less restrictive than the federal statute. Local laws, as well as any collective bargaining agreements made on behalf of the employees by labor unions, may supersede the federal regulations.

WHAT YOU NEED TO DO
You must file certain documents according to the specified deadlines (opposite). Under the restrictions laid out in the FMLA, you need to write to your employer at least 30 days before you start your maternity leave, stating that you are pregnant and giving your estimated delivery date. You must also state in writing if you intend to return to work after the birth and whether you are asking for more than the minimum 12 weeks' leave.

MATERNITY PAY

The payment you receive while you are on maternity leave varies widely, from none at all to whatever you and your employer have agreed upon. Under the provisions of the Family and Medical Leave Act, your employer must maintain your health coverage under whatever group plan you are using, whether you have chosen the group medical insurance or a health maintenance organization (HMO), for the duration of your maternity leave. At the employee's or employer's option, certain kinds of paid leave may be substituted for unpaid leave. For example, if you have not taken all of your annual paid vacation time or sick leave, you may be able to apply it toward your maternity leave. More than half of all employed people in the US also receive some temporary disability benefits from their employer through private insurance plans.

STATE TEMPORARY DISABILITY INSURANCE PROGRAMS

In five states, New Jersey, Rhode Island, California, New York, and Hawaii, as well as Puerto Rico, temporary disability insurance programs are available to working women. These programs are funded by employers and/or employees, either through taxes or contributions. In order to be eligible for disability benefits, a physician or certified nurse-midwife must verify that you are disabled and therefore unable to work as a result of your pregnancy or the birth of your baby. Disability benefits are available for up to six months within any consecutive 12 months.

REGISTERING THE BIRTH

The birth must be registered in the county in which your baby was delivered. The form is available at the hospital; if you give birth at home, the midwife will be able to give it to you. If possible, return the form to the hospital before you leave, or to the department of health within a day or two of your baby's birth. The information required on the form varies from state to state. Obtain several copies of the notarized birth certificate.

You can apply for your baby's Social Security number at the same time as the birth certificate. In order for your child to be claimed as a dependent on your tax returns, you must include your baby's Social Security number.

161

RIGHTS AND BENEFITS SUMMARY

WHEN	WHAT YOU NEED TO DO	WHY YOU NEED TO DO IT
BEFORE YOU ARE PREGNANT	Check with your employer to determine the company's maternity leave policies.	To maximize your employee benefits.
AFTER 12 WEEKS OR AFTER AMNIOCENTESIS RESULTS ARE BACK	If you are working, inform your employer.	To maximize your employee benefits.
ABOUT 12 WEEKS BEFORE YOUR BABY IS DUE	Discuss your maternity-leave plans with your employer.	To negotiate the best maternity-leave package possible.
ABOUT 10 WEEKS BEFORE YOUR BABY IS DUE	Give your employer a letter summarizing your maternity-leave plans and what you have agreed upon.	To clarify your expectations as well as those of your employer. This gives both of you time to fine-tune plans.
AT LEAST 30 DAYS BEFORE GOING ON MATERNITY LEAVE	Inform your employer in writing.	To protect your rights under the Family and Medical Leave Act.
ONE MONTH BEFORE DUE DATE, OR LATER (OR EARLIER FOR A MULTIPLE BIRTH)	Leave work.	To give you time to rest and prepare for the birth.
1–2 DAYS AFTER BIRTH	Submit information for birth certificate; apply for Social Security number.	Easier than if you wait until later.
2–3 WEEKS AFTER BIRTH	Purchase copy (copies) of baby's birth certificate.	To facilitate recordkeeping.

HEALTHCARE PROFESSIONALS

You'll be looked after by a series of professionals throughout your pregnancy amd after the birth.

YOUR FAMILY DOCTOR

If you do not have a gynecologist, see your family doctor as soon as you suspect you're pregnant. She'll confirm your pregnancy, if needed, and refer you to a obstetrician/gynecologist.

THE CERTIFIED NURSE-MIDWIFE

A midwife may be responsible for your prenatal care and may run a prenatal class. If you choose a midwife-assisted or home birth, she will be with you during labor, will deliver the baby, and will monitor you and the baby for two weeks after the birth.

THE OBSTETRICIAN/GYNECOLOGIST

Obstetrician/gynecologists are physicians who are specially trained in women's health issues, especially concerning the female reproductive system.

THE PEDIATRICIAN

Pediatricians are specially trained in health issues affecting children.

162

LOW-INCOME BENEFITS

During pregnancy and after the birth you may qualify for benefits if you are on a low income:

■ Food supplements are available for women and children through the WIC program. Consult your local government and welfare office for other benefits, such as Medicaid, welfare or workfare, and food stamps.

■ Immunizations may be offered by your community at a low cost. You may be required to show proof of certain vaccinations before your child is allowed to attend school.

HEALTH INFORMATION

Your baby's health will be closely monitored so that any problems can be picked up as early as possible. To protect your baby from certain illnesses, you will be advised to have him immunized from when he is two months old.

HEALTHCARE RECORDS

A record of your pregnancy, labor, and delivery is kept as well as anything from your medical history – or your family's – that could affect your child. Details of your baby's growth and development are recorded and updated at the regular checks (see p. 133); charts are used to record his weight, height, and head circumference to check that he is, on average, developing at the correct rate. You will be given a copy of your child's health records.

IMMUNIZATIONS

Some parents are anxious about the possible side effects that may occur as a result of a vaccination. If you have concerns, it's important to talk these through with your pediatrician. The risk of complications in all cases is extremely small; the risk of harmful effects from the diseases themselves is much more serious. Your baby will not be immunized if he was premature or when he has a fever. If he has had side effects from a previous vaccination, the pediatrician may delay or stop further immunizations, depending on the severity of the reaction. If you test positive for hepatitis B at the time your baby is born, your baby should be vaccinated for the disease within 12 hours of birth and at one, four, and six months; otherwise, vaccination at two, four, and six months is optional.

IMMUNIZATIONS IN THE FIRST YEAR

AGE DUE	VACCINATION	HOW GIVEN	SIDE EFFECTS
NEWBORN	Hepatitis B	• Injection	• None
ONE MONTH	Hepatitis B	• Injection	• None
TWO MONTHS	• Polio (IPV) • Hib • DTP (Diptheria, Tetanus, and Pertussis)	• Injection • Combined injection	• Possible lump at injection site; fever; slight risk of high fever and convulsions.
FOUR MONTHS	• Polio (IPV) • Hepatitis B • Hib • DTP (Diptheria, Tetanus, and Pertussis)	• Injection • Injection • Injection • Combined injection	• None • Possible lump at injection site; fever; slight risk of high fever and convulsions.
SIX MONTHS	• Polio (OPV) • Hepatits B • Hib • DTP (Diptheria, Tetanus, and Pertussis)	• By mouth • Injection • Injection • Combined injection	• None • Possible lump at injection site; fever; slight risk of high fever and convulsions.
12–18 MONTHS	• MMR (Measles, Mumps, Rubella)	• Combined injection	• Fever; rash; slight risk of high fever and convulsions.

USEFUL ADDRESSES

HEALTH AND SAFETY INFORMATION

American Academy of Pediatrics
141 Northwest Point Blvd., PO Box 927
Elk Grove Village, IL 60007
Tel: (800)-433-9016
Website: www.aap.org

American Red Cross
430 17th St. NW
Washington, DC 20006
Tel: (202) 737-8300
Website: www.redcross.org

Consumer Product Safety Commission
Publication Request
Washington, DC 20207
Tel: (301) 504-0580
Website: www.cpsc.gov

National Health Information Center
PO Box 1133
Washington, DC 20013
Tel: (800) 336-4797
Website: www.nhic-nt.health.org

National Lead Information Center
Hotline Tel: (800) LEAD FYI
Website: www.nsc.org/ehc/lead.html

CHILDREN WITH BIRTH DEFECTS

The Cleft Palate Foundation
1829 East Franklin Street, Suite 1022
Chapel Hill, NC 27514
Tel: (800) 24CLEFT
Website: www.cleft.com

National Down Syndrome Society
666 Broadway, 8th floor
New York, NY 10012
Tel: (212) 460-9330/(800) 221-4602
Website: www.ndss.org

Spina Bifida Association of America
4590 MacArthur Blvd. NW, Suite 250
Washington, DC 20007
Tel: (800) 621-3141
Website: www.sbaa.org

PARENT SUPPORT

ACCH (Association for the Care of Children)
710 Woodmont Avenue, Suite 300
Bethesda, MD 20814
Tel: (800) 808-2224
Website: www.acch.org
(premature and high-risk infants)

Childhelp USA
Tel (800) 4-A-CHILD
(parents in crisis, child abuse prevention)

Depression After Delivery
PO Box 1282
Morrisville, PA 19067
Tel: (800) 944-4773

La Leche League International
1400 Meacham Road
Schaumberg, IL 60173
Tel: (800) LA LECHE
Website: www.lalecheleague.org

Adoptive Families of America
2309 Como Avenue
St. Paul, MN 55108
Tel: (612) 535-4829

Mothers at Home
8310-A Old Courthouse Rd.
Vienna, VA 22182
Tel: (703) 827-5903
Website: www.mah.org

Parents Without Partners
401 North Michigan Avenue
Chicago, IL 60611
Tel: (800) 637-7974
Website: www.parentswithoutpartners.org

Stepfamily Foundation
333 West End Avenue
New York, NY 10023
Tel: (800) SKY STEP
Website: www.stepfamily.org

CHILDREN WITH SPECIAL NEEDS

National Information Center for Children and Youth with Handicaps
PO Box 1492
Washington, DC 20013
Tel: (800) 695-0285

Federation for Children with Special Needs
95 Berkley St., Suite 104
Boston, MA 02116
Tel: (617) 482-2915
Website: www.fcsn.org

Association for Retarded Citizens
500 E. Border St., Suite 300
Arlington, TX 76010
Tel: (817) 261-6003/(800) 433-5255
Website: thearc.orgwelcome.html

Council for Exceptional Children
(special education)
1920 Association Drive
Reston, VA 20191
Tel: (703) 620-3660
Website: www.cec.sped.org

Children and Adults with Attention Deficit Disorders (CH.A.D.D.)
499 NW 70th Ave., Suite 109
Plantation, FL 33317
Tel: (800) 233-4050/(954) 587-3700

National Autism Hotline
Prichard Building
PO Box 507; 605 9th Avenue
Huntington, WV 25710
Tel: (304) 525-8014

American Council of the Blind
1155 15th St. NW, Suite 720
Washington, DC 20005
Tel: (800) 424-8666
Website: www.acb.org

American Foundation for the Blind
11 Penn Plaza
New York, NY 10001
Tel: (800)- AFBLIND/(212) 502-7600

United Cerebral Palsy
1660 L St. NW, Suite 700
Washington, DC 20036
Tel: (800) 872-5827
Website: www.ucpa.org

Alexander Graham Bell Association for the Deaf
3417 Volta Place NW
Washington, DC 20007
Tel: (202) 337-5220
Website: www.agbell.org

International Dyslexia Association
Chester Building, Suite 382
8600 La Salle Road
Baltimore, MD 21286
Tel: (410) 296-0232
Website: www.interdys.org

National Assocation for Gifted Children
1707 L Street NW, Suite 550
Washington, DC 20036
Tel: (202) 785-4268
Website: www.nagc.org

Stuttering Foundation of America
PO Box 11749
Memphis, TN 38111
Tel: (800) 992-9392
Website: www.stuttersfa.org

CHILDREN WITH CHRONIC CONDITIONS

Asthma and Allergy Foundation
Consumer Information Line
1125 15th St. NW, Suite 502
Washington, DC 20005
Tel: (800)- 7-ASTHMA

Cystic Fibrosis Foundation
6931 Arlington Road, # 200
Bethesda, MD 20814
Tel: (800) FIGHTCF
Website: www.cff.org

American Diabetes Association
PO Box 25757, 1660 Duke St.
Alexandria, VA 22314
Tel: (800) 232-3472/(703) 549-1500
Website: www.diabetes.org

Juvenile Diabetes Association
120 Wall Street
New York, NY 10005
Tel: (212) 785-9500
Website: www.jdfcure.com

Epilepsy Foundation of America
4351 Garden City Drive
Landover, MD 20785
Tel: (800) 332-1000/(301) 459-3700
Website: www.efa.org

Sickle Cell Disease Association of America
200 Corporate Point, Suite 495
Culver City, CA 90230
Tel: (800) 421-8453

BEREAVEMENT

The Compassionate Friends
PO Box 3696
Oak Brook, IL 60522
Tel: (630) 990-0010
Website: www.compassionatefriends.org

Pregnancy and Infant Loss Support
St. Joseph's Health Center
300 1st Capitol Drive
St. Charles, MO 63301
Tel: (800) 821-6819/(314) 947-6164
Website: www.nationalshareoffice.com

SIDS Alliance
1314 Bedford Ave., Suite 210
Baltimore, MD 21208
Tel: (800) 221-SIDS

163

INDEX

168

ACKNOWLEDGMENTS

THE PUBLISHER WOULD LIKE TO THANK:

For their kind permission to reproduce photographs:
(c=center; t=top; b=bottom; l=left; r=right)
AKG: 10crb; Collections: Anthea Sieveking 46bl, 59b; Sally & Richard Greenhill: 42b, 45b; Science Photo Library: Ron Sutherland 50b.

For help in producing the book:
Sue Callister, Keith Davis, Glenda Fisher, Mae Hau, Ian Merrill, and Robert Newman for design assistance; Adam Moore and Rajen Shah for DTP work; Andy Crawford and Steve Gorton for additional photography; Elizabeth Burrage and Liz Jones for makeup; Joanna Moorhead for research; Claire Cross, Jen Dorr, Ray Rogers, Iris Rosoff, Clair Savage, and Anna Scobie for editorial assistance; Caroline Green for proofreading; Hilary Bird for the index.

For help and information:
Habitat, Early Learning Centre and Mamas and Papas for loaning props; the National Stepfamily Association and the British Association for Adoption and Fostering for advice.

For modeling:
Jacqui and Rosalyn Burton; Luke and Ziz Chater; Louise Clairemonte, Karl and Thomas Clowes; Rosie and Sarah Crouch; Lisa and Richard Czapnik; Angie and Chloe Elstone; Meredith and Tim Ericson; Ann and Kealey France; Imogen, Phoebe, Rohan and Sophie Harris; Oulimata Jagne; Joanna, Morgan, Niall, Rosie and Sarah Johnson; Kerry, Georgina and Sam Joseph; Nazrin, Neda and Nassar Khalili; Guenevere, Micheal and Suzanne Kiely; Adele King; Amber and Amelia Lecoyte; Maggie and Rebecca Mant; Jo Marceau; Cathy and Felix Miles; Claire and Thomas Moore; Alfie and Juliette Norsworthy; Darcie, Eva, Marea, Zak and Pat Oyrzynska; Katie Paine; Alastair, Linda and Matthew Partner; Ragen and Tina Patel; Vicky Phillips; Tim Pilcher and Megan Pilcher-King; Caroline and Marco Pinit; Ian and Kathy Redington; Jo and Shekinah Reuben; Nathan and Marvin Sackey; Ann and Joshua Simpson; Annabel Storr; Amanda and Zachary Stuart; Lawrence and Harry Taylor; David and Zachary Ward; Max and Sonia Whillock; Martin Wilson; and Emilie Woodman.